THE OTHER PLAYS
AND THE CHANGELING

Keith Eckert

ROMECK

First Edition

© 2020 Keith Eckert

All rights whatsoever in these plays are strictly reserved and applications
(professional or amateur) for permission to perform them, etc., must be
submitted to the author at kaxeckert@gmail.com before rehearsals begin.

ISBN: 978-1-7358361-1-9

Romeck Publishing

keitheckertcommunications.com/works

For Deana

CONTENTS

THE CHANGELING

*Loosely based on the play
by Thomas Middleton and William Rowley.*

CHARACTERS

Lord Nicolás DeFlores, physically deformed, humpbacked, the
Changeling
Lady Beatrice Sandoval, only child of the Duchess
Diana, Beatrice's personal servant
Duchess, Beatrice's mother, duchy ruler
Duke Alonso de Piracquo, suitor for Beatrice
Alfredo Tristan Velazquez, actor and confidante hired by DeFlores
Duke Alsemero Sabatio, suitor for Beatrice

Various lord, ladies, servants and players

SCENES

Beatrice's Apartments
Common Area/Ballroom of the Castle
Castle Garden
Various Unnamed Parts of the Castle
Tavern

TIME/LOCATION

Circa 1615, Spain

ACT I SCENE 1

(The curtain opens with DeFlores, Beatrice and Diana on stage. DeFlores sits or stands at the end/side of the stage, looking at Beatrice. Beatrice, center stage, sits before a makeup table and mirror as Diana prepares her to go out. Beatrice and Diana do not see or hear DeFlores as he speaks the following lines.)

DEFLORES. *(looking toward Beatrice)*
 She — she frames the sun; its light —
 It does not tint
 But through her eyes dispersed
 Our flowers blaze;
 It does not warm
 But by her convex smile our hearts unfreeze.
 Ah, Beatrice, Beatrice!
 Light transforming, eyes and lips aglow —
 The morning's iridescent streams
 Pour forth!
   (to the audience)
 I and you and all of us are but pale moons
 In orbit 'round her lustred eyes —
 We're but cold stones in obeisance
 Bowing to the weightful force of her beauty!
 See her move — ah!
 Like a gleam a'glance the water's face,
 Currenting graceful, breath-like waves.
 Ah, Beatrice, I could look on her all day.
 She and I —
 But look at me —
 See what I am.
 A beastly shape in human dress —
 Bent backed and gnarled, face uneven,
 Skin ablaze and festered.
 My name is Nicolás DeFlores.
 By royal blood, a lord,
 Second in line to be the Duke!
 But because my vessel is befouled
 I'm made the menial of these minors —
 The go'fer, chaser, messenger of choice
 For all and any.

Malformed as I am,
The ash and wormwood of beauty, as such
Who will look on me?
On me, a melted cherub,
A flyblown, rotting angel?
Who dares to look upon the Gorgon
And have their heart turned into stone?
Few —
And those who will
Will bite their lip and scrunch their nose,
Lean back in repulsive agitation.
Ah, the worse for me.
For we feed upon the eyes of others,
Find nourishment in loving looks,
And sustenance in sympathetic gaze.
Thus mistwisted, I am starved.
Who will look into my eyes and see the man?
The human? Born with sense and season, feelings,
Dreams ...
Although my frame is cracked, my mind
Is formed as handsomely as any man's.
Yes, I feel love, and too the loneliness at night,
The groaning pit of rainy days, the lilting bounce of hope,
The tears of choking laughter, yes —
I feel the same — the same as you
Though trapped inside this broke-back body
Through no sin nor crime
But my birth.
   (looking back at Beatrice)
Beatrice — Beatrice —
Even the rankest sinner wants to peek the gate
And watch the angels play.
She was so beautifully sad back then — she was.
It was another of my stinging misfortunes
That she could not abide my presence.
Watch.
   (DeFlores walks toward Beatrice.)
Excuse me, my lady.
BEATRICE. You? You fen-grown monster!
  Why d'you hang those ugly looks around my neck?
  Go back beneath the rock from which you crawled
  And die!

DEFLORES. I'm sorry, lady, that my looks offend you.
 Could I mend them I would.
BEATRICE. Could I banish you, I would.
DEFLORES. *(to the audience)*
 The scorn, it never ended.
 Fate would have her shake abuse upon my head.
 "Well," I thought, "fates do your worst!"
 I was pleased enough within her sight
 To endure the spittle of her rage.
 I knew she'd rather see me dead than living, yet
 I assure you,
 She had no cause for her complaints, none
 But a peevish will and my own peevish ugliness.
   (to Beatrice)
 But I come on order of your mother
 With a message.
BEATRICE. Then a plague on her for bringing such
 A reeking mouthpiece in my presence!
DEFLORES. Your mother is a fine —
BEATRICE. She's a fine pain in my ass — now out with it.
DEFLORES. What's that?
BEATRICE. The message, fool! What did she want?
DEFLORES. Ah, well, you know the Duke Signoir Alonso,
 Son of the —
BEATRICE. You festering sore of a beast, get to the meat
 And cut the appetizer. I know who Alonso is,
 You dog-faced baboon, I'm engaged to marry him.
DEFLORES. *(to the audience)*
 Ah, the abuse! But I take it with a smile —
 To drink her presence is a joy!
BEATRICE. Now, you spider-backed monkey,
 Reveal the gist and then be gone.
DIANA. *(to Beatrice)*
 I don't know why he comes around.
DEFLORES. Your mother — the duchess —
BEATRICE. Yes! Yes! The fly, you toad!
DEFLORES. Alonso comes for dinner and he will be here soon.
BEATRICE. It's understood. Now fast as your left feet
 Will hobble you away, go tell my mother
 To jump from the highest parapet.
DEFLORES. *(laughing)*
 I'll take my leave, but keep your message
 To myself.

BEATRICE. I'd rather that you shared the message
  But kept yourself to yourself. Now be gone!
DEFLORES. As you wish!

(DeFlores steps to one side of the stage, then addresses the audience.)

  The insults and invectives —
  To say they didn't hurt would lie,
  But Beatrice, I'd soon learn, had problems of her own,
  Ones that soon would turn the wheel of fortune
  Upside down!
BEATRICE. That ill-formed monster! How I loathe his sight!
  He shivers me with unnatural dread.
DIANA. He is a witch's child, I say.
  I lose my appetite when I see his garbled face!
  But come — he's gone, and now we must prepare
  For your Alonso. Look in the mirror.
     (Beatrice angrily turns away.)
BEATRICE. Ugh! Don't stale the air with his name. Ah!
DIANA. Now, now. Is he that bad?
BEATRICE. He's worse.
DIANA. Yes, but he's rich, and from an ancient family —
BEATRICE. He's a pig and a fusspot! I can't abide his sneering
arrogance
  And his pedantic advice.
  The man is all quibbles and quips,
  Carefully rehearsed and performed, on cue or not.
  He knows nothing but his own voice
  Echoing drearily into his hairy ears.
  And he's old — so old and crusty,
  Decrepit, heavy and musty,
  Stiff and dull and gray.
DIANA. Now now — he's only thirty-four.
BEATRICE. That's almost twice my age.
  He's twice put wives in graves,
  No doubt from his ceaseless tedium.
    (Beatrice look at herself in the mirror.)
  How will it look for me, so young and fresh,
  With one so bland and moldered?
  How am I to stand with such a dotard?
  The man is time's fool and a clown's tool. Besides,
  It seems that he was born a grey-haired man —
  Why as a child I bet he smoked a pipe.

He probably slept in his slippers,
Complained about his indigestion
And drank weak cognac
While sitting by the fire in a jacket!
                    (They both laugh. There's a moment of silence.)
Ah, Diana — what am I to do?
Am I to spend the unwound ribbon of my days with him?
To feel the weight of a thousand tics
Landing on my heart
One after another after another
Until Fate's scissors clip off this gloom
And agéd death succors me?
Why should one like me — alive and bold and free —
Bend 'neath a man like him — emasculate, old and fusty?
DIANA. That's the duty of a duke's daughter.
DEFLORES. Ah, my poor, poor Beatrice.
                    (to the audience)
Soon we'll fix all that.
BEATRICE. You don't know how lucky you are to love —
To love for love, and not for duty —
To feel the spray of passion, rather than the dust of inheritance.
Maybe I should jump off the highest tower.
DIANA. Don't be silly, my lady!
Come, let's go outside a bit. That will cheer you up.
                    (Beatrice and Diana exit.)

DEFLORES. *(to the audience)*
My poor, poor Beatrice!
You'll find love — but what a twisted road it will be!
You'll find love — and it will be me.

(A loud, raucous banging is heard offstage — as if several people are pounding on a door with their fists and feet. DeFlores moves to the front of the stage as the curtain closes behind him.)

VOICES OFFSTAGE. *(amid shouts and grunts)*
DeFlores! DeFlores! He's in here! Here! Let us in!
DEFLORES. Ah! D'you hear them call my name? Ha ha!
It's music to my ears! Who's called my name before?
No one! As if my name were some profanity
To be spit in hoarse desperation.

Now everybody screams my name!
They want me — more than anything!
VOICES OFFSTAGE. *(more pounding offstage)*
DeFlores! We're going to get you! We've got him!
DEFLORES. *(almost laughing)*
You shall! You shall! And thus our time is short.
VOICES OFFSTAGE. DeFlores! Someone get an axe! DeFlores!
DEFLORES. *(to the offstage voices)*
Patience! Patience!
The hunt tastes better than the catch,
So savor the anticipation! The wetting mouth!
> *(to the audience)*
Forgive me for their interruption.
We'll meet with them at the end of my tale —
Which we'll get to soon enough.

ACT I SCENE 2

DEFLORES. But to my tale! Hmm, where'd I drop the thread?
> Ah yes! You saw my life, such as life was:
> Derision's prince, a leper laid among the roses.
> Such was my life, until that night.

(As DeFlores speaks, the curtain opens revealing a party — people mingling and talking, entering and exiting the stage. Music starts playing softly in the background. DeFlores walks into the scene still talking to the audience.)

> That night! The engagement celebration!
> The bride and groom to be, enthroned and feted
> In a festival of light.
> Among those holding place or power in the duchy
> All were here:
> Flowering skirts and glistening bodices,
> Silk and satin ribbons banding glimmering hair.
> And musicians from Seville were going to sing!
>> *(A man and woman walk by. DeFlores bows.)*
> My lord! My lady!
>> *(The man and woman grimace and keep walking.)*
> Soon, everything would change.
> For this was my moment-making day,
> And those glistering candles formed
> The light of a transfiguring dawn —
> I awoke fate's slave, but went to bed good fortune's prince.

(DeFlores begins mingling among the people — he nods or bows, but they turn away from him. Beatrice particularly sneers at him and walks away.)

> Beatrice was especially glowing,
> A gleaming star among the night
> Of minor constellations.
> Ah!
>> *(Duchess walks by.)*
> A lovely party, Duchess.
DUCHESS. Ah, Lord DeFlores. Thank you.
> It reminds me of your mother's wedding party,
> Rest her soul. She was so beautiful.
DEFLORES. I hear. I hear.

DUCHESS. The most beautiful woman I ever knew.
     Breathtaking. But then ...
DEFLORES. Yes, she died giving birth to me.
DUCHESS. Yes. It was unfortunate.
     Well, I must prepare the players.
DEFLORES. Ah, players! How fun!
               (The Duchess exits.)
     You wouldn't know by this preposterous mug
     That my mother was a dazzling beauty —
     Renowned in all the land. She was!
     At least that's what I'm told.
     By everyone.
     But giving life to me, her life was snatched away,
     Her beauty too.
     And so my father, broken hearted, profligate,
     Drank himself to an unseasonable grave,
     And I was raised a stranger.
     That so much ugliness could be the spawn
     Of so much beauty's just another irony
     Of this afflicted life.
     It's said, you know, that fairies sometimes switch
     One baby with another; they replace
     A perfect newborn with a sickly tempered changeling.
     Sometimes I think I am the changeling,
     Replaced at birth and tossed upon this stage
     Ill-fit to play the scene.
     If so, who was my mother? Where's my home?
     Perhaps there is a land where everyone's as me,
     And there I'd be the handsomest of all!
     But I'm not molded for such lolling,
     My daily struggles leave me little leisure to dream.

(Beatrice walks up, but seeing DeFlores frowns and lowers her eyes.)

DEFLORES. *(cheering up)*
     Congratulations, my lady.
BEATRICE. Congratulations on what?
DEFLORES. Why your soon-to-be nuptials.
BEATRICE. Why would you congratulate me?
DEFLORES. To wish you well.
BEATRICE. I'd rather that you cursed me, you pig.
     Your praise is sickly prey for wolves.
     Better you howled a full-throated, damning imprecation

And went away forever than wished me well
And hung upon my leg.
I'd rather that your foul tongue spit barbed glass
And bitter curses;
For certain you do good ill
And fevered misfortune licks your heels.

DEFLORES. I only mean you well. I am, after all, your humble servant.

BEATRICE. If so, then go impale yourself upon your sword,
And if you prove too cowardly for that,
The next time you wish to talk to me, impale me instead.

DEFLORES. Ha ha! My lady —

BEATRICE. Over there's my mother — go pester her.

(Beatrice pushes DeFlores away. DeFlores goes to the side of the stage.)

DEFLORES. At the time I didn't know of Beatrice's
Loathing of Alonso. Yes, poor girl!
Trapped in loveless duty,
Sundered from her heart's desire — from love.
Poor girl, little did I think to pity her.
To pity her — ah, then it would have seemed absurd!
But then this night — this night ….

(Diana enters and approaches Beatrice.)

DIANA. What a joyous day!

BEATRICE. I'm so happy I could crumble to dust and blow away.

DIANA. Why, my lady?

BEATRICE. Alonso? Really? What a troll he is.

DIANA. Still that? He's not so bad. You'll want for nothing.

BEATRICE. Except for love. And what is life without love?
I want the same as every peasant girl.

DIANA. Most would give up love for good food and fine clothes.

BEATRICE. But for love ...

(The Duchess re-enters with Alfredo and two singers/musicians.)

DUCHESS. Lords and ladies, friends and guests!
I'm pleased introduce the Seville Players.
They come here highly recommended
And tonight they will perform a song for us.

(The people applaud while Alfredo's musicians play a flourish. Then Alfredo steps forward.)

ALFREDO. My lords, my ladies, my name
      Is Master Alfredo Tristan Velazquez,
      Of the late Seville Players.
      I say the "late" for several weeks ago,
      Amid the century's greatest storm
      We were ensnared atop the Alps for weeks
      Without support or food except each other.
      And of that once and lively troupe
      This threadbare threesome that you see before you
      Are all who have survived unstarved.
      But we are overjoyed to be with you tonight,
      Bestowed a second chance on life,
      Knowing now the gentle mercies of our lord,
      And the saving graces of our god.
      And so tonight we will perform for you
      A song — a tragic tale of love achieved.

(The music starts. Alfredo and his troupe sing.)

      A wife and a husband happily made,
      A comfortable marriage, a comfortable bed.
      Sharing the sunsets, they go 'bout their days
      With little undone and little to say.
        And never a need stop to ask,
        "What would love do?"

      But rivers can suddenly leap from their way
      And the best laid plans are swept away.
      And thus in a look, in a smile or a thought
      A passion is loosed and a fever is caught,
        And then someone wonders
        What would love do?

      So felled by love's dart, so stung by love's bee
      The young woman's life 'comes a tumbling sea
      And feelings of passion set to fire her soul —
      Feelings she cannot explain or control.
        And she asks of herself,
        What would love do?

The husband discovers an unguarded note,
Learns of her feelings — unfulfilled, passionate;
He reads of the fire, the love so estranged,
Consuming her soul in a wondrous new pain.
   He reads and he wonders
   What would love do?

The passion he reads of fills him with fear,
It fills him with envy and wonder and tears:
To see how he's lived, how he's loved and he's lied,
It unleashed on his heart a poisonous tide.
   He knows then the answer
   What would love do?

With his knife it is settled, his hand it is run,
With his blood, his very life, the lesson is done.
By trading his heart for the hearts of two lovers
He's made the path clear for true love's discover.
   And answered the question,
   What would love do?

(People applaud and come up to congratulate Alfredo.)

ALFREDO. *(bowing extravagantly)*
     Thank you! Thank you! Thank you!
DEFLORES. *(coming up Alfredo)*
     Well done sir, I —

(Pushing DeFlores aside and grabbing Alfredo rather roughly by the sleeve.)

BEATRICE. You must tell me —
ALFREDO. What? Ah, the bride to be!
BEATRICE. That story — is it true?
ALFREDO. Story? What story?
BEATRICE. The story in your song. That story. Is it true?
ALFREDO. My lady, all great art is as true as the sun is warm.
BEATRICE. And love is that strong? It can be
     That powerful?
ALFREDO. My lady, love's the pith and pinnacle of life.
     What else is there, but love?
BEATRICE. Love?
ALFREDO. What else?

19

(Beatrice let's go of Alfredo's sleeve and walks away deep in thought.)

DEFLORES. That story, yes, quite nicely done.
ALFREDO. But this, what's this? This crumpled flesh
    Discarded here?
    My god, a man! But what? A victim of a hard, blunt axe!
    What? Had your face caught fire?

(The people laugh at Alfredo's jokes.)

DEFLORES. No sir, I was born a little homely.
ALFREDO. You lie! You're not the least bit homely, sir,
    Why you're completely hideous!
DEFLORES.　　*(painfully embarrassed)*
    It's true! Ha!
ALFREDO. Yours is the kind of face a girl dreams of at night,
    Because it's better than seeing it in the light!
DEFLORES. Ha ha! It's true! It's true!
ALFREDO. But you've a sympathetic face, my Lord,
    Believe me you've my sympathy.
DEFLORES. I thank you, sir. I am but child of loving nature.
ALFREDO. And still you love dame nature, after what
    She's done to you?
DEFLORES. But what am I to do about it?
ALFREDO. There's but one problem with your face, my lord,
    It shows.
DEFLORES. But one must live and work and eat and socialize.
ALFREDO. And one must die. But that's no excuse
    To walk and talk just like dying man
    In ash and a shroud bedecked!
    Come here, come here, my Lord.

(Alfredo leads DeFlores aside.)

    My lord, my heart does feel for you, and for your
    Strange affliction. So let me give you some advice:
    Do not just snicker and say "I'm ugly, true!"
    Look up, look out!
    Yes, by god you've been dealt a gargoyle's face,
    A possum's body, and a box's gait,
    But do not let your ugliness reek from within,
    Let the strength, the fortitude shine out
    And confound the scorn-weaved eye of fate.

You play the wart with a guffaw — that will not do!
Play it with a meaning — play it with anger, with resolve,
With beauty!

DEFLORES. *(intrigued)* Beauty?

ALFREDO. Hmm, yes, with beauty!
Yes, you can play your ugliness with beauty!
The ugly duckling is the beautiful swan —
The ugly wench with a heart of gold —
Thus there is beauty 'neath the ugliness to shine
And shower all.
But to play ugly with ugly, my my! What good is that
But to rain down on you snarling boos and hisses?
This is your moment on the stage,
The exits and the entrances loom forever either way.
We must move and captivate our audiences,
Or else perish in boos!
This is your time, your stage, your part,
Play it with a gusto and imagination worthy of the greats!
What's Orestes have on you? What's Oedipus?
You've been given a part — unique in all the land, I say.
Now play it! Play it to your heart's excess!
Now stand up straight, and turn and look.
And wipe the impish grin from off your face.
Imagine you're the star.

DEFLORES. The star?

ALFREDO. Yes, the star in view and scope of everyone.

DEFLORES. But how do I become the star?

ALFREDO. By doing it!

DEFLORES. What? You'll show me how?

ALFREDO. My lord, I'm cast from humble means
And I must serve my art unless I starve.

DEFLORES. Not for a one-hundred florins a month?

ALFREDO. For that sir, I'm your teacher and your light —
Lean on my instruction, child, until you walk upon your own.
(turning to his other players)
My friends, the time has come for us to separate
And each our own true paths find out.

PLAYER 1. What? You're discharging us?

ALFREDO. You've learned so very much from me, my children.
Now spread your wings and fly the nest.

PLAYER 1. After all that happened on the Alps?

ALFREDO. Especially after all that happened on the Alps!
    What profounder lesson can be a taught?
    Upon the Alps you feasted on the very heart of man!
    Take those lessons to your art.
PLAYER 1. It is as well. I've no more appetite for you
    Or for the rest our old troupe.
    Come Miguel, we'll join the brothers
    And pray there is a merciful god.
            (to DeFlores)
    Good luck, sir. May Master Alfredo's tastes
    Not turn to you.

        (The players exit. Alonso walks by.)

DEFLORES. Lord Alonso — Lord Alonso, congratulations
    On your wedding!
    Did you hear, I've hired Master Alfredo
    To join my house?
ALONSO. Lord DeFlores, why in heaven would you want
    Such actor-vagabonds to share your meals?
    They bring no value but to primp and prate,
    They know no skill but empty, childish talk.
ALFREDO. Sir, I can tell you are an educated man —
    The University of Seville perhaps?
            (Alonso nods)
    Then well you know the value of these empty shells,
    For what's a king's decree but winnowed wind?
    The word of god but wispy breath?
    What's all the world, then, but our speech?
    But I pity the philosopher scholar —
    At worse, you learn no practical skill
    To put some food upon your table.
    At best it teaches you feel
    The hunger all the more profoundly.
    And you don't want to have scholar for dinner.
DEFLORES. Because they eat too much?
ALFREDO. Au contraire! They eat too little!
ALONSO. I've given my advice, my lord,
    Do as you please. I wash my hands of this.

(Alonso exits.)

ALFREDO. Behold the man!
DEFLORES. My friend, come see me in the morning
    And we'll talk some more of this.
ALFREDO. *(with a flourishing bow)*
    I am your most obedient service.

(Alfredo exits with the rest of party guests.)

ACT I SCENE 3

(The stage clears as DeFlores speaks until he is alone on stage. As he nears the end of his speech, Beatrice enters and stands at some distance, her back to DeFlores.)

DEFLORES. It was a light delicious party,
    Made whole by the night, made true by vows
    Made soft beneath the shimmering cape of stars.
    For later on that night I chanced to see
    Dear Beatrice by herself among the garden paths.
    Although I risked a lashing of her tongue
    I couldn't help but stare at her.
BEATRICE. *(turning as if hearing something)*
    Lord DeFlores — is that you?
DEFLORES. *(to the audience)*
    What? Shall I run mad with joy!
    She's called me by my name — DeFlores!
    Not "rogue" nor "rat."
               (nervously walking toward her)
    My lady?
BEATRICE. What have you done to your face, my lord?
    I don't recall you ever looked so handsome.
DEFLORES. I haven't done a thing, my lady,
    Why every prickly hair and creasing blemish
    Is unchanged from yesterday.
BEATRICE. Come nearer, man.
DEFLORES. *(to the audience)*
    I'm up to the chin in heaven!
BEATRICE. Turn, let me see.
        (stroking his face)
    Something is definitely different.
    You look stronger, bolder, more assured.
    You have a hard resolve about you.
DEFLORES. *(to the audience)*
    Her fingers' touch — they smell of violets!
BEATRICE. Hardness becomes the visage of a man quite well;
    It argues valiantry, strength and resolution —
    All traits valuable in the service of others.

DEFLORES. These are qualities I'd happily show you, my lady,
    If ever you had a need for them.
    I do but wish the honor of serving you.
BEATRICE. *(moan-like)*
    Oh, my DeFlores!
DEFLORES. *(to the audience)*
    Again my name!
            (to Beatrice)
    What is it, madam? You sighed such torn anguish.
BEATRICE. I did? I did. It's nothing.
    Oh!
DEFLORES. There it is again, the fellow of the first!
BEATRICE. You have the eyes of Argus, sir. I can't hide
    A thing from your all-knowing gaze.
DEFLORES. I've heard it twice now, madam:
    That sigh would have its speech. Take pity on it
    And give your sorrow words. I hear the murmur yet
    Beat within your bosom.
BEATRICE. Ah, Lord DeFlores, I am — I am troubled —
    Trapped …
DEFLORES. Yes, my lady?
BEATRICE. Ah, would creation —
DEFLORES. Yes, out with it!
BEATRICE. — Had made me a man.
DEFLORES. Oh, don't say that!
BEATRICE. Oh, it's but my desperate cry for freedom!
    Oh DeFlores, why should I be forced to marry one
    I hate beyond all depths? Yes, one whose cold
    Would freeze my loving heart to icy death.
    Were I a man I'd have the power of my arm
    To shatter all my loathings — yes, destroy
    Them from my sight forever.
DEFLORES. *(kneeling)*
    Make your wish of me without unmaking your sex.
    Make your claim of the man in me.
BEATRICE. In you, DeFlores? You have no stake in this.
DEFLORES. Do not take it from me; it's a service
    That I kneel for.

(DeFlores kneels.)

BEATRICE. You're too blinded by passion's glare
    To mean that faithfully;
    There's horror in my service — blood and death:
    Are these the kinds of things to sue for?
DEFLORES. If you knew how sweet it were for me
    To be employed in any act for you,
    You'd ask me those and more.
BEATRICE. Rise.
DEFLORES. First I'll have the charge.
BEATRICE. If you — if you insist.
    I need a man extracted from my life —
    And all of life.
DEFLORES. I'll do it.
BEATRICE. One who would not sacrifice for love,
    Must then be sacrificed to it.
DEFLORES. I am the man to do it.
BEATRICE. You will take him to your bloodshot fury?
DEFLORES. I will crush his bones to dust!
BEATRICE. When you take hold, you will not let him go?
    You'll not feel pity or remorse though he would beg?
DEFLORES. I will be the feral beast. And once engaged
    I'll lock my teeth upon his neck and drink his blood.
    Just say his name and he's no more.
BEATRICE. Alonso de Piracquo.
DEFLORES. *(rising)*
    His end's upon him; he'll not live to see
    A second dawn.
BEATRICE. How lovely now this face appears to me!
    Never was a man more dearly admired.
DEFLORES. It is a happy service for me.
BEATRICE. Now be careful in the execution.
DEFLORES. Are not both our lives upon the cast?
BEATRICE. Then I throw all my fears upon your service.
DEFLORES. They will never rise to hurt you.
BEATRICE. When the deed is done, I'll furnish you
    With all the things for flight; you'll live a kingly life
    In another country far, far away.
DEFLORES. We'll talk of that a later time.
BEATRICE. So then goodnight, my dear DeFlores.

(Beatrice exits. DeFlores steps forward and the curtain closes behind him.)

DEFLORES. Oh, my blood, my friends! My blood ran thin
    I thought that I would faint! Yes, me
    In Beatrice's employ!
    Oh, I knew it was a bloody service
    Which she uses me as her fool.
    And when the job is done, she'll seek a way
    To crumple me upon the heap.
    But I have plans myself, I do!
    And she may yet grow warm to this weird face.
    ☐

ACT I SCENE 4

DEFLORES. But to the deed: The door was opened soon.
    Alonso's starving ego made it all so easy

(*The curtain opens behind him showing a small, empty tavern. There are a couple tables and chairs. A bottle, glasses and a long knife or sword lay on or beside one of the tables.*)

    But I'm too loud. Here comes the man
    Who supperless will go to bed, and yet
    Be serving breakfast by the morning.

(*Alonso and the Alfredo enter.*)

ALONSO. This seems quite out of the way.
ALFREDO. It's much too dangerous to be in the way, my lord,
    Why, one gets run over that way.
ALONSO. Hmm, I suppose so.
DEFLORES. What do we need of others, eh? A quiet drink
    'Mongst friends without the rabble to disturb us.
ALFREDO. Quite. We don't need the groundlings hawking us
    Or stepping on our toasts with "We are hungry"
    Or "Spare a penny?"
ALONSO. Ah yes. The poor, it's sad to say, don't understand
    The better things in life, or their betters.
    To think they'd even dare to beg of us —
    Have they no self-respect? No pride?
    Peasants aren't as hardy as they used to be.
    Now every voice believes it needs an ear.
DEFLORES. True. So true.
            (*to Alfredo*)
    Come, my friend. The drinks! Where are our drinks?
ALFREDO. Here. Here.

(*Alfredo pulls out a bottle and glasses, then pours drinks.*)

    My lord. My lord.
DEFLORES. Ah yes, that's better, yes.
            (*awkward silence as they sip the wine.*)

ALFREDO. *(eyeing his glass)*
    I am suspicious of this vintage.
    I fear some crime had been committed on the grapes.
ALONSO. Hmm. Hmm.
                (more awkward silence)
ALFREDO. I hear the Black Death's come to Valencia.
    The streets are lined with the dead.
DEFLORES. Is that the best topic you can come up with?
                (another awkward silence.)
    How about a toast?
ALFREDO. Ah yes! To the groom to be. Shall I?
DEFLORES. Oh please!
ALFREDO. Ah, yes — let me see, let me see.
                (standing and raising his glass)
    My lord, I'll never forget the first time we met
    (Though I keep trying).
ALONSO. What?
ALFREDO. My Lord, when people told me that
    You were a perfect fool, I did protest —
    Most heartily I protested! Yes!
    I assured them you were far from perfect.
ALONSO. Now!
ALFREDO. Nay, I said our lord is very smart, he is!
    Why he has brains he's never used!
    My lord, I said, is no one's fool, that is for sure,
    But maybe someday someone will adopt him.
ALONSO. What's this?
ALFREDO. And so we raise our glasses — raise them high
    To Lord Alonso de Piracquo on his nuptials
    To the beautiful Lady Beatrice.
    To a decisive, charismatic, brave man,
    A man of pith and gall, of vigor and vim,
    Of wisdom, graciousness and wile,
    We would give a toast — but since that man's not here,
    We'll toast instead out Lord Alonso, who,
    Were he a bit less boring, he might entertain
    A thought. Cheers!

(Alfredo and DeFlores drink.)

ALONSO. *(standing up, angry)*
    Sir, I've never been so insulted!

ALFREDO. *(sitting down)*
    Then you should clean your ears, my lord.
ALONSO. Why you — you are a villainous liar and whoreson!
    I'll take no more of this roguery!

(Alonso gets up to leave, but DeFlores, laughing, holds him.)

DEFLORES.   *(laughing)*
    Come now, Lord Alonso, sit — yes, sit!
    I put Alfredo up to this prank. I said
    "I will suggest a toast and you insult him,
    Then we'll laugh a hearty laugh!"
ALFREDO. It's true my lord. He put me to it. Please
    Accept my abject apology!
ALONSO. *(reluctantly sitting down)*
    It's a quirky humor that you twist.
DEFLORES. But you're the groom — tradition has us prank
    The groom! It is a sign of fellowship.
ALONSO. *(becoming cheerful and chuckling to himself)*
    Well, since you put it that way — it was a funny joke.
    How droll! Yes, me a boor!
DEFLORES. *(rolling his eyes)*
    You said it, my Lord. Ha!
ALONSO. Yes, a man's reputation is the most important
    Thing he has.
DEFLORES. What do you think of one who murders another's
reputation?
ALONSO. Why that's worse than murder proper!
ALFREDO. Or improper.
DEFLORES. Have you ever killed a man, my Lord?
ALONSO. Me?
ALFREDO. Yes, have you ever pressed the knife into a child's chest?
    Fed poison to an unsuspecting rival?
    Pushed a pregnant woman down the steps?
ALONSO. My god, sir! I have never done such black-souled things!
    I say, you have the most disturbed imagination.
               (to DeFlores)
    But to your point, sir. Yes, I've killed a man
    In battle.
DEFLORES. What was it like? Were you afraid? Did you
    Regret it later?

ALONSO. Well, I never gave it that much thought.
    I was young, and it was war, and he —
    He was the enemy.
ALFREDO. You don't give much thought to thinking, do you?
DEFLORES. *(before Alonso can respond)*
    Is there anything that you would kill for?
ALONSO. Why certainly — my reputation for example.
        (to Alfredo)
    You, sir, damn near met my fury with your joke.
ALFREDO. Heaven forfend! Well, I'm glad it needn't come to that.
ALONSO. You should be.
DEFLORES. Would you kill for love?
ALONSO. What do you mean?
DEFLORES. Would you lay in ambush for a rival?
ALONSO. Most certainly not — that is a dastardly deed!
DEFLORES. I suppose.
    But for love?
ALONSO. Not for anything. It is dishonorable.
DEFLORES. But for love, for love —
    It seems that any deed be possible.
    To hold the woman of your dreams —
    To spend your days in bliss entwined,
    To feel her breath upon your neck as morning dawns.
    Wouldn't you risk everything? Dare anything?
ALONSO. My man, you clutch a puerile view of love.
    No doubt caused by your most unfortunate ugliness.
    You've no experience. And thus should speak no word on it.
DEFLORES. Perhaps, perhaps. I am quite ugly, not?
ALFREDO. Hideous. Rude. Unstinting —
DEFLORES.   *(cutting him off with a smile)*
    We've got it.
ALONSO. Look here: I've been married twice and so I know
    Of what I speak. A good marriage
    Is not built on love or passion or starry looks, but duty:
    Each knowing their role, fulfilling their obligations.
    Why, my wives I hardly saw. And if I did,
    What was I to do with them?
    They had their friends, they had their interests,
    And I had mine. A day of hunting would be marred
    By bringing my wife. Why would I do that?
    Yes, a good marriage is a mutual agreement.

It should be comfortable like a jacket
That fits so well you don't even know you wear it.
That defines a happy marriage.
ALFREDO. That sounds so ... business like.
DEFLORES. There's no place for passion? Earnestness?
Secrets shared beneath a harvest moon?
ALONSO. My lord, you've listened to too many songs.
Poets, sir, should be enjoyed but not believed.
DEFLORES. But take this sword, for example.
(*standing and picking up a sword from a neighboring table*)
With the power of love, what is not possible
With this sword? What kingdoms could be brought down?
What worlds overturned? What fast-bound fates beguiled?
ALONSO. DeFlores, you are embarrassing yourself.
DEFLORES. Am I?
ALFREDO. Quite. Bring to him the point — the point!
He's bored my soul to tears.
ALONSO. I beg your pardon!
DEFLORES. (*ignoring Alfredo*)
Would you kill to be better looking?
ALONSO. DeFlores, I fear you've lost your mind!
If you insist on talking so foolishly,
I will leave.
DEFLORES. I guess it's pretty foolish, isn't it?
ALONSO. Preposterous, more like. How can a man
Change the way he looks? Especially one
Like yourself. God has made you so,
You've better come to peace with that.
ALFREDO. But a man may tailor his appearance
Without mending of his face in the least.
ALONSO. I have no idea what you mean.
You're near as mad as our homely friend here.
What is a man but his eye, his nose and his chin —
God made us so, and some like me he's blessed,
No doubt for my virtue.
DEFLORES. Hmm. No doubt I've been a sinner --
And if I've not the hero's cut
Then I am more the villain.
ALONSO. Well — that's not exactly what I meant.
You know what I mean.
This is a most unusual conversation —
The strangest I have ever had, I say.
Murdering to look better — absurd!

ALFREDO. The more stranger the better, my lord.
DEFLORES. But if the chance is one in a million,
    At least it is a chance.
ALONSO. Have you gone mad?
DEFLORES. Yes, I'm mad. I'm mad with love.

*(DeFlores stands up and stabs Alonso in the chest and pulls out the sword.
Alonso stands up, shocked, knocking over his chair. DeFlores steps back
hesitantly while Alonso collapses and dies, gasping, with a quizzical look on his
face — as if unsure what he should say or do. Alfredo steps to Alonso.)*

ALFREDO. A terrible, terrible thing this is!
    To die — to die in such a way,
    It's an embarrassment, my man.
    You are embarrassing, my lord.
    A thousand times I've died,
    By poison, sword, sickness, age,
    By fall, by accident, by hanging —
    I felt the graying cold o'erdrape my eyes.
    And lashed out at my cruel murderers,
    Cursed my fate, lamented my own loss,
    Denied it in an ugly tantrum.
    But you, you do not know of death,
    You never saw the specter peek across your shoulder.
    What emotion did you show? What was that?
    What eye would that have moistened?
    What howl for blood's atonement would it ring?
    What gasp, what cry, what cringing self-recognition
    Would your performance have wrought?
    An amateur!
    One should never be surprised by death!
    It lurks about us at all times. But how
    Can one unknown to life put thought in death?
    Ah, shallow, shallow man.
    They'd boo you hoarse from the boards for that!
DEFLORES. Then my fate is cracked beyond repair.
    Yet I didn't feel the Earth shake open.
    Why — that was easier than I thought.
    And I feel handsomer already!

ALFREDO. It was well done, my lord. Well done!
    In bold, dramatic fashion. Nicely done!
    "Mad with love." It was wonderful line!
    It's just too bad he did his part so —
    So inanely.
DEFLORES. *(stepping toward the front of the stage)*
    Dispose o' the body.
ALFREDO. As you wish, my lord. I'll season him
    According to my tastes.

(Alfredo drags Alonso's body offstage. The curtain closes behind DeFlores.)

ACT II SCENE 1

DEFLORES. *(to the audience)*
>As I wished, my wish comes true. Although
>It's framed upon a death, a callous murder,
>Cold and cutting, I feel no weight for the deed;
>It's but light a sinful load to bear
>To be with Beatrice.

(As DeFlores finishes his last words, a pounding offstage starts.)

VOICES OFFSTAGE. DeFlores! DeFlores!
DEFLORES. *(looking offstage)*
>Patience, friends! My my — you hurry along my tale.
VOICES OFFSTAGE. Let us in! DeFlores! Listen!
DEFLORES. There's time! I hear you. Savor the desire!
>It makes the end more sweet!
VOICES OFFSTAGE. Damn you, DeFlores — let us in!
>We'll knock the door down!
DEFLORES. Come, my friends, you crowd my story.
>>*(to the audience)*
>Now where was I?

(The pounding stops, and the curtain opens. Beatrice enters as DeFlores speaks, looking around cautiously.)

BEATRICE. DeFlores.
DEFLORES. Ah, my lady!
BEATRICE. Your looks — they promise cheerfully.
DEFLORES. Though marred, my face brings good news.
BEATRICE. It's done?
DEFLORES. It is. Alonso — he's no more.
BEATRICE. My joys start at my eyes; our sweetest delights
>Are born weeping. Here sir —
>Here's three thousand golden florins;
>I haven't poorly thought upon your merit.
DEFLORES. *(angry)*
>What's this, a salary? Now you move me!
BEATRICE. How so, DeFlores?

DEFLORES. Do you rank me 'mong the verminous fellows who,
  For gold enough, would spike the orphans' broth?
  Do you see no higher rank for me?
BEATRICE. I don't understand.
DEFLORES. You could have hired a dozen cutthroats
  With that gold, men who would have done the deed
  Indifferently, and my own hands would be
  Unstained by guilt.
BEATRICE. *(visibly confused)*
  I'll double the sum, sir.
DEFLORES. Then you'll double my vexation!
  What's a few gold florins, diamonds, gems?
  What are these when there is more?
BEATRICE. For my fear's sake, then flee with all due speed.
  And if you're still too modest to pronounce a sum,
  A letter does not blush. Send your demand
  And it will follow you, you have my word.
  But now, I beg you, take your flight.
DEFLORES. Then you must fly, as well.
BEATRICE. Me?
DEFLORES. Yes, you.
BEATRICE. What do you mean? Why me?
DEFLORES. Don't the wrathful waters rise on you as me?
BEATRICE. Foul villain!
DEFLORES. Fair murderess!
BEATRICE. Me? I didn't hold the blade!
DEFLORES. One hand held the blade, but another steered the thrust!
  You can't so easily hide your sin from god or man.
  We both did this, and to this act we both account.
BEATRICE. No, no! You did it!
DEFLORES. Our sin is one —
BEATRICE. It's not!
DEFLORES. — Is whole, is shared by us
  For all eternity — a shade upon our damnéd souls.
BEATRICE. No! No!
DEFLORES. No surgeon can untie our tangled up perdition,
  Excise the cancer from the clean. We're one,
  Entwined one crime, enwrapped one love.

(DeFlores puts his hands on Beatrice's arms. She pushes him away.)

BEATRICE. What the — what are you doing? Monster!
  You foul spewing toad! You sharp-toothed ape!

DEFLORES. What makes you act so strange? What venom's
    Spit from these fair lips? These lips that formed
    The pledge that's twinned us one? These lips
    That breathed the fire of our forever?
BEATRICE. You rave like a madman! Mad!
DEFLORES. A man that's mad? Perhaps. Forgive my roughness —
    I've been unloved so long, I am unpracticed.
BEATRICE. Here, take your money and be gone! Go Judas!

(Beatrice throws the money at DeFlores' feet. DeFlores ignores it.)

DEFLORES. Why fight the truth? I thought you understood this
    When we made our pact,
    When I went down on my knee,
    When you solemnly plead,
    When I rose with deadly purpose,
    When you pointed out the lamb,
    And when I stabbed Alonso.
BEATRICE. You'll have us both accused if you don't leave!
DEFLORES. I won't. We'll both be safer if I stay.
    How would it look for me to leave so suddenly?
    Suspicion's eye would surely turn to you.
BEATRICE. Then — ?
DEFLORES. Then I must stay, and we as one must live
    This secret sin, our bond.
BEATRICE. My god! My god!
DEFLORES. The god who will sore punish us for murder,
    Will forgive us for our love, and all
    This ugliness will dim beneath beauty's thrall.
BEATRICE. You are a monster — a monster!
    What have I done? What devil am I sold to?
DEFLORES. A devil who will always love you and protect you.
BEATRICE. A madman! A madman!
DEFLORES. Mad with love, mad with love.

(DeFlores tries to get closer to Beatrice, but she pushes him away again.)

    Don't you see, it's meant to be?
    Nothing can undo this stark finality.
    We're one, we're one!

(DeFlores puts his hand on Beatrice's shoulder and she pushes him away
forcefully.)

Don't worry though, you'll grow accustomed
To my face. With constant use
The roughest features smooth and soften.
And so it is the hand and eye.
You'll love me. Yes, I warrant it.

BEATRICE. And — and if I won't?

DEFLORES. Then I will rest from all love's plagues.
I live in pain: that shooting eye of yours
Will burn my heart to cinders.

BEATRICE. Oh, sir, hear me!

DEFLORES. She who in life and love refuses me, in shameful death
Will sway beside me on the gallow's post;
A pallid end to what our love could be.

BEATRICE. *(weeping)*
What have I done?

DEFLORES. You've cast off the bulky coat of marriage
For the warming heart of love.

BEATRICE. What have I done?

DEFLORES. You've shed facile mask of beauty
For the pink and cheek of passion.

BEATRICE. What have I done?

DEFLORES. Kiss me.

(Beatrice runs offstage. DeFlores turns as if he hears something from the other direction, then picks up the purse of gold. The Duchess enters.)

DUCHESS. What's that, my lord?

DEFLORES. The wages of sin.

DUCHESS. What? Have you seen Alonso anywhere?
He's missing completely.

DEFLORES. Last night he said he planned to go to Valencia
To buy a gift for Beatrice. Something special
I took it for, but he would not say what it was.

DUCHESS. Valencia? The plague is there. Why
On Earth did he go there?

DEFLORES. I warned him, Duchess. But you know his manner.
He's too well bred to catch the plague.

DUCHESS. He's quite the stubborn man. Well if you see him,
Let him know I wish to speak to him.

(The Duchess exits. DeFlores moves to the front/side of the stage while the curtain closes behind him.)

ACT II SCENE 2

DEFLORES. What? My tale does not conform
    To the raw-worn lines of thrice-told tales of love?
    No moon-soaked pleas, no starry looks
    Lost in shimmering pools of each other's eyes?
    No witty flirt? No vows of love undying?
    Not here. Not in my play.
    Just look at me — whose every line
    Distorts — then you should know
    My tale will not tell straight.
    But love you'll see — you will! You will!
    My wooing's just begun and my art
    Is not yet spun.

(The curtain opens. Beatrice sits motionless, covered in blankets and looking out the window.)

    My poor, clipped angel — see her nesting there.
    Ever since Alonso was — well, disappeared,
    She's sat in knots of gloom.
    One would almost think she loved him.

(Diana enters.)

DIANA. Enough o'this foolishness —
    It's time that you get dressed.
BEATRICE. It's time —
DIANA. I'm glad you agree.
BEATRICE. It's time, past time, time that's passed me:
    Too late to cry repent, too early death's
    Enfolding brace.
    My wandering thoughts my torturers become.
    Around each corner, stumbling on a reeking corpse. Ah!
    These unstrapped thoughts, these one-time dreams
    Now stink to make the stars that once led me wince,
    And if I could I'd bury them like unwanted children, deep.
    But like a virulent germ they spread,
    They split and twice the fever I endure.
    My mind's a playground of ash and heat,
    A volcano lip to which I'm pressed beneath a stone

Of error, beneath the monotonous hum
Of hourly death, unyielding way.
The hammer's struck, the midnight rung, my soul
Is gone with Faustus — is dying with fading toll — too late.
If but the blacksmith's glowing blade
Could sear these black rags from my mind,
And burn them from eyes, I'd glad accept
The blank and silent solitude of nothingness.
But I'm to be forever wracked by what
I could have been if —
What I could have done if —
"If," you foulest, fricative fiend of all the words, ah!
If! If! Re-playing scenes again, if!
Again with different outcomes — If!
But life's an ink that cannot be erased, the page torn out —
The author-god does not allow for second drafts.
And we must play out our contracted plot,
Toe our marks and from there call out our lines to empty seats
Until the bored, desultory applause
Should cease to echo in our ears and we are done.
DIANA. I didn't understand a thing you said.
BEATRICE. It was nothing but the wind. Ignore it like the rest.
DIANA. I suppose, but let's get dressed.
BEATRICE. It doesn't matter.
DIANA. It will matter when the Duchess comes.
BEATRICE. Wine spilled cannot be drunk,
    Nor death's cold touch untipped.
DIANA. Look: You've been moping here for days.
    It's time to dress, get up, get out, get moving.
    I didn't even think you liked Signor Alonso,
    But ever since he's disappeared,
    You've sat there staring out that window,
    Leaking sighs and tears.
    I thought that you'd be happy he was gone.
BEATRICE. This country's a narrow place,
    A narrow space between the earth and sky
    In which to live soul-heaving lives.
    I am shrunk, pressed on each side — I once
    Stood tall, stood wide, but neither the world
    Nor I are large.
DIANA. What — ?
BEATRICE. When I was a little girl I used to climb that oak.

DIANA. Ah yes, I do remember. And I remember
>How your father would complain.
BEATRICE. I swept my eyes across the far horizon.
DIANA. *(taking out a dress)*
>And ripped your clothes to shreds, as I recall.
>How about you put this on?
BEATRICE. And now the tree stands without me, taller than before.
>But gone is the curling horizon,
>Gone the distant closing roads
>Unspooling every imaginable corner.
>Gone the dreams of distant lands.
>And now there's just here. Tight. Small.
>Nowhere. Nothing. Now.
DIANA. Now you're just depressing.
>>*(Beatrice sighs deeply)*
>To see the way you act, one would think
>Your suitor's disappearance was your doing.
>I swear.
BEATRICE. What? What?
DIANA. Well, you're acting so foolish.
BEATRICE. What did you say?
DIANA. I said you're acting like a fool!
DEFLORES. *(to the audience)*
>A fool? That's much too harsh!
>As if one's will could will away the granite of despair
>And all would be lights airs, cool winds.
>But the stone is too heavy.
>One needs help with such a crippling weight.
>I will see her.

(DeFlores makes a knocking noise.)

DIANA. Let me see who it is.

(Diana walks to DeFlores. They pantomime a discussion with Diana shaking her head "no" while DeFlores persists.)

BEATRICE. *(sings quietly)*
>Little bee buzz buzz buzz!
>What's it all about?
>Pretty little daffodil
>Pretty little — *(hesitates as if lost or distracted by thought)*

Pretty —
Pretty little daffodil
Wants to take you out.

(Diana returns to Beatrice.)

DIANA. It is Lord DeFlores. He wants to see you.
BEATRICE. *(pulling the blankets up to her neck)*
	No! Him! No, no, no! No!
DIANA. All right. I'll tell him.

(Diana goes to DeFlores again. They pantomime talking with Diana emphatically shaking her head no.)

BEATRICE. Not him! Not him! No, no, no!
	Run — hide — road —
	No! No! Ruin! Ruined!

(Diana returns.)

DIANA. That man is deafly persistent.
	And coming here — it's quite unheard of.
DEFLORES. *(to the audience)*
	True, true. But I'll not be packed away
	Like winter boots.
BEATRICE. Is he gone?
DIANA. I told him you couldn't see him.
BEATRICE. Hmm. Just here. Just now. Just here.
	Everything else? Nothing.
DIANA. I'm sorry?
BEATRICE. Go tell the Duchess I'm not well
	And won't be down to see her.
DIANA. But she —
BEATRICE. "But she" nothing! Go — go!
DIANA. Yes, my lady.

(Diana exits.)

BEATRICE. Enough of her badgering!
	What chance have we against the pounding tide —
	To hold back the leaning ocean?
	It is a folly grinding us to sand.

(DeFlores enters unseen by Beatrice.)

DEFLORES. My lady, I assure you it's not all so bad.
BEATRICE. *(surprised and shrinking from him)*
    What are you doing in here — my chamber!
    Did anyone see you come in?
    What do you want? What — what do you want?
DEFLORES. Come, my lovely Beatrice.
BEATRICE. I'm your lovely nothing. Nothing!
DEFLORES. But you lock me out — and plug your ears to my pleas.
    What am I to do?
BEATRICE. What — what do you want? What do you want?
DEFLORES. Need I want anything but your presence?
    You make it sound so — so unseemly.
BEATRICE. You'd better leave before you're seen.
DEFLORES. Seen? What do I care?
BEATRICE. Well — well — Diana, she sounded suspicious.
DEFLORES. She did?
BEATRICE. She did. And wondered if I had anything to do
    With Alonso's disappearance!
DEFLORES. *(becoming grave)*
    She did?
BEATRICE. She did. I don't know what to do.
    Perhaps you'd better leave —
    Yes! Take the money that I gave you —
    It's more than enough —
    You should go. You must!
DEFLORES. This is bad — quite bad.
BEATRICE. It is! So you had better go.
DEFLORES. Stop it. We've had that conversation
    And I'll never leave you here, this way.
    I'll never leave you vulnerable
    Yes, something must be done.
BEATRICE. Go — go! I can handle it.
DEFLORES. And have that stupid girl hold this
    Over you forever? No. No, you needn't worry.
    I'll take care of it.
BEATRICE. What?
DEFLORES. I will.
BEATRICE. No! You can't do that!
DEFLORES. Yes, I can and will. I must.
    I've had the prick of blood, and now
    I am immune to conscience.

Don't you see? I'll do anything, my dear, to protect you.
As I have breath, no one will hurt you.
BEATRICE. But she might have been joking — or something.
DEFLORES. It's a chance we cannot take.
Don't worry. I'll take care of everything.
BEATRICE. No! No!
DEFLORES. Ah, my broken angel! You're too trusting.
What we've done yields not a drop of milky forgiveness,
And the acrid stream from which we drink
Will suffer no remorse. Not anymore.
I'll take care of everything — and I'll take care of you.
Don't worry!

(DeFlores exits.)

BEATRICE. *(fearfully)*
No! No! No!

(The curtain closes.)

ACT II SCENE 3

(The curtain opens with DeFlores walking back and forth while the Alfredo closely watches him.)

ALFREDO. My lord, your gait is much improved!
    You sweep the floor like a prince! My hammer's wrought
    A most amazing metamorphosis.
DEFLORES. Master Alfredo, I walk on air of late —
    Fate and gravity, my natural oppressors, elevate me,
    And what was grounded by a downwind
    Now leaps into the sky with a breath.
    I'm cured and rise from my crippled bed
    To feel the world light upon my shoulders.
ALFREDO. *(showing him how)*
    Keep your toes pointed in the direction you go.
    Shoulders lower, head up.
          (pause, watching)
    Yes, yes.
DEFLORES. There is an easement to my life, I'm raised
    Upon the surge and carried by the wind.
    My hands — they move with plain facility,
    They move unfiltered toward their goal.
    Yes, all I do is easily done, from thought to deed.
    Like Diana, silly girl, was done —
    Or should I say undone?
    Choked upon the golden chain of her desire.
    Yes, easily done!
ALFREDO. My lord, although it's goodly murder, it's bad theater.
DEFLORES. How so?
ALFREDO. Chin up. She was a shallow puddle of a girl.
DEFLORES. She was dangerous.
ALFREDO. Good. Good. But a well-known fool,
    A one whose word was never heeded.
    Were she to say the sun was shining,
    Most would bid each other goodnight.
    But don't misunderstand me —
    I'm not one to over-price this life,
    But one must dole one's sins proportionately.
    Don't spend them all at once.
DEFLORES. Well, never mind you. The deed is done.

ALFREDO. With each step, wing your body, rise and float —
  You are as light as cloud, as lithe as water —
  Let this Earth take spin beneath your feet.
  Close your eyes and feel it — rising, rising.
  What you can envision, you'll become.
  What you feel, you do. Have purpose and pride.

(DeFlores closes his eyes as he walks.)

DEFLORES. I see ...
  I feel ...

(The Duchess walks in and DeFlores, his eyes closed, walks into her.)

DUCHESS. DeFlores! Be careful where you're going!
  Why in heaven's name do you walk with your eyes closed?
DEFLORES. I'm practicing my posture, lady.
DUCHESS. Yes, well, that is very strange. Practice it
  More carefully.
DEFLORES. *(bows)*
  As you wish, Duchess. How's the Lady Beatrice?
DUCHESS. Not good, not good. I fear Alonso's — situation
  Has unbalanced her. She hides within her room,
  Not getting dressed. Curtains drawn.
  Mumbling to herself.
  I think she cries. It breaks my heart.
DEFLORES. What kind of man would leave like that,
  Without a word. A scoundrel, wouldn't you say?
ALFREDO. His departure was most ruthless.
  No doubt he's caught in the plague in Valencia
  And we shall never see his face again.
DUCHESS. Enough of him — I don't even want to think of that man.
  What Beatrice needs is someone to take his place —
  Another suitor to for her heart.
DEFLORES. A wonderful idea, my lady.
DUCHESS. A new man to win her heart and restore her mind.
DEFLORES. Just what she needs! And may I say,
  Instead of looking far and wide,
  Why not look within the dukedom? Here?
  Where many men of breeding, class and kind
  Would love the lady as she well deserves.
  Someone like myself.

DUCHESS. You? Really, DeFlores, you?
    You're full of such absurd ideas today.
    You. My god, sir. I don't know
    What's got into you of late.
DEFLORES. *(deflated — resuming his old form)*
    I — I —
DUCHESS. I've someone that I've written: Lord Alsemero.
    He's a man that she could proudly stand beside her
    And rule the duchy.
DEFLORES. *(further deflating as he speaks)*
    I'm sure. I'm sure he is.
    No doubt he's tall and handsome,
    Clear of eye and soft of feature,
    With curls cascading from his head
    To grace shoulders broad and straight.
    One deserving all respect, called on and called out.
    Gentle on the eyes and hearts of all.
    A man 'mong men, a leader 'mong nations.
DUCHESS. Why — why, yes — you are most strange today, DeFlores.
DEFLORES. I am, my lady?
DUCHESS. You seem more open with your views
    And I don't know if I like that.
    You used be so reserved and so obedient.
DEFLORES. Yes, the court pup. I am sorry, Lady.
DUCHESS. Hmm. I don't like it when you act this way.
           (aside to DeFlores)
    I fear this actor is a bad influence on you.
           (resuming her normal voice)
    Alsemero will be here in a day or so.
    I trust you'll curb your strangeness for him.
DEFLORES. Most certainly, madam.
DUCHESS. Good.

(The Duchess exits.)

DEFLORES. *(slumping)*
    I am hopeless, Master Alfredo.
ALFREDO. Look at you. You let her slump your shoulders,
    Bend your back, sag your eyes. Be shamed!
    He who but a minute past had thought
    His words would bend the world around his thumb.

What? So you're not a god! So do not be a dog.
Now raise your chin and stuff your spine.
That's better! When life would crush you,
Then — then you must stand all the taller.
That's better. Keep your focus.
DEFLORES. You're right. I lost my focus. Lost my place.

(Beatrice enters, looking about as if trying to stay concealed.)

BEATRICE. (hissing)
　　DeFlores!
DEFLORES. Ah, my lady!
BEATRICE. Shush! Have you seen Diana?

(DeFlores approaches Beatrice.)

DEFLORES. I have, my lady. And you need not worry
BEATRICE. Worry? About what?
DEFLORES. The gangrene has been removed. The body's healthy.
BEATRICE. Removed?
DEFLORES. Yes, removed. Excised. You needn't worry.
BEATRICE. You didn't — Diana —
DEFLORES. You, too? It had to be done.
BEATRICE. No!
DEFLORES. Fear not. No one will know what happened.
BEATRICE. Diana!
DEFLORES. You are safe now. You need not worry.
BEATRICE. Diana!
DEFLORES. Your mother, the Duchess, was just here.
BEATRICE. Mmm.
DEFLORES. She thinks you need a new suitor.
　　I proposed myself.
BEATRICE. You — You?
DEFLORES. But she most rudely shot me down,
　　And poured invectives on my wound.
BEATRICE. She did? Oh my god — she did?
DEFLORES. Am I not a man of breeding? Gentility?
　　Am I not but two steps from the crown?
BEATRICE. You're not going to —
DEFLORES. We'll have to deal with her another time.

(DeFlores leads Beatrice offstage.)

BEATRICE. Not my mother, DeFlores — Not my mother!
DEFLORES. Don't give it any worries. We'll talk later.

(DeFlores guides Beatrice offstage. Alfredo follows. DeFlores stops but motions Alfredo to continue with Beatrice. DeFlores steps forward as the curtain closes behind him.)

ACT II SCENE 4

DEFLORES. The court all swooned on handsome Alsemero —
    The women oohed and men he moved.
    Tall and handsome, charismatic,
    Perfectly complexioned:
    He walked as if walking with the gods,
    And had so rich a baritone that none
    Would dare to question what he said.
    But I — well, I was unimpressed of course.
    For he was everything that fate denied to me.
    But we have our flaws, yes, all of us,
    And some, like mine, glare harsher on the eyes.
    And though we try to smother them inside
    They will not be denied the air.
    And so I watched, I trailed the lauded Alsemero,
    Knowing somewhere he would stumble.
    But oh, how meanly he was felled.

(*The curtain opens to a room in the palace. Several chairs are spread around the room. Alsemero, drinking, enters with Beatrice, Duchess, Alfredo, several lords and servants. DeFlores joins them next to Alfredo.*)

DUCHESS. (*laughing*)
    Lord Alsemero, you show uncommon wit!
    I am so grateful that you visited our home.
ALSEMERO. (*sitting*)
    Thank you for inviting me here, my lady.
    You have a wonderful home and, need I say,
    A beautiful daughter. More wine.

(*A servant fills his cup. He drinks it down.*)

DUCHESS. Dinner soon approaches — do not spoil your meal!
ALSEMERO. Bah! Wine expands the appetite for life!
BEATRICE. (*sitting next to Alsemero*)
    Why don't we walk the gardens — it's so lovely now.
ALSEMERO. Some other time. I want to finish my drink.
BEATRICE. I think you did and filled it up again.

(*Alsemero, in defiant glee, drinks down the cup.*)

ALSEMERO. Then more!

(Alsemero raises his cup and waves it around. The servant fills it again.)

BEATRICE. That drink will never finish if you keep on filling it.
      Let's see the garden and get some air.

(Beatrice stands and takes a few steps to the side.)

ALSEMERO. Ah, I've not the taste for flowers and virgin moons.
      I'll tell you what I'd like. Come sit upon my lap.
      I'd like a kiss!

(The Duchess and the lords titter.)

BEATRICE. My lord?
ALSEMERO. If I'm to choose a wife, it's only natural then
      I know what she will taste like. No?
            (awkward laughter)
BEATRICE. *(walking next to him, laughing)*
      That time will come, my lord, yes, soon enough!
      Tonight we've guests to entertain —
ALSEMERO. I tell you I've no practice at this waiting game,
      And I don't plan to learn it now.
DUCHESS. My lord —
BEATRICE. *(in a friendly, motherly way)*
      I think you've had enough to drink, my lord.
      Give me your cup and let's enjoy the garden.
      The evening air —

(Beatrice reaches to take the cup from Alsemero, but grabs her arm and stands up.)

ALSEMERO. Don't touch my cup! And never tell me
      I've too much to drink!
BEATRICE. *(wincing)*
      My lord, you're hurting me.

(DeFlores starts toward them, but Alfredo stops him, signaling for him to wait a moment.)

DUCHESS. *(laughing nervously — nodding to the servants)*
      Lord Alsemero, I think the dinner's ready —

(The servants quickly exit.)

ALSEMERO. I am your lord and duke, my lady — I do
    As I am pleased. And no one — no one — tells me "no."
BEATRICE. *(angrily)*
    My lord, let me go!
DUCHESS. I'm sure it's ready now — yes, dinner is served!
ALSEMERO. Come here!

(Alsemero pulls Beatrice to him and forcibly kisses her. She angrily slaps him.)

DUCHESS. Yes, we'll all feel better after we eat —
ALSEMERO. *(standing)*
    You little bitch! You need to learn some discipline!

(Alsemero angrily strikes Beatrice several times. She screams and he pushes her to the ground. The Duchess and the other lords look away.)

    I am your lord and you'll obey!

(Alsemero starts to pull up Beatrice by her hair while raising the other hand to strike her. DeFlores runs in and pushes Alsemero away from Beatrice before he can strike her again.)

DEFLORES. Stop it, you coward!
ALSEMERO. *(recovering himself)*
    What? How dare you — you! The bug-faced ape!
DEFLORES. No one strikes the lady — not especially you.
ALSEMERO. Not especially me, eh?
DEFLORES. Not especially a drunken ass.
ALSEMERO. *(laughing)*
    Well! Well!
    I think the Beast has eyes for Beauty! Ha!
    The ugly duck woos the graceful swan.
            (laughing loudly and coarsely, then stopping)
    You — you pig! — you are a monstrosity!
    An insult to my sensibilities!
    You should stand exhibit at a circus freak show
    By the bearded ladies and the half-fish men —
    But never here among nobility.
    I cannot fathom why they give you standing,
    Let you laugh, let you eat, let you talk with them.
    You don't belong. You are a freak!

Who says you've royal blood? It can't be true.
I say your mother was a lousy whore
Who must have screwed an ape to turn out you!
>   *(pulling out his sword)*
But now it's time I do what these rank fools
Have seemed afraid to do, and end this mockery.
Now, my ugly fiend, you'll die an ugly death,
And leave us nothing but an ugly corpse.
DEFLORES. I won't deny my form, my lord,
>   But we have seen true ugliness tonight.
>   Your mouth is bold.
>   Let's see if that coward's blood you slurp
>   Gives courage to your arm to strike a man.
>   We've seen it's bold enough to strike a lady.
DUCHESS. We've got quite a nice dinner ready, please —
ALSEMERO. Those words will be your last!

(Alsemero swings at DeFlores, narrowly missing him, starts stalking him around the room. The others retreat out of the way.)

DUCHESS. DeFlores — stop this!

(Alsemero swings at DeFlores several more times, slightly wounding him.)

DUCHESS. Alsemero! He's unarmed, my lord! Put down the sword
>   And we will make this right.
ALSEMERO. Be quiet, woman, and stay out of my way.
>   *(roughly pushing her away, knocking her down)*
>   I'll make this right myself, and then I'll deal with you!
>   Stand still you grotesque pig.
DEFLORES. Do your best, I'm not afraid.

(Alsemero swings several more times at DeFlores, but misses. DeFlores, though, does not run away. Alfredo takes a sword from one of the lords and throws it to DeFlores.)

ALFREDO. Here my lord.
DEFLORES. *(taking the sword from Alfredo)*
>   My odds improve. Let's see how brave's that wine.
>   I am ready to die. And to kill.

(Alsemero, enraged, lunges at DeFlores, but misses. More people enter to watch. They fight and DeFlores kills Alsemero.)

DEFLORES. *(standing over Alsemero)*
    No one harms Beatrice. It has been learned!
DUCHESS. DeFlores — I'm — I'm — I'm speechless in gratitude!
                (DeFlores helping her to her feet)
    Your bravery was amazing. Thank you!
    Thank you! I thought he'd kill me, too.
BEATRICE. *(recovering)*
    Alsemero — the blood?

(The Duchess goes to Beatrice and kneels down, helping her.)

DUCHESS. He's dead.
BEATRICE. Dead? How dead?
DUCHESS. Lord DeFlores stopped his hand from beating you.
    They fought and Alsemero was killed.
    The man was in a homicidal rage!
    Who would have thought a man so handsome
    Could be so violent?
BEATRICE. DeFlores? Saved me?
DUCHESS. He did, my beauty, he most bravely did!
    He took on Lord Alsemero unarmed.
BEATRICE. *(looking at DeFlores)*
    DeFlores?
DUCHESS. Come now, you need some care.

(The Duchess and others help Beatrice get up and exit. The other lords congratulate DeFlores. The curtain closes.)▯
    ▯

ACT III SCENE 1

(Garden. The curtain opens and DeFlores stands alone, but near the end of his opening speech Beatrice enters. She has bruises on her face, and her hair and makeup are not completely done, as if she'd left in a hurry.)

DEFLORES. After that, my reputation took a healthier sheen,
    And I was laud a hero. Feted and congratulated,
    Even admired by some, though secretly I'm sure.
    No more monster, no more beast
    To beck and burden with their trivialities.
    Yet some still gnawed their lips to praise
    The upstart changeling who had earned
    And equal place among them.
    For now I sat within the inner circle,
    And stood at shoulder on the council.
    I'd finally earned the privilege of my birthright.
    But Beatrice — I didn't see her for a week,
    No one did. She ministered her wounds
    In solitude, and shared her thoughts with no one,
    Until I saw her in the garden.
BEATRICE. My lord, a minute please.
DEFLORES. Ah, my lady. Yes?
BEATRICE. I want — I wanted —

(Beatrice walks towards him.)

DEFLORES. Oh my! Your face still wears the bruises,
    Are you okay?
BEATRICE. These? There but an outward scuff, a dull and trivial blot —
    But we must talk. I want to tell you —
DEFLORES. There — say no more. Rest your voice.
    Were all Apollo's poets to shower me
    In golden verses of praise, they could not
    Match your eyes.
BEATRICE. It must be spoke, and I must say it else
    It's but a dream, and has no life with us.
    The world is full of chutes and pockets
    In which we're turned and harshly twisted 'round,
    And yet the most of men remain unchanged,
    And topple rigid in the face of harder facts.

DEFLORES. We are who we are.
BEATRICE. Yes, but more surprisingly:
     We're not always who we think we are.
     Our face is unfamiliar and our voice unrecognized.
     The world's colored differently than the painting in our eyes.
DEFLORES. Our lives are full of surprises.
BEATRICE. *(laughs lightly)*
     Surprises? Yes, and shocks and quakes and thunder.
     And now my sight has been restored —
     The scales are torn away.
     And I can see — can see how foolishly
     I've trifled with rippling surface shimmers
     Yet ignored the swelling light beneath.
     And not just the light of saints, but also evil's glare.
DEFLORES. We swim among them all.
BEATRICE. We do! We do. And they 'mong us, and they
     Within us. So we paper them with fashionable forms
     And painted etiquette. We paste the front
     Of beauty top this teeming, untamed soil.
     As if that paper-thin veneer will save us
     From the beautiful horrors rising up from underneath.
DEFLORES. What are we do to then?
BEATRICE. We — We are to strip away the masks, take off
     The gloves and thrust our hands into the fertile bowels
     Of the Earth, neither pinching our noses
     Nor letting ecstasy intoxicate us.
DEFLORES. My lady —
BEATRICE. *(cutting him off)*
     DeFlores, my lord, your bravery the other day —
     I want to thank you. Thank you.
     While all the servants, lords and ladies
     Fearfully tugged upon their masks,
     You stepped in, unmade, unarmed and unafraid.
     And I, upon the tip-toe of horror,
     Had the winding drape torn from my eyes
     And light — light edged and hard and hot — burned over me.
     I saw the bare-faced actors all unmade,
     Their hideous looks, their festering eyes.
     And I saw you — for the first time
     Saw you, knew you, understood you.
     Not as the changeling, not as a cripple or a freak,
     But as a man,
     A man unyielding, unafraid of life's unseemly stench.

A man hard pressed by fate, and yet unbowed,
Whose heart is bigger than his mask.
For the first time I realized how fortunate I am.
For the first time I realized the gift I'd been given.

(As Beatrice speaks she approaches DeFlores, then takes his hands.)

And I realized that I love you.

(She kisses him. They embrace.)

DEFLORES. My lady — my love —
A gift is not one person's, but it is shared
Between them. And so is love, so ours.
I am, I always was, and always will be yours.
BEATRICE. And I will always be yours, my beloved.

(They kiss.)

DEFLORES. Now I must go to a council meeting.
BEATRICE. We shall meet tonight.
DEFLORES. We shall. We shall.

(Beatrice exits. DeFlores walks to the side of the stage.)

ACT III SCENE 2

DEFLORES. Ah, what happened next? So much, so much!
    The Duchess, Beatrice's mother, died
    Of a most peculiar fall —
    And I was first to find her.
    "A most peculiar thing this — this peculiar fall,"
    They said, "And DeFlores finding her."
    It was. It was peculiar.
    But they could do no more than think,
    Their hands were tied to their uncertainty.
    And then, yes, more peculiar yet
    Was fate's next roiling twist —
    Unbelievable to some — unthinkable to most —
    Unpalatable to all —
    Being next in line was I made the Duke.

(A pounding sound is heard offstage again, accompanied by shouting.)

VOICES OFFSTAGE. Pig! Open this door, god damn it! DeFlores! You
    monster!
DEFLORES. Again? You spoil my telling!
    And just as it was getting good!
           (laughs)
    There's time — I told you, friends.
    Have some patience, cool your heads and hear me out.
VOICES OFFSTAGE. I hear him talking in there. Who's he with?
    Someone — get an axe! Yes, an axe! Go, go!
DEFLORES. Yes, go find an axe, and let me finish my story!
    Where was I, ah yes, I was named the Duke!

(Servants carry a robe and crown and dress DeFlores as he speaks. Also, they bring two thrones and set them on the stage.)

    Beatrice said she wouldn't have it any other way!
    And so,
    DeFlores, wretch and runt, society's fart,
    Was named Duke of all the land!
    The sun 'round which all planets orbit. And now
    Their eyes could no more look away,
    But must squint upon my majesty.

Shield their eyes, they may
But stare upon my glaring power they must.
But better — oh, there's better! Yes!
As diamonds heaped on gold —
Beatrice and I were married! Yes, made one!
And it was all her idea.
Was ever man made luckier than me?
Was ever man raised higher, faster?

SERVANT. My lord, the chamberlain asks
If he should pack our things for travel.

DEFLORES. Where are we going?

SERVANT. I don't know.

DEFLORES. You don't know. But he wants to go.

SERVANT. The plague, your majesty.

DEFLORES. A plague upon the Chamberlain!

SERVANT. No, your majesty, the chamberlain
Thought you'd want to leave the plague.
It's coming nearer.

DEFLORES. The plague?

SERVANT. Yes, my lord. The city's in a panic.

DEFLORES. A panic 'bout the plague.

SERVANT. Yes, my lord. It's been reported just outside the city.

DEFLORES. Well then. Tell the chamberlain we will not cower,
Nor will we run from the plague.
We live a charméd life, and whether age
Or plague should kill us, we will not quail
Before our monstrous fate.
Tell him to be at peace with himself,
And the plague cannot hurt him.
It infects the ugliness within the soul,
And mostly the beautiful are caught.
Be gone.

SERVANT
Yes, my lord.

(The servant exits as Beatrice and Alfredo enter. Beatrice's fac is healed, but her hair and makeup are more eccentric than before.)

BEATRICE. Duke, come here and learn our newest game,
They call it mirrors.

DEFLORES. It sounds delightful.

BEATRICE. One person leads, the other mirrors,
And the goal's to be as one.

DEFLORES. Show me! Show me!

(*DeFlores sits on his throne. Beatrice and Alfredo start playing mirror.*)

ALFREDO. It teaches observation and concentration.
BEATRICE. Can you tell who's now the leader?
DEFLORES. I can't! That's very good!

(*Several Lords enter.*)

     Why I can't tell at all, you're both so good!
RAFAEL. Ahem. Excuse us, your Excellency.
DEFLORES. One moment, my lord.
     You'll teach me this mirror game, Alfredo?
ALFREDO. Myself or the Duchess — she's mastered it completely.
DEFLORES. Very good! And now my lords. Come in, come in.
     We're playing. It's important to grow and learn.

(*Beatrice stands next to DeFlores and looks grimly on the lords.*)

LORD 2. Yes, yes, we see. It's very good.
     How do you do, Duchess?
BEATRICE. Better, my Lord, better.
LORD 2. Better? Have you been ill? You don't look yourself.
BEATRICE. Whose face do I borrow, pray?
LORD 2. I merely thought you looked — you looked — uh — pale.
BEATRICE. I suggest you cease from judging by our looks,
     You're awful at it.
     You're like a child with a sextant, hopelessly lost.
     Our faces are but doors to shield our motives
     And blunt the edged ambition of our sins.
     I am a mask that shouts its name, and now
     I see through masks. I see we're more than we will seem
     And less than we will look and everything we're not.
     So looks make warping yardsticks of our height.
LORD 2. Well, uh, I simply meant —
BEATRICE. Why? Don't you like my mask? Still,
     You cannot see it, can you? Ha!
     Perhaps you'd have me in a different mask?
     A mask more pleasing, deferential?
     Perhaps you'd have me someone else?
LORD 2. No — I — I —

BEATRICE. Look — look harder! Peel away the papier-mache!
    Dig in the flesh! It's still not there?
    The beauty's hid, if it's there at all.
    But what is hid will be exposed.
    No oil or powder will shield the nakedness,
    Nor clangor mute its scream, nor herb
    Benumb its pain.
    But lord, I'll share with you a secret:
    The world's a dangerous place where beauty flits
    Before the eye, but ugliness turns on every lip.

LORD 2. I —

RAFAEL. I heard the ladies practice needlepoint together
    In the parlor and I know they miss you.
    Perhaps you'd like to join them, Duchess?
    We have important topics to discuss now
    With the duke.

BEATRICE. The ladies? They're well to stick to quilting.
    They've let you make them useless.
    And now what use are they except to wear
    The greenest fashions and competing jewelry.
    What use have I for these poor sleeping souls?

RAFAEL. I don't understand, my lady.

BEATRICE. What do you know of women's thoughts?
    Not much, I suspect. They're just like you
    Though you are unfamiliar to your mind.

RAFAEL. I'm sure the ladies are quite content, my Duchess.

BEATRICE. Content? We're all content with our lives,
    From leper to lord. But what are they worth?
    Life is thrown away quite easily, our own and others.
    Ask Alonso! Unloved, unwanted, unmissed,
    But content.

RAFAEL. Alonso?

BEATRICE. You are hopeless dunces. Why do I bother
    Trying to teach you anything!
    What do you say, Master Alfredo?

ALFREDO. I most heartily agree, your highness.
    Teaching them is hopeless.

LORD 2. I'm not sure what you're asking of us.
    If you'd excuse us while we talk our business —

DEFLORES. Spare us your stuttering ignorance, my lords.
    The duchess and I share everything.
    D'you find that strange?
    She is as wise as beautiful, and smarter than any man here.

So no more of this. What you speak to the Duke
You speak to the Duchess. Understand?
Now tell us what occasion brings you here. You've been a stranger
To our eye. Give voice to your petition.

RAFAEL. Very well my lord; it is about the taking of my land
Near Santa Faz. I come to humbly beg for its return.

DEFLORES. And why should I not take it? It's a lovely tract
And I will build a castle on it to defend the city access.

RAFAEL. My lord: Such seizure's without precedent.

DEFLORES. Precedent? What's that?

RAFAEL. Why, in a thousand years no Duke has taken land
From a Lord in such a way.
It's not been done before.

BEATRICE. This duke's rule is unprecedented, fool.
Without peer, without parent,
He's risen to the pinnacle of power
Heir to nothing but uneven fortune.

RAFAEL. But tradition —

BEATRICE. Tradition is a sop for weak-kneed fools
And a blanket for wizened old men.
Do we not hold power, is not our rule
Absolute?

RAFAEL. My lord and lady, it is. Your power's absolute.

DEFLORES. But — ?

RAFAEL. But it is graciousness and generosity
That makes absolute power absolute good.

DEFLORES. My esteemed lord,
My path has been most rocky, you'll agree.
And on that rumbled, rutted journey
I've used up all my generosity and graciousness.
I used it up when you, sir,
Would lock me out of doors overnight as a jest —
When you, my lord Mendoza, when you
Would call me goat and try to ride me like a pig!

RAFAEL. My lord, to bring up childish things —
We're sorry for our acts, but we were children.

DEFLORES. Remember how I grunted like a pig for you?
I remember it quite well.
Why don't you grunt like a pig for me?

RAFAEL. Pardon me?

DEFLORES. You will oink like a pig.

RAFAEL. What, my lord?

DEFLORES. You heard me quite well.
>   Is my elocution not clear, Alfredo?
ALFREDO. Quite clear, my lord.
DEFLORES. And you understood me, no?
ALFREDO. Perfectly, my lord. Your words are eloquent.
BEATRICE. Then like a pig you'll grunt, my lord. Dare you defy
>   My husband? My love? Our Duke? This man
>   Is ten times the man of any one of you!
DEFLORES. You are too kind, my love.
BEATRICE. You'll no more warp us with tradition
>   Into unnatural shapes not of our own making.
DEFLORES. So let me hear you grunt like pigs, eh?
>   You'll lead us lord? Can't you do that?
>   *(DeFlores starts grunting like a pig)*
>   Like this. Ah? Like this?

(Beatrice joins him. DeFlores continues grunting while the Count smiles nervously. DeFlores stops suddenly.)

>   You think this is funny, eh?
>   A joke? A laugh? Are we your jesters?
RAFAEL. My lord —
BEATRICE. Do we entertain you, lord?
DEFLORES. *(shouting)*
>   It's not funny! I'm not here for your amusement!
>   I'm the Duke! And she's the Duchess!
>   And now it us who will be amused
>   And you will grunt like a pig! A pig! A pig! A pig!
RAFAEL. B-but — my lord — please —
DEFLORES. Take this man away! *(no one moves)*
>   I said take this man away and have the jailer
>   Twist his spine until he learns to grunt like a pig!
>   *(the guards start taking the count away)*
>   I want him squealing like a pig! Squealing, I say!
>   Listen all! I am the Duke,
>   Your lord and master. Grow accustomed
>   To the sound of it and bear it meekly.
>   I will not be played the fool nor be tagged with insults!
>   Now be gone! Be gone! Get out!
LORD 3. Your excellency!
DEFLORES. Do you have a complaint, too?
LORD 3. No, my Duke.
BEATRICE. Then leave our sight. You sicken us.

ALFREDO. *(herding the men out)*
  My lords, my lords, this way.
BEATRICE. *(as they are leaving)*
  My lords, we are your betters — in character
  And in breeding. Do not trust your eyes,
  They lie to you! Power needs no beauty
  To break the proudest beam.
ALFREDO. *(returning)*
  My lord, some advice if you will.
DEFLORES. I will.
ALFREDO. Sometimes a sweet deed or word
  Will loosen stone. But a sharp tongue
  May cut off one's own head.
DEFLORES. You think so, eh?
ALFREDO. I do, my lord.
DEFLORES. You think that I should be more — more restrained?
ALFREDO. Restrained is a fine word. The performance
  To the scene, if you will.
DEFLORES. I see.
  I see. Well — it's duly noted. Duly noted.
  Leave us.

(Alfredo bows and exits.)

BEATRICE. We've lost the actor, I fear.
  His love grows a distant, unmoored look.
DEFLORES. I've noticed a cooling of his fire.
BEATRICE. It's just as well. His act grows stale.
  His pupils outdo the teacher.
DEFLORES. You are wise! We'll keep our eye on him.
  But now, my light, my love — why don't we walk the garden
  And we shall walk in beauty?
BEATRICE. I love the garden, my brave lord.
  I'll meet you there.
DEFLORES. Wonderful.
        (to the audience)
  Looking back, I guess I was too harsh.
  Perhaps I wielded too heavy a mace,
  Went too quick to the lash, too harsh with the sentence.
  Yet, I must be forgiven.
  The firstling of power went to my head
  And I was floating with evanescent bubbles.
  It was intoxicating ecstasy.

Anyone who tells you different is a liar.
Who has ever been so low, and risen so high?
Who else has scraped the ocean floor then leapt
The coldest peak — it's bound to make one dizzy.
Perhaps a gentler word would — ah,
Those words were foreign to my ears.
But as I was to find out later,
My rise did raise much talk of me, and not the good.
Although unknown it was not unsuspected.

(DeFlores walks to the side of the stage. The curtain closes.)

ACT III SCENE 3

(The curtain opens revealing an old woman crouching along a wall. DeFlores enters and stands along the wall, unseen by the woman or the others that enter.)

DEFLORES. *(to the audience)*
    Poor woman! The time has not been kind.
    Ah, but here come the faces that I know.

(Enter two lords talking quietly among themselves, occasionally looking around. They notice the old woman.)

LORD 1. Who's this? You there — old woman!
    Why cower here within the hall?
    What brings you to the castle?
WOMAN. Death.
LORD 2. *(smiling oddly at the other lord)*
    What's that?
WOMAN. The end of time, return to dust, the dreamless sleep.
    If you don't know of death, you will — and soon.
LORD 2. D'you have a book of spells that see the future?
WOMAN. One needs only eyes. Though mine are weak, they see.
    It's here. Its black and ravened fangs are locked
    Upon the torso of the country —
    Men and women, babies, children, all. Insatiable.
    It is hunger. And it's here. Outside the door.
    The monster's here.
LORD 1. You mean the plague.
WOMAN. I mean death. Unmerciful fate. Unwaking sleep.
    Our land is cursed. The Devil's stretched is hand,
    And on our shoulder laid his rotting finger.
    Now the flesh is dead and molders on our bones.
LORD 2. Yes, yes.
WOMAN. We are reviled in gods' great eye, repulsive
    And disfigured. Our ugliness a mote upon his sight.
    And if the itch be rubbed, we're all destroyed.
LORD 1. Hmm. Yes.
WOMAN. This plague attacks us from the outside,
    But the real disease ferments within.
DEFLORES. She speaks wisely. True, yes, very true.
    Listen to her lords.

LORD 1. *(to the other lord)*
     It's getting bad — quite bad.
LORD 2. It seemed to come just days before Alonso's disappearance.
WOMAN. We must destroy the graven images
     Within us, and repent our heart's false idols;
     Yes, kill the ugliness within our midst
     And the loathsomeness before our eyes
     Unless it suffocate the beauty in our souls.
     But I am old, my bones are wearied. And death's
     An old acquaintance that I'll soon embrace.
     I've lost my husband and my children all,
     And I am too exhausted to pretend it otherwise.
     But you — will you let the vile disease live on?
     And let it eat you from within?
     Cut it off! Cut it out! Pull it out by the roots
     And smother it. Or you will die.
     Will die. You'll die!
LORD 1. Enough there, woman. That's enough!
     We won't be threatened. Move along.
     If you must die, then die another place.
     Not here.
WOMAN. *(as she leaves)*
     Though I may leave, the seed will spread,
     Disease will grow, the ugliness will be fed.

(The woman exits.)

LORD 2. Ah, her words! She says strange truths
     That pour a scalding shame.
     My heart dissolves to tears for our sickly nation!
     Burdened by a double plague, a double ugliness —
     This rank disease, and this worse DeFlores.
     The one, we're helpless without god to stop,
     The other, though, we have our hope in our hands.
LORD 1. Yes. How much longer will we absorb the ox's lash?
     How much longer eat his threat and curse
     And meekly smile upon the bounty? How much longer
     Bow to evil? Smile on sin?
     We are the shadows of our former selves!
LORD 2. DeFlores must die! And soon.
     Just look at us!
     Yes, what's become of us? What accident has marred us?

Why, I don't recognize myself within the mirror!
We're unfamiliar to each other!
LORD 1. We're not ourselves — made monstrous by the monster!
LORD 2. Then we must be ourselves, and be those men
We see within our inner mirror, yes, resume those noble looks
That are a stranger to ourselves.
LORD 1. Now's the time to act. Confusion reigns —
DeFlores stands with half his guard.
LORD 2. He has no allies, not a friend, not one
Who'd 'change his life for him — except the Duchess.
LORD 1. And what of her? We can't just kill her, too.
She's so belovéd by the people
That her death would cause a riot.
And yet she's too devoted to the Duke
To quietly let him fall. What can we do?
LORD 2. She must be
Removed. For her own good,
We'll have her put away, yes, some place far.
The people haven't seen what we have seen.
She's clearly lost her mind.
LORD 1. And wears that queer, outrageous face.
LORD 2. She's mated with the beast — what else would you expect?
He has diseased her mind and now his sin,
It seethes within her blood.
DEFLORES. *(to the audience)*
Now, really, that's too much! Don't you think?
They can slander me, but now to say
Such things of Beatrice — that's too much!
LORD1. Who could believe it? Turned away for him. Him!
LORD 2. He must have cast a spell on her —
Played the darker arts, or bought a potion.
DEFLORES. No magic spell but love without condition.
LORD 2. Wait — someone comes! Ah, it's just the actor.
LORD 1. Yes. I want to talk to him.

(Alfredo enters and the Lords grab him, one holding a knife to his throat.)

Look here, you boot-licking dog! We know
You're nothing but a charlatan, a mountebank.
So watch your step. It's quite enough to take
Abuse from that beast DeFlores and the Duchess,
But from you, we won't abide it!
LORD 2. What was the Duchess saying about Alonso?

ALFREDO. My lord, I assure you I know nothing.
LORD 2. Ha! Your lying's worse than your performing!
  Who'd have thought it possible? Well, never mind.
  You'd better come to peace with Jesus, clown.
  You and your friend are going to see the curtain close,
  And you may get the first bad notice.
ALFREDO. My lords, the Duke, I'm sure, is quite insane.
  He holds us in thrall of his stark madness,
  And were I to find my own escape, I'd be out.
  But unlike you I am a prisoner of his love
  And not a convict of his hate.
DEFLORES. *(to the audience)*
  And this is how my love's repaid?
  And from an actor, nonetheless! Ha!
LORD 2. *(laughing and pushing Alfredo away)*
  The rube's pathetic even in allegiance.
  He has no center. Let him go.
  Why swat at rats where lions crouch?
LORD 1. Stay clear of us, you clown. Stay clear.
  And share no word of this with anyone — or else.
  Now go — get out! Go!

(Alfredo exits.)

  Come, we'll call a council of the other lords.
  Like doctors, we must cut away the tumor
  Festering on the nation's head, or else
  We lose the patient. And ourselves.

(The Lords exit.)

ACT III SCENE 4

(*A servant enters and hands DeFlores book, while another brings in a throne. DeFlores moves to the center of the stage.*)

DEFLORES. Ah, here I am, yes —
                (*reading from a book*)
    "Would I had been my mistress gentle prey,
    Since some fair one I should of force obey.
    Beauty gives heart, Corinna's looks excel,
    Aye me why is it known to her so well?

(*As DeFlores reads, Beatrice enters and sits. Alfredo enters and paces as if deep in thought.*)

    But by her glass disdainful pride she learns,
    Nor she herself but first trimmed up discerns.
    Not though thy face in all things make thee reign,
    (O face most cunning mine eyes to detain) —"
    A most strange poem.
BEATRICE. It seems Corinna knows her mirror better than her mind.
ALFREDO. (*continuing to pace, not looking up*)
    Yes, keep reading. Don't hit the meter quite so hard,
    Let the music come out on its own.
    And focus on pronunciation.
    Use your entire mouth. Speak from your diaphragm.
DEFLORES. (*flips to another page*)
    "Such chance let me have: I would bravely run
    On swift steeds mounted till the race were done.
    Now would I slack the reins, now lash their hide,
    With wheels bent inward now the ring-turn ride.
    In running if I see thee, I shall stay,
    And from my hands the reins will slip away.
    I that ere-while was fierce, now humbly sue,
    Least with worse kisses she should me endue.
    She laughed, and kissed so sweetly as might make
    Wrath-kindled Jove away his thunder shake."

(*While DeFlores reads, Alfredo pulls a sword on DeFlores and has him seemingly cornered.*)

DEFLORES. What's this? Our fencing lesson is tomorrow.
ALFREDO. Yes it is, my lord. But tomorrow you'll not see.
  For it is with much solemn thought, my lord,
  That I, Master Alfredo Tristan Velazquez,
  Have decided that I must kill you. Yes,
  I must bring this troubled act to a close,
  For it is clear, my lord, that you have gone quite mad,
  Quite mad, along with your lovely wife.
  So mad, indeed, that I am thrust in danger's eye myself.
  If I kill you, I figure that the counts won't bother
  Chasing me down. They want your corpse
  More than my death.
DEFLORES. Your sense of self-preservation is always finely tuned.
ALFREDO. It is, my Lord, one of my gifts. But I shall miss you.
    (to Beatrice)
  My lady, stand back. You are but a woman
  And I mean you no harm. Your husband's death
  Suffices me.
DEFLORES. It will? Then play your part, and I will mine!
ALFREDO. I will, and I will kill you like Hector did
  Brave Patroclus on Ilium's plain —
  Boldly and decisively as one killing a god!
  Goodnight sir!

(DeFlores cleverly escapes from Alfredo's initial thrust. Beatrice pulls a long knife and stabs Alfredo in the back.)

BEATRICE. You, Master Alfredo, make the same mistake as the rest,
  I am surprised!
ALFREDO. *(with a smile)*
  A plot twist, ah —
DEFLORES. Thank you, my love!

(He takes Beatrice's hand and kisses it, then turns to Alfredo.)

  You shouldn't have tried to kill me like a god,
  But like a dog — we're all but dogs.
ALFREDO. Ah, true, true! I overplayed the scene, eh?
  That will teach me.
  My Lady — I apologize! I see how blind I was.
  But how shall this be played?
  With vengeance-spitting rage? With timorous quaking?
  No — with sad farewell.

(to the audience)
Sad world, I sadly leave you.
Turned upside down upon ourselves
We twist upon our leash of hapless sorrow.
But I will miss the lights, the makeup and the roles
From kings to beggars — Great roles all!
In them we're all a star to blaze the shuttered stage.
Ah! Goodbye my troupe,
Goodbye my crew, goodbye my audience.
I fear you die with me! The curtain falls!
To darkness!

(He dies. DeFlores and Beatrice clap politely.)

DEFLORES. Well done, my friend.
BEATRICE. The practice is rewarded.

(A servant enters.)

SERVANT. What's that, my lord?
DEFLORES. That? It's but a prop.
                    (Beatrice laughs)
SERVANT. *(examining the body)*
        No, it's a man — and he is dead.
BEATRICE. I say it isn't a man.
SERVANT. No, my Lady, it is a man. I'm sure of it. Look!
BEATRICE. It *was* a man, you fool. Can't you tell the difference?
SERVANT. Should I call a priest?
DEFLORES. You should call the stage manager, he's too late for a priest.
SERVANT. I don't understand, my lord.
DEFLORES. Fret not — the script is lost on you.
        Here's what I'd have you do:
        Take his corpse and have it cut to little pieces
        And when you're done, feed him to the dogs.
SERVANT. How can that be done?
DEFLORES. I'd feed him to the Lords, but they're being
        Quite recalcitrant. Now, do as I say.
SERVANT. Certainly not, sir!
DEFLORES. *(angrily grabbing the servant by the shirt)*
        What? You'll deny my final tribute to my friend?
SERVANT. You can't do that!

DEFLORES. *(slapping the servant)*
    Don't tell me what I can do, you cur.
    Do what I say or I'll have you eat him yourself!
SERVANT. Yes, my lord.
                (starts to drag the Alfredo offstage, but stops)
    My lord, I almost forgot: I came to tell you the lords
    Are gathering outside the royal residence.
    I wasn't aware of a meeting.
DEFLORES. Thank you, boy. Take good care of our friend.

(The servant drags Alfredo offstage.)

    Then it's begun.
BEATRICE. It has. I'll make sure Alfredo's wishes are fulfilled.
DEFLORES. Thank you, dear.

(Beatrice kisses DeFlores and follows the servant offstage.)

           (to the audience)
    The end is near. The sands soon rest.
    Yes, that would be the last sweet kiss we would enjoy.
    I think she knew it also. All things pass,
    All judgments final.

(DeFlores picks up Alfredo's sword and looks at it.)

ACT III SCENE 5

(Several lords enter cautiously with their swords drawn.)

LORD 1. *(quietly)*
> Here he is. Lord Vallejo,
> Tell the rest: The monster's found.

(One man exits. The others walk toward DeFlores.)

> Duke, surrender your sword.
> We're here to snatch the crown from your brute brow
> And press it on a head more humankind.

DEFLORES. *(laughs)*
> A face more human, though less kind, I'll bet!
> Don't let the human mask conceal the beast
> You'll find within. My mask is more transparent,
> That's all. I wear my secrets on my face.

LORD 1. Lord —

DEFLORES. *(suddenly angry)*
> Don't nettle me, my lord! No, not today.
> I've blood washed hands, still warm with hate.

LORD 2. We do not jest, DeFlores.

DEFLORES. What's this? "DeFlores?" — no "Duke"?
> What of my noble blood, god's will?
> What of the sun-bright majesty that through me flows
> And demands obedience?

LORD 1. The sun has set upon your reign.

DEFLORES. They say my looks improve at night.

LORD 1. Come, no more play.
> We're taking back the crown from one
> Who never should have filled it.
> But for your lies and murder
> You would not be wearing it.
> Now let us have it, lord.

DEFLORES. Upon what grounds? Upon what murder?

LORD 1. The Duchess.

LORD 2. And on the grounds you are an unnatural beast,
> Deformed in the eyes of god and law and man.
> Yes, all you touch is torturously disfigured

And fouled in form and soul.
Just look at Lady Beatrice —
You've molded her a monster!
DEFLORES. Oh, you blind, blind fool!
You understand so little, see much less.
Why, she now shines more radiantly than ever
Because she is her mirror, her mirror her.
The face you'd graft on her is gone — it never was!
And now the mask's undone, discarded.
And now — now you see her:
Untranslated and inviolate, unblemished and unspoiled,
Pure in nature and in feature, and this —
This you call a monster.
Oh, I pity you your blighted eyes —
But I will still that slanderous tongue of yours.
LORD 2. Threat on, you foaming cur.
We've come to cure what ails the state
By cutting off that queer growth upon its head,
And wresting that gold crown from your diseased hands.
DEFLORES. These hands are the hands of a man-made beast,
Formed by the scorns and prejudice of men.
For what? That I looked different.
That my face and figure don't conform
To your idea of man and lord and duke and angel?
Oh, vain and ignorant men! Unwrap your eyes!
This crown was a gift of god,
A vengeance on your sins, and a wrath
Upon this purblind nation.
Look from yourselves and feel the weight of hell
Upon your necks!
LORD 1. My lord, my lord — by force or free you'll give the crown —
From your hand or head it will be plucked.
The castle lays beneath our sword;
Your followers — few and futile —
Are bound by chain or bound toward hell.
The crown is ours but for its weight upon our hands.
One question waits your answer:
Will you give it straight and painless,
Or will you make it otherwise?

DEFLORES. I see, my lord. A choice. A choice!
>As one star-bent, I've never known unblemished paths.
>So full of curves and twists I am
>The straight and quick are quite impossible.
>In other words: My lady and I do object.

(DeFlores lunges at them and they fight. He kills Lord 2, sorely wounds Lord 1. They flee.)

>Be gone, you pretty ones! Be gone! I hope
>Those wounds improve your looks!
>>*(to Lord 2's body)*
>And you, who dares call beauty beast —
>Your lips will never breathe a curse on love again.
>I hope the worms enjoy your handsome features.
>And now to Beatrice —

(A servant rushes in.)

SERVANT. Duke! There's a coup!
DEFLORES. *(pointing to the body)*
>This I know, Tiresias.
SERVANT. *(seeing the bodies)*
>But — but —
DEFLORES. But what, hangdog? Men with knives for teeth
>And swords for hands are coming for me.
>I've not much time.
SERVANT. The Duchess is dead.
DEFLORES. Is dead?
SERVANT. She is, my lord. Like you,
>The rebels cornered her.
>They promised to spare her life for yours,
>To which she answered with a sword,
>And struck down Lord Vazquez and wounded Lord Palmero.
DEFLORES. Ha! Good for her!
SERVANT. But trapped her inside her room
>She said she'd rather die than be their prisoner
>And so she leapt out from her window to her death.
DEFLORES. Dead? Ah? She died — she died then as she lived,
>Well.
>Yes, the endmost wick
>Must in time expire and the midnight win.
>To flay against the night is wasted sweat.

Thus the gentle hands to hard winds bend,
And then it's over, sleep. Forever.
And all this, all the sweep and compass,
The rise and rapture of success, of love,
It was all for you. For you, my love. For you.
To quake for more would make all less.

VOICES OFFSTAGE. He's here — up here.

SERVANT. My lord —

DEFLORES. Go, fool. It's over. Yes, it's over.
And now they come for me.

VOICES OFFSTAGE. *(pounding on the door)*
DeFlores — Are you in there? We just want the crown —

DEFLORES. *(to the servant)*
Did you bolt the door? Good.
Let them work for it. Ha ha!
Now leave the back way and lock that door.
Our friends will learn that expectation's more than half the prize!

SERVANT. As you wish.

(The servant exits.)

VOICES OFFSTAGE. It won't open. It's locked! Let me try. Open up in
there! Get the axe.

DEFLORES. *(to the audience)*
And so, my friends, my tale is told.
And now the closing curtain nears.
But who am I to mourn?
To rub the dust into my hair and tear my clothes
In histrionic sorrow and regret?
Born a beast, born bent and gnarled,
Born a freak of form — the other —
I have vaulted from the swampy mire to the sky-edge of power!
I've seen my grimace shake the knees of noble men.
And I have felt the air of love's wing upon my face,
The breath of loving lift, the rise
Of warmth and blood. Ah love! Sweet love!
How many men upon their bed of death
Can say the same as me?

VOICES OFFSTAGE. *(the pounding on the door gets louder)*
DeFlores! DeFlores!

DEFLORES. My friends! My lovers!
    Here I am! For you!
VOICES OFFSTAGE. What the — he's gone mad! Don't stop — knock it
    down! Let's go. Come on! Yes!

(Several, repeated loud crashes on the door.)

    DeFlores! Open up the door! DeFlores! We won't hurt you — open
    up the door!
DEFLORES. *(to the audience)*
    Do you hear how I'm wanted?
VOICES OFFSTAGE. *(frustrated)*
    Damn this door! DeFlores — Open the door! Open the door!
DEFLORES. *(looking at his sword)*
    In Beatrice's death I find my map. Be you
    The ploughshare that will open up the Earth for me.
               (throws down his sword)
VOICES OFFSTAGE. DeFlores! Open the door or we'll kill you! I know
    he can hear us. Look — it's starting to give!
DEFLORES. I, who none would touch or see, now fires their passion!

(The pounding is louder and steadier.)

    Ah, love. To want, to need, to have.
    To hold and look into the eye.

(A loud crash and men storm on the stage with swords drawn — they see the body of Lord 2 and pause a second. Then they start to encircle DeFlores.)

    Before, I was the runt, the whelp, today
    I am the mighty lion that you hunt!
    Look at me and tell me what you see! Am I not beautiful?
    The object of your desire? Look at me!
    Don't you want me? Yes! Yes!
    How I enjoy your eyes feeling me over!
    And soon your hands! Into my blood!
    Gorge yourselves upon my blood, my friends —
    Enjoy the zest you feel! I feel it too!
    The unalterable act, the unforgiving blow,

The warmth and zeal of living!
Taste the blood — you want it! Taste it!
It's good — it's good. Yes, life is good!
I am your desire — have at me!

(They all lunge toward DeFlores and he is blocked from view as he collapses.)

Feel it! Feel it. Ugh! It's — good! It's good! Good!

(The lords stand back revealing DeFlores' lifeless, bloody body. The curtain closes.)

FINIS

THREE SHORT PLAYS PHILOSOPHICAL:
The Song of Miriam
The Cave at Hope's End
A Miracle Too Many

THE SONG OF MIRIAM

With a Prologue/Epilogue Puppet Show:
The Story of Golad and Badel

And the anger of the Lord was kindled against them; and He departed. And the cloud departed from off the tabernacle; and, behold, Miriam became leprous, white as snow: and Aaron looked upon Miriam, and, behold, she was leprous. (Numbers 12:9-10)

CHARACTERS

Golad and Badel
Golad — male, generic Old Testament figure
Badel — male, generic Old Testament figure
God — female, Silicon Valley techie geek/entrepreneur

The Song of Miriam
Miriam — middle aged or older, sister to Moses, singer and prophetess
Chorus of Women Elders — at least four middle aged or older women, the Chorus leader (Chorus 1) does most the speaking
Aaron — younger brother of Miriam and Moses
Miero — young Ethiopian/Cushite wife of Moses
Messenger — Male or female wearing a distinguishing yellow sash or belt
Guard — middle aged or older man

SCENE LOCATIONS

Golad and Badel
A hilltop

The Song of Miriam
A cave in the desert near Hazeroth where the Hebrew people have set up tents.

TIME PERIOD

1300 BC

THE STORY OF GOLAD AND BADEL:
PART ONE

(The stage is dark except for a spotlight on the puppet theater center stage. The curtain of the puppet theater opens showing a backdrop of a pleasant summer day with a tree, sun and several billowing white clouds. The sound of chirping birds is heard. As Golad and Badel are introduced, they appear.)

NARRATOR. The story of Golad and Badel, Part One. Once upon a time in the land of the south, high in the hills of Edom near the nation of Uz, there lived two upright, righteous and right-thinking men, Golad the Just and Badel the True. Of all men, Golad and Badel were the most pious, and they deplored the multitudinous wicked things of the world — like universal health care. Every day they went to the high holy places and there implored almighty God to help them straighten this hopelessly crooked world.

BADEL. Oh lord! Only you can cure us of this evil malaise infecting us! Only god omnipotent can right what's wrong, show us the path to virtue and save us from the temptations of government postal service.

GOLAD. Oh lord, hear us!

BADEL. Oh hear us, righter of wrongs, wronger of wrongers, wringer of swingers and stoner of stoners!

GOLAD. Remove from your ancient ears, oh lord, the wiry hair that blocks our pleading voices! Rub from your eyes the sleepy sands that blind you to our misery!

BADEL. Dear lord on high, the sodomites rise up around us and force us to make cakes for them, and the unclean invade our nation and multiply! Find us a way to stop them!

GOLAD. But please keep them doing our interior decorating and mowing our lawns, oh mighty one!

(The clouds part in the background and God appears. She hears Golad and Badel, but doesn't see them, and they don't see her right away.)

BADEL. Yes! Give us your help, my lord! Our tongues grow weak with making gloomy predictions that never come true — our voices grow hoarse with denunciations!

GOLAD. Yes, omnipotent one, lend us your lightning that we may strike down many evil doers and their motor voter laws! Give us your power to show them what's what!

GOD. *(looking around unsure)* Uh, did somebody say something? Is there someone out here?

BADEL. It is god! *(falling prostate to the ground)* It's god him — herself?

GOLAD. You heard our prayers, oh mighty lor — *(surprised to see god is a woman)*

GOD. What the — who are you? What are you doing here?

GOLAD. Oh mighty one, we are your servants!

GOD. Stand up! I can't hear a thing you're saying when you lay on the ground like that.

GOLAD. Oh, yes, great one. We will stand.

(Golad and Badel turn away and lower their gaze.)

GOD. Now what are you doing?

BADEL. Averting our eyes, oh powerful one.

GOD. Don't do that. It's weird.

BADEL. Whatever you wish my — lord.

GOLAD. Oh great one, we are confused. All our teachings did not prepare us for such … femaleness. Shall we call you lord? Or lady?

GOD. Hmm. I like the sound of "lord."

BADEL. Then as you wish, our lord.

GOD. Who are you?

GOLAD. We are your creations, my lord. From the moist clay you breathed life into us. I am Golad, and this is Badel.

GOD. Out here, in this desolate part of the universe? Well, I guess that's just a serendipitous result of the algorithm. How long have you been here?

BADEL. Your people have lived here thousands of years, my lord. Many generations of men have come and gone, risen from the earth and returned to the dust.

GOD. Huh, I never knew. I came out this way looking for a place to dump some toxic waste. I never imagined this third-rate galaxy would produce sentience.

GOLAD. No, my lord. We are orthodox. We await your command.

GOD. Hmm. *(brief pause)* Well, I've got nothing. There's really not much you can do for me, you know. It was nice meeting you, but I've got to go. I'm watching the creation of a double quasar over here — it's super rare. I want to see how it all goes. Good luck —

BADEL & GOLAD. No! No! No! Don't go! Please! Lord please stay!

GOLAD. We need your help, all powerful one! Our world is wicked with evil, sin and death! And the barbarian Marmuks threaten us with invasion, murder and progressive taxation!

GOD. Well, I guess I could help out.

BADEL. Oh, yes, dear Lord, help us destroy the envious!

GOLAD. And the unbelievers!

BADEL. And the envious unbelievers!

GOD. Well, I am known for my social justice. I separate my recycles, you know.

GOLAD. Then you will help us, oh great one?

GOD. *(pauses for a second thinking)* I'll do it! I've created you. You deserve a just world that can be a shining example to all — a city on a hill!

GOLAD & BADEL. *(dancing around)*

Oh, thank you, Lord! Thank you, lord! Oh glorious world to come! Praise the lord! Oh, happy day!

GOD. Let us bring justice and peace to the world. Let us make this land a beacon for all living beings, a glittering example of progress and prosperity where the good are rewarded, and the evil punished; where god is real and the hands of the righteous are lifted!

(The puppet theater curtain closes and it is pushed off stage. The lights go down.)

THE SONG OF MIRIAM

(Scene: An outcrop of rocks in the desert with a cave opening stage left. Surrounding the opening is a semi-circle of small boulders. To the right and rear, there is a rise in the rocks where sits or stands a guard with a spear. The stage is dark for a while, then a light slowly rises, with the guard little more than a dark silhouette against the backdrop. The Chorus of Women Elders, in separate groups, enter and stop on either side of the stage. As they begin to chant, dancers perform across the entire stage. The Chorus and the dancers are softly lit. The Chorus chants.)

CHORUS 1. Who stands the brittle black of night?
    Who shudders 'neath the owl's arced flight?
ALL CHORUS. Without god, there is darkness.
CHORUS 1. Who gropes the midnight-sealing face
    And falls into the Earth's cold 'brace?
ALL CHORUS. Without god, we are blind.
CHORUS 1. Within the murmuring slate we quail,
    And sightless reckon hazard's veil.
ALL CHORUS. Without god, our way's lost.
CHORUS 2. But there, to the east, the shadow breaks,
    The lid of sky awakens, quakes —
CHORUS 3. And dawning day makes morning's awning —
CHORUS 4. Dapple-hued horizon rising —
    As light floods o'er the lip of night.
ALL CHORUS. The day! The day! God's light!

(Dawn-like soft lights rise up as if from the stage floor, rising behind the guard and gradually over the entire stage. The Chorus exits before the lights come up fully.)

GUARD. At last, at last, dawn's shaping hand. Praise god
    I'm soon released from my watch, and from the waste
    And wild of night — grave-blind enfolding me —
    I'm soon discharged to blankets warm and sleep
    Untroubled.
        All night I stood my orders, slumb'ring eyes
    Leaning heavy on the threshold of that cave.
    So I was ordered, so I did. Who dares

Match eyes with the splitter of the seas? What hands are these,
Worn rough from bricks pulled hot from smoth'ring ovens,
To rein the course of days or shape the arts
Of reason or why?
   Not me — I am a simple man yet wise enough
To bend beneath the whirlwind's blow, to know
We lay defenseless 'gainst the power of god
And fate, fate and god.
   Who shutters their hot breath from the door?
Or with this clay-clad body softens their wave?
Who quiets their foaming sea with their tongues? Not I.
Nor you nor any — none but him, the bringer
Of plagues.
   All else who shout upon the louring sun
Tosses his seed into the crackling flame — or worse
He draws the fiery light upon his nakedness.
Better to lower one's eyes to the pressing beam,
Unnoticed and unseen, than meet its stare
And be scorched blind.
        (looking toward the cave opening)
   And yet heartsick I leaned upon my spear
And stared into the yawning cave last night;
Saddened to know that, in this blinding night
Unbound, she lay but steps away — but steps from me
And yet, as far as the stars' unyielding glint,
Untouchable.
   I wonder if she wakes, or if she ever slept.
I saw no light like mine to keep her warm.
Nor did she venture once to peek outside
The rictus of that natural tomb. And yet —
And yet she's queerly quiet, curiously unmoved,
Undiscovered in the night, unrisen at dawn.
        (music comes from offstage)
What's that? The women elders come.

(The Chorus enters from the side opposite the cave entrance. They carry and use several percussion instruments to keep their time, possibly accompanied by music playing offstage. Some carry pitchers and covered trays. Several dance to the rhythm. They chant.)

CHORUS 1. To what a desolate, desperate home
   Are we led? Is this the place
  To wrestle injustice with fate
   And measure out one's final days?
ALL CHORUS. Ah Miriam! Miriam! Our poor, poor friend!
   Who knows the hand of the lord?
   Who fathoms his end?
CHORUS 2. Plucked from the bosom of the people,
   From her family's tent cast away —
  To never wrap arms 'round her grandchildren,
   Or press them to her lips in play.
ALL CHORUS. Ah Miriam! Miriam! Our poor, poor friend!
   Who knows the hand of the lord?
   Who ravels his end?
CHORUS 3. Ah, Miriam, prophetess, singer —
   Our voices, our voice — is it lost?
  Our sorrows coil up to the sky,
   Our tears fall and blacken the dust.
ALL CHORUS. Ah Miriam! Miriam! Our poor, poor friend!
   Who knows the hand of the lord?
   Who knows his end?

(As the Chorus completes their song, the Guard comes down from his perch and stands between the cave and the Chorus.)

CHORUS 1. Guard, we come from the encampment.
GUARD. I see. What leads you here far from the pillowing fires of our tents?
GOD. To see the Prophetess Miriam, we come.
GUARD. The staff bearer's sister, yes. But come no closer.

(He holds the spear in front of them to block them.)

GOD. But surely we can see her, no? We've come
  To share her grief, to bring her drink and food.
GUARD. She's not been seen — perhaps she's not awake.

(The Chorus Leader steps toward the cave.)

CHORUS 1. Then let us closer and we'll see.

GUARD.   Stay back!
    My charge is keeping all away from her,
    And her from all. You understand?
CHORUS 1. We do not wish to get too close, but only
    See her and speak. We will obey.
GUARD. That's good. Now see those sentinels there? Those stones?
    They're death to cross. None can pass them either way.
    So I'm ordered, so I will ensure.
CHORUS 1. We understand. Thank you, guard.
    (steps toward the stones but stops)
    But now — a disheartening dread weighs down my feet.
    What desperate mood's she in? What anger seethes in her?
    (to the guard)
    Guard, have you seen her here since yesterday?
GUARD. She's not come out. Nor has a whisper.
CHORUS 1. Hmm. How unlike our candid friend who grinds
    Fire and bone upon the head of injustice.
    Oh, poor friend! To clasp the leper's shroud.
    Oh, what's become of her? God's will it is.
GUARD. God's will it is.
CHORUS 1. And so he's touched her — so she's touched. For what?
    For calling out to hear god's voice — speak mouth
    To mouth with god. Strange sin it is.
GUARD. What's strange? Who would demand of god who's all?
CHORUS 1. She'd have no more or less than any man
    Or any brother. Yet here the judgment's struck
    Upon the woman's flesh, but not the man's.
    Such is the fate of women who'll be heard.
GUARD. God's will it is. This world's of his design.
    There's nothing to be done.
CHORUS 1.   What? You've no faith
    In us or in our prayers? You don't believe
    Our words rise up like incense to the heavens?
GUARD. I doubt that my words do. Who am I
    To tug the hem of god? To beg a favored eye
    From he who paints the stars upon the black,
    Who makes the waters toss, the mountains rise,
    Fires the oven inclement on our brows?
    What voice have I for him? What ear has he
    For me? And if he'd hear, what question dare I ask?
CHORUS 1. Whatever your heart desires to ask of him.

GUARD. Perhaps. The wiser course, I think, is fearing god —
    His love as well as inattention. How's
    A piece of straw petition the flame-lipped sun?
    The ask would make him ash.
CHORUS 1.   We'll pray and we'll
    Petition for our friend — and god will hear. You'll see.
GUARD. Do as you please, my friends, but be prepared:
    God's scale may weigh more than your backs can bear.

(The Guard returns to his original post atop the crop of rocks. The Chorus starts to play their instruments and chant.)

CHORUS 1. Dear lord, hear our sad and suppliant voices,
      Let our pleas rise and their urgency robe you;
    For our friend, our Miriam, our voices call out —
      Unwind your mercy so that all men may know you.
CHORUS 2. Why unshutter on Miriam this reckoning frown?
     Why unpent your eyes' searing blazes?
    Why close your smothering hands upon her
    Who so long sang your glories, your praises?
CHORUS 3. Poured music from out of the heavens?
CHORUS 4. From visions, translated your will?
CHORUS 3. Gave movement and music to your words?
CHORUS 1. Made hearts with your melodies upswell?
CHORUS 1. Hear, lord, our hoarse and disconsolate pleas,
      Let your love foam like the bubbling spring
         And quench our throats of this parched sorrow
    So that from ev'ry hillside our praises can ring.
ALL CHORUS. So that from ev'ry hillside our praises can ring.
CHORUS 1. *(speaking)*
    Lord, hear our prayer!
CHORUS 2. There's movement at the cave! She comes!

(Miriam enter the stage from the cave and steps gravely toward center stage. Her skin is startlingly white and powdery. The women gasp and whisper at her appearance.)

CHORUS 1. Dear lord! Her skin is white as snow! Rinsed of color!
MIRIAM. *(as she stops near the line of stones)*
    My friends! My friends! Like the dawning sun
    Your faces raise the warming light of love.
    I wish that I could take you in my arms
    And sing our songs as we've done many times.

CHORUS 1. Ah Miriam! Dear friend, Miriam! Your flesh! Your skin!
    Our poor, dear prophetess. We've come to pour
    Our tears upon the senseless earth with yours!
MIRIAM. Save up those tears, my friends, our sorrows come
    In bundles. Save them for a better cause.
    Recall the fate of all mankind:

(Miriam's words are accompanied by the musicians.)

    We're like the glistening grass come morn
        Which flourishing grows tall
    But by evening we are cut and withered,
        Broke beneath god's steely scythe.

    Our years are but an eye-blink's time,
        A single night's ungainly watch.
    And then the lord carries us away as with a flood,
        And drowns us in rememberless sleep.

    Selah.

(The Chorus perform a flourish with their percussive instruments each time "Selah" is spoken.)

    By fate's thresher we are consumed,
        And by its fury tormented.
    The tempest cracks and howls at night,
        The hinges of our souls all shudder;

    The fiery blast of fate wilts the sky,
        The darkness bends our knees.
    For all our days are passed in turmoil:
        Our years spent in toiling murmur.

    Selah. *(flourish)*

CHORUS 1. Oh Miriam,
    Will the Lord cast you off forever?
        And smile on us never more?
    Has the well of his forgiveness gone dry?
        Has his anger locked tight mercy's door?

MIRIAM. Who knows god's will? Yes, we may shake his veil,
 His face, although, remains unglimpsed — a void.
 Last night I stared into the thoughtful dark —
 I crept inside that space afflicted — now, but now
 Today embrace the morning sun — my spirit raised.
 Yes, like the proud unyielding ox unyoked
 I've looked beyond the plow's broke rut to see
 Anew — so my disease became my cure.
CHORUS 1. But you were once a favorite of the lord!
 To suffer now like this — it's unimaginable.
MIRIAM. Didn't you hear what I just said? To the lord
 All is imaginable.
CHORUS 1.   Your sun-bronzed skin —
 It's turned to ash.
MIRIAM.   Like Lot's wife, yes, I'm turned
 To salt. I've seen the awful power of the lord,
 I've witnessed his destruction — the sight of which
 Has seared my flesh to ash. And now I wear
 Death's coat with pride, and wouldn't choose another.
CHORUS 1. Oh, Miriam, our hearts lay broke upon the stones.
MIRIAM. Be strong, the path is there. But not where you
 Expected it.
CHORUS 1.   But this — it seems so meaningless and so unjust.
MIRIAM. Suffering is suffering. If god will shield his face
 From us, then how are we to hear his words
 Of justice? Read his lips? This much I learned
 Last night: We're not born to understand,
 But to endure. And finally, to endure no more.
CHORUS 1. Harsh fates will breed harsh words.
MIRIAM.   So be it. Selah.

(A flourish of the instruments, then a brief pause.)

CHORUS 1. We've brought you food and wine. Guard,
 What should we do?
GUARD. You, Miriam, step back toward the cave.
 You women, lay the food there by the sentinel stones.

(Miriam steps backs and the Chorus lays down the food and drinks. Then to Miriam he continues.)

 Now you may take it.

MIRIAM.   Thank you, friends for these
    Kind gifts. I'll lay them in my shelter.

(She takes the food into the cave. The Chorus then begins to chant.)

CHORUS 1. Meekly she lays herself down,
    Quietly rests her head —
ALL CHORUS. Here on the sundering dust.
CHORUS 2. How coolly she turns and she speaks,
    How indifferently she looks and she grins
ALL CHORUS. Here on the flames that engulf her.
CHORUS 3. Without a complaint she continues,
    Neither sigh nor a moan leave her lips
ALL CHORUS. Here 'mong the thundering judgment,
      Here 'mong the poisonous summons.

(Aaron enters from the side opposite the cave.)

AARON. My sister — is she here? D'you women know?
CHORUS 1. Yes, Aaron — she's gone inside the cave.
AARON. *(stepping forward)*
    I must speak to her!
GUARD. Stay back! Stay back behind the stones!
    I'm ordered by the tablet breaker that no man
    Or woman cross, even you, his brother, Aaron.
CHORUS 1. What brings you here? You both petitioned god
    But she alone has borne his awful curse.
    Why come to taunt her, a mirror unspoiled
    Before her fouled reflection?
AARON.   You don't think
    The pois'nous gall recoils inside of me?
    We both demanded that our brother
    Not wed the Cushite woman. Yes, we both
    Demanded to be given voice to speak
    To god. And yet — yet god reached down to spoil
    Her flesh, and cast me out untouched among
    The tents — reprieved but not absolved — burnt sore
    Beneath the crackling glare of others' eyes.
CHORUS 1. You let her take the front of god's harsh breath,
    But never raise a count'ring voice, a coward.

AARON. When god's deaf thunder jars the vacant air,
    One doesn't cross or quip — one bends or breaks.

(Miriam reappears from the cave.)

    Ah, Miriam! My beautiful sister? What's happened?
MIRIAM. Aaron! Brother, look! See god's art!
    Upon his flaming altar I am turned to ash.
AARON. Oh Miriam, I had to see you.
MIRIAM.   Then quench your eyes
    And learn, my brother. See what I've become.
    But also hear what I have learned.
AARON.   Miriam,
    Rain down your curses on my head. They are
    Deserved — all of them and more.
MIRIAM. Why should I curse you, Aaron? What's your sin?
    This is the judgment of our god. His will's
    Unbendable, his words unquestionable.
    Our bitter portion must be drained t'the lees.
CHORUS 1. He should have spoken for you, plead for your
    Forgiveness 'fore the court of god?
MIRIAM. God's not a council to be swayed by lawyers.
    Yes, who are we to lecture god on justice?
    His breath and act, his will and want are just!
CHORUS 1. But surely he could let god know —
MIRIAM.   What god
    Is god that doesn't know? Does he walk blind?
    Or deaf? Go half omniscient? Does he sleep
    Death's sleep unknowing? Which of our thoughts
    Doesn't he overhear? At what grave sin
    Doesn't he peek? Toward what hope doesn't he nod?
AARON. Then you — then you'll forgive me, Miriam?
MIRIAM. Why must you ask for my forgiveness?
AARON. I'm wrecked by grief — I failed to stand for you.
MIRIAM. You failed no one. Be strong. If it will help,
    Then I forgive you. I've forgiven all.
AARON. Then come with me — we'll ask our brother's help.
MIRIAM. I cannot leave.
AARON.   Then I will bring him here.
MIRIAM. I can't — I won't ask anything of him.
    God's will it is.
ALL CHORUS.   You can and must! Why not?

AARON. What? Surely you don't mean that, Miriam!
>   *(to the Chorus)*
>   I'll go myself — at my brother's feet I'll throw myself
>   For Miriam's restoration.
MIRIAM.   If pleading dulls
>   The pain you feel, so be it. But I do not
>   Ask to be more than I am today.
CHORUS 1.   Go now, Aaron!
MIRIAM. I will not be restored as I was, but as I am.
AARON. Strange words you speak —
MIRIAM.   A language I can't teach.
AARON. It is your illness speaking now. Fear not —
>   I'll make you whole again — you wait. You'll see!

(Aaron exits. The Chorus chants.)

ALL CHORUS. Sing ye to the lord, for he will reign triumphant,
>   We will be heard, and Miriam restored!
CHORUS 2. For god can do no man unjust,
>   He can touch no person but for good.
ALL CHORUS. Sing ye to the lord, for he will reign triumphant,
>   We will be heard, and Miriam restored!
CHORUS 3. He can say no thing but the truth,
>   And think no thing but it is so.
ALL CHORUS. Sing ye to the lord, for he will reign triumphant,
>   We will be heard —

(Miriam grows increasingly agitated as they chant, until she angrily shouts.)

MIRIAM.   Stop that blasphemy! Stop it now!
>   What can we, clay shells, conceive of god
>   And justice? Did we weave the Earth, pin stars
>   Upon the night? Does our shuttle bring
>   Down trees? Our hands unroll the endless sky?
CHORUS 1. We only plead for your health! And justice!
MIRIAM. Who wears the eyes of god? Sees his view?
>   If in god's eye, I should be struck, it's just.
>   If in god's eye, I should be cured, it's just.
>   To live, it's just! To die, it's just! It's all god's will.
CHORUS 1. Where comes this fire? We don't understand!
MIRIAM. *(after pausing and calming herself)*
>   I'm sorry. These are the riddles of a restless night.
>   It's not your fault.

CHORUS 1.   Miriam — we fear you're not well.
GUARD. Someone comes. Who is it?
CHORUS 1.   The Cushite woman,
     Wife of the bringer of plagues, Miero.

(Miero enters.)

CHORUS 1. What brings you here, Miero, gentile slave,
     Bringer of sorrows! If you think you've come
     To taunt our friend, then be forewarned:
     We'll stand for none of it!
MIRIAM.   Friends, sheathe your threats.
     She comes alone, unguarded. Let her speak.
MIERO. Women, why turn your scorn on me?
     What wrong have I done you or Miriam?
     I'm subject of a curséd fate like her —
     Caught while drawing water from a far-flung well,
     Brought here among a race that I don't know,
     Torn from my family, lands and gods.
     Carried from familiar hearths and smiles
     To strange and ugly faces leering over me.
        Oh, how I prayed to Maweth to return me home,
     To crush you all within his fearful jaws.
     I even prayed for my own death so I'd
     No more endure the slanted looks of strangers,
     Feel their lascivious touch upon my skin.
     And yet he did not hear, nor aid, nor act.
     "Oh Maweth," I moaned each night in pain,
     "Why do you ignore my pleas, my salt-bitter streams?"
        Yet nothing grew from all those welling prayers —
     I was forgot, alone, unwanted, cast
     Upon the barren sands. And so I tell you all —
     It's best to curse the gods! A blight upon them all!
     They have no use for us but telling lies.
CHORUS 1. Such heresy — yes, even for a gentile!
     God metes out what each deserves. Your fate's
     Tugged hard by words like that.
MIERO.   All useless words.
     Your bromides reek of shallow suffering.
     Someday knowing worse you may know better.
CHORUS 1. Enough! Say your mind, but know we hear.

MIERO. *(to Miriam)*
    I've come, my sister, from your brother's tent
    To tell you that my hands are clean of this foul deed,
    And never wished this loathsome ill on you.
    As one whose fate is also cursed, I come
    To share your suffering, and pour our tears
    Together in confluent grief. You must believe me.
MIRIAM. That's kind of you, Miero. I know you're blameless.
    Rather, let me ask for your forgiveness.
MIERO. What? Mine?
CHORUS 1.   How so? For what?
MIRIAM. I spoke against your marriage to my brother —
    Not for who you are but what you are.
CHORUS 1. A gentile, yes, and as the law is written
    Their marriage is forbidden.
MIRIAM. *(to the Chorus)*
                 Yes, it's written, it's the law.
    So what? The clouds' indifference shades both Jew
    And gentile. Yes, we either die of thirst
    Or drown in their too much.

(The Chorus looks at each other in speechless confusion. Miriam turns to Miero.)

                 You've suffered much,
    My new-made sister. Maybe you'll find peace
    In marriage. I hope it's so. Within the cloying chaff
    Of this brief life, yes, if we look for it,
    We sometimes glean a slender seed of joy.
    But we must look for it, it won't find us.
MIERO. *(pause)*
    Oh, Miriam, whose suffering far exceeds my own,
    Your gentle words of hope dissolve the stone
    Grown 'round my aching heart. Thank you, sister.
MIRIAM. You're welcome, Miero. Go back to the bringer of laws.
    You're now his wife and hold a noble seat.
    Much they will demand, and much you'll give.
MIERO. Thank you, Miriam. I'll leave you now, but know:
    I'll beg my husband to restore your health.
MIRIAM. Do what you will, but do not grieve my fate.
    It will be whatever god will choose.

(Miero exits.)

CHORUS 1. You speak such baffling words, Miriam.
      From you, who once stood firm as Ararat
      Upon each word of law. From you, who was
      Its eyes, its breath, its voice — who was the weight
      And hew of its great sword! But now, unless
      Our aging ears deceive us, you say the law
      Is so much breath, no more. No more. I fear
      A burning fever sweats your thoughts.
MIRIAM. Perhaps, my friends, I've changed, or I've been changed.
      The number of my days are counted out,
      A period put upon this living sentence.
              (looking up to the sun, shielding her eyes)
      The sun begins to climb the peak of sky,
      The light leans hot upon our necks and soon
      We must retreat to quiet shades and cool.
      But now, before you leave me, let us sing
      One final time our song of mourning,
      That song we've sung so many times before.

(They chant. Miriam chants two lines, the Chorus responds with the next two.)

MIRIAM & THE CHORUS

      Why do you cast me down, my lord,
        Let turmoil rage upon me?
      We hope in god; for we shall again praise him,
        Our salvation and our god.

      As a deer pants for flowing streams,
        So pants my soul for you, O god.
      Ours soul thirsts for god,
        For the word of the living god.

      Deep calls to the deep
        At the roar of your waterfalls;
      All your breakers and your waves
        Smash over our withered frames.

      In the swirling turmoil I am tossed,
        And my breath it is lost.
      And we say to god, our rock:
        "Why have you forgotten us?"

Your anger lies hard upon me,
    I am counted 'mongst those in the pit:
We're set among the dead,
    Like the slain that lie in the grave,

You have laid me in the lowest pit
    In the darkness, in the deep.
What good are your wonders to the dead?
    Will they rise up and praise thee?

Why are you cast down, my soul,
    In turmoil roiling within me?
We hope in god; for we shall again praise him,
    Our salvation and our god.

MIRIAM. Selah.
CHORUS. Selah.
MIRIAM. Thank you, friends, for joining me in song
    This one last time. (*looking offstage*) Who's this? I see
    Another visitor — and from the yellow sash
    I know he's sent by order of the freer of slaves.
CHORUS 1. What does he portend?

(*The Messenger enters. The guard gets up.*)

GUARD. Stop, no closer! State your business here.
MESSENGER. I'm sent by the deliverer to share
    A message with his sister, Miriam.
GUARD. She's there, but do not cross the stones.
MESSENGER. (*to the Chorus standing in front of Miriam*)
    Miriam?

(*The Chorus separates revealing Miriam.*)

MIRIAM.   Here I am. Please share your news.
    These are my friends.
MESSENGER. (*turning to her*)
    I come by order of our leader, mouth
    And ear of god, divider of the seas,
    Giver of laws: From him I bring these curing words:
    For his esteem and love for you, his sister,
    One worthy of the highest place in all
    Men's eyes, he has petitioned god to disavow

His curse, and begged him on his knees to shine
His mercy. And toward this grave request,
Our lord has nodded; and on the sixth sunrise
You will resume your former health. God be praised!

(The Chorus chatters happily.)

CHORUS 1. The lord be praised! Our prayers are heard! Our voice
Has wafted to the ear of heaven's height,
And there been heard! Yes, justice has been done.
MIRIAM. My brother appealed for me? He spoke to god?
MESSENGER. He did, my lady. And god has listened, yes,
And answered the tablet maker's prayers for your cure.
MIRIAM. *(quietly bitter)*
So then my words were seeds cast on stone,
My breath but lavished on the arid sky!

(Miriam pauses for a second, everyone is confused and quieted by her downcast mood. She continues to herself.)

Why this astonished mind, Miriam? This —
Isn't this what you learned last night?

(She sees everyone staring at her, forces a smile and continues to the Messenger.)

Express my deepest thanks to him, my brother.
And say I hope to live as worthy as his love.
These coming days I'll fill with meditation
And prayer.
MESSENGER.   As you request. I'll share your words.

(The Messenger exits.)

CHORUS 1. Miriam, oh what heart gladdening news!
Like a rain upon cracked lips, we drink god's grace!
You must be so relieved! In just a couple days,
You'll be returned among your family
And your slaves. What? Aren't you happy? What's the matter?
MIRIAM. What reason's this for celebration? Why?
God's will be done. So be't. What once may cure,
Another time may kill. Indifferently,
We huddle to them both. One day we walk

The Red Sea's ragged seam, another drown
Upon the dark and dust of Sheol.
CHORUS 1. But god's not deaf, he hears and answers us.
MIRIAM. God hears all prayers — of pagans and believers both.
But listens only to Moses — speaks only to Moses.
Don't you see? Our pleas dissolve like tears
Within the vast, colliding tide of fate.
From which blue patch will god refill his cup?
We'll never know. His motives are as shadows
And light, walked through but yet unknowable.
Last night I bent to hear the voice of god,
But he was mute — no words assured, explained
Or comforted — unrippled stayed the glassy dark.
I heard no voice except the scratch of voles
Upon the sandy waste, the yowls of jackals
Tackling prey, the whispering leopard's slink,
The wind-face scraping on the desert rose.
So closer in I leaned — and heard the voice
Of creatures large and small, warm blooded, cold,
The walking and the crawling, myriad beasts
And birds and insects — each voice struggling to be heard
Above the clamor. Then, amid their howls,
There I heard the voice of nations — people —
Women and men — bent and young — who shook
The mountains with their desperate pleas,
Who then themselves awoke and called; and too
The oceans cried, and then the stones and Earth
Conclamant, the sky and stars, the heavens all
Around me clanging, calling, shook the ground!
And then the truth appeared to me: I thought, yes,
Yes! What single voice amid this screeching din
Presumes to rise above god's terrible whirlwind?
CHORUS 1. Miriam! Your words — your words are blasphemous!
MIRIAM. Hmm. Blasphemous perhaps, perhaps the truth.
ALL CHORUS. God gave to man dominion, we are the lords
And stewards of the world, and hold with god
A special counsel. Yes, he hears our voices,
Answers our prayers. Look what happened to you!
MIRIAM. (smiling wearily)
I'm sorry. Who am I to shake your bed?
You won't be woke for all the suffering world.
Man is a many wondered thing, a dreamer stirred,
A font of hope, a gleaming spark in the night.

And yet he sees himself a great colossus
Shaking dust upon the mountains,
Wiping oceans from his lips, tying ropes
Around the stars! He'll be no less than more
Than all!

(Miriam laughs lightly.)

But now I weary, friends, the sun
Glares down unmercifully upon my rankled flesh.
Thank you all for your considerate words,
Your loving hopes, your food and drink.
I must inside my tomb take my repose
Where I will pray, until the seventh dawn has rose.
ALL CHORUS. Good rest, god's strength with you, our friend.
God makes him whole whom he will rend.

(Miriam exits into the cave. The Chorus chants.)

CHORUS 1. The sun now rings the long horizon round
And the day calls us to duty and obligations bound.
CHORUS 2. Yet we in somber hue return to our employ,
Though god answered our suit, and there is no joy.
CHORUS 3. Miriam, is it the illness that speaks so strange?
Or has something else within you changed?
ALL CHORUS. Miriam, may you find peace to bring you cheer —
Lord, grant this wish, and keep our voices near.

(The Chorus exits to the playing of their instruments. The lights go down and the puppet theater is pushed back to center stage.)

THE STORY OF GOLAD AND BADEL:
PART TWO

(After the puppet theater is pushed back on the stage, the curtain opens to the same scene as before, but now fire and smoke billow in the background. The tree is bare and burnt. The clouds are black and ominous. The sounds of sword battles and screaming can be heard in the distance. Golad and Badel look visibly beaten, dirty and tattered.)

NARRATOR. The story of Golad and Badel, Part Two.

GOLAD. *(weeping)* Ah! The misery! I eat nothing but my own tears!

BADEL. Why? Why? Why? What sin have we done to deserve all this?

GOLAD. Oh lord! Oh lord! What's happened to us?

(God appears.)

GOD. What's up? Oh my — what happened here? Sorry to be gone awhile. I'm watching the creation of a Black Hole. It's really quite interesting. It starts with a star swelling to ten-times its size, then collapsing under the weight —

GOLAD. Oh lord, we don't care!

GOD. *(surprised)* What? Oh, I — uh — guess not. What's the matter?

BADEL. Just look at us! At our land! We are destroyed!

GOD. Wow, this is messed up. Sorry about that plague of mosquitos. Are those things still around?

BADEL. *(swatting at something)* Yes, our lord.

GOD. Who'd have known that killing the snakes would cause a plague of frogs? And when I killed the frogs, it caused a plague of mosquitos. And those things totally took over. I was like "Wow!" That was my bad. Sorry!

GOLAD. Oh, lord! We are a hundred times worse off.

GOD. Don't blame me for the flare up with the Canaanites. They told me you guys started that.

BADEL. And now they burn our crops! How are we to feed the many children we now have?

GOD. *(frustrated)* You said to cure all childhood diseases. I thought you'd be happy!

GOLAD. And now we starve!

GOD. Well, didn't I get rid of the Marmuks for you? No more teachers' unions threatening you — eh?

BADEL. But without the Marmuks counter balancing the Phoenicians, the Phoenicians have the upper hand. And now they rape our livestock and price fix our prescription drugs.

GOD. Price fixing? That's an outrageous assault on creativity and free enterprise! I'll take care of that!

BADEL & GOLAD. No! No! Don't do anything!

GOD. But I —

GOLAD. Don't touch a thing!

GOD. If —

BADEL. Just leave us alone, oh mighty one! Please!

GOLAD. Oh lord, oh great sky leader, I don't know how to say this — how to express this — but you're killing us down here.

GOD. I'm what?!

BADEL. We are a thousand times worse off since you arrived! Everything you touch has horrendous unforeseen consequences. You are a curse — a blight — a pestilence!

GOLAD. Is there anyone else up there we can talk to?

GOD. (angrily) No, it's just me!

GOLAD. Are you sure? Is there a man we can talk to?

GOD. Errr! Now you're pissing me off. Look — I'm just trying to help you people. I'm busy, you know. I've got stars to make, comets to launch, planets to form — I've got other things I could be doing.

BADEL. Oh mighty one, then please do them and let us, your lowly servants, drop from your attention.

GOLAD. Great omnipotent one, make your holes of black, spin your planets and stir milk into your galaxies, but please: leave us vessels of clay without your loving attention.

GOD. Man, you guys know how to hurt a girl.

GOLAD. It's not you, it's us. Really.

GOD. (hurt) Fine. I've got other universes I'm cultivating — better universes than this one, by far. I'll give them my love. You guys are way too needy. This wasn't working out for me anyway. I don't need you.

(God exits. The clouds close behind her sounding like a door slamming. Badel and Golad watch the clouds for a second, then look at each other.)

BADEL. Thank god, god has left!

GOLAD. Praise be to god that god's not here to praise!

(Golad and Badel dance around as the narrator speaks.)

NARRATOR. Thereafter, the land of the south, high in the hills of Edom near the nation of Uz, endured war and prosperity and virtue and ignorance, poverty, crime, epidemics and whimsical twists of fate like every other nation. And Golad and Badel lived precarious lives like all humans, struggling each day to survive indifferent happiness and paralyzing dread. But they never stopped thanking god for not being there for them. And so they lived their days until they died of the flu because they thought vaccines were socialized medicine. The end.

(Badel and Golad sneeze and then collapse. The curtain closes. The lights go down.)

FINIS

THE CAVE AT HOPE'S END

Based on a story in Book 1, Canto 9
of Edmund Spenser's The Fairie Queene

CHARACTERS

Narrator, a speaker.

Hermit, a haggard old man wearing rags.

The Knight, a man, 25-35 years old.

Fellow Knight, a woman, 25-35 years old.

TIME

Although the characters and setting are ostensibly medieval, the time and place should be approached allegorically rather than literally. Costume and time period are up to the discretion of the director.

PERFORMANCE NOTES

When the narrator speaks of the owl, he or she should take on a different tone. They may want to look offstage or above the audience as if they are watching the owl — to return their attention to the audience when discussing the Knight and the Hermit.

☐

(Scene: A cave with a small fire built in the middle. The cave is strewn with the bones of men and animals, ashes and blood. A wizened, ashen-faced man sits before the fire, staring at it. His hair is long and disheveled. He wears rags. On the wall behind him is the shadow of a man hanging by a rope, swaying ever so slightly. The narrator enters and stands to the one side of the stage.)

NARRATOR. Folded deep in the tangled heart of the forest
    Opens a cave — this cave. A cave
    Sought out by knights and maids in grief,
    Or stumbled on by those
    Of somber, solitary reflection.
    And all who slump toward this grim mouth
    Meet a Hermit, clad in rags and dirt,
    Staring blankly into a cool, glimmering fire,
    Waiting the next pilgrim's arrival.
    Whilst outside, the great horned owl perches.
          (looking offstage)
    Unblinking stare his eyes
    Inside the ebbing twilight tides.

    From his pitiless gaze no creature 'scapes,
    The flesh halts and quakes.

    Prey and hunter,
      Object and will,
    Dance unending
      Toe to heel.

    And so, the rising nighttime lays
    Its weary shoulder on hunter and prey,

    And neither from their heaving breath
    Finds solace till comes thoughtless death.

(The Knight enters the stage, sword drawn, and stops at the entryway to the cave.)
          (looking back to the audience)
    Ere long the Knight comes, the setting sun
    On fading man. He comes

To this rough cave, this dreaded hole,
Comes in search of a man — a friend,
But only hears the baleful horned owl's shriek —

(The shriek of the horned owl is heard offstage.)

And there, the Knight set eyes upon his friend —
There, upon the knotted rope-end hanged. He looks
On death's face, the wide-eyed awe,
Grief's swollen cheeks, fate's salt-streaked lines.
KNIGHT. It's true — just as that fearful stranger described.
He told me of their visit here,
To this dread cave —
He came with my friend
Who hangs here now,
And here they met an ancient who,
With wounding words
Plucked from their breasts all hope
And so persuaded both to put an end
To living sorrow in ceasing death.
My friend, he said, without delay
Gave up his breath upon the rope.
And seeing this horrific deed, the stranger panicked
And ran until I stopped his writhing legs.
Yes, everything he said
Is true!
NARRATOR. *(looking offstage)*
The horned owl shrugs its speckled coat,
(then turning to the Knight)
While the Knight's face pales —
Grief twists to frowns of rage.
He steps inside the squalid cave,
The air of rotting flesh,
Corrupted breath. He falters
At the curdled fume, but just a moment —
Then leans ahead, this everyman,
In spite of every instinct:
For he must seek, must know, must look,
For he must challenge all. Even purpose.
His eyes come down upon the cavern's homely lord —
And with rising anger, raises his sword.
KNIGHT. You there, wizard — don't move!
NARRATOR. Commands the Knight.

KNIGHT. You stole this knight's last breath,
    And now I come to read your judgment — death!
NARRATOR. The Hermit turns his eye upon his surly guest.
HERMIT. Strange man. Why come sword drawn?
NARRATOR. He growls, annoyed.
HERMIT. What threat am I to you? To you, steel draped,
    In weapons wrapped, while I in rags and dust sit here
    Unarmed, unarmored. One. Alone.
    You in manhood's bloom, and I in stiffened age.
    You, who wear the vestments of authority and power.
    And I who wear the scabs of poverty.
    What fell stroke am I to harm you with?
            (returning his gaze to the fire)
    Strange mortal!
    Who fears me's a fool!
KNIGHT. It was no man that killed my friend, but an enchanter!
HERMIT. What magic wields this impoverished frame?
    No devils wait upon me here, no witches brew.
    What mystic ring do I possess?
    I've none —
    None but eyes and words to see and say.
    To explain what men already know,
    That's all I do.
    Therein's my magic, all of it.
NARRATOR. The Knight, confused, lowers his sword
    And stutters.
KNIGHT. But I —
NARRATOR. The Hermit points to the empty seat.
HERMIT. Fear not and sit. I see you've travelled far.
KNIGHT. I have.
HERMIT. But gotten nowhere.
KNIGHT. I have traveled far across this world,
    I've seen the New Jerusalem, and sipped
    From the well of life.
    I've tasted the fruit of the House of Alma,
    And slew the dragon at Radegone.
    I've sat at the elbow of King Arthur,
    And spoke to the enchanted trees.
    Many sights and customs strange I've gleaned,
    And many a wondrous man and maid I've seen.
HERMIT. And you have climbed great peaks, withstood
    Harsh storms, crossed raging waters,
    Fought horrid beasts to a hot death.

But little you've accomplished, friend,
And less you've changed.
The world goes on no better for it all.
The orphan still cries out at night for a parent's love
While you thrash recklessly at ghosts in the forests.
Here, sit with me.

NARRATOR. *(as if watching offstage)*
From his perch, the great bird's tufted hood
Pivots o'er the tangled wood.
His dismal outcry shakes the air.

(The shriek is heard offstage. Then the Narrators turns to the audience.)

The Knight jumps, heart-pounding, reels —
The fetid odor, Hermit's voice
Press his throat — he cannot breathe.

KNIGHT. I must be going — I must —
Keep moving. Breathe —

NARRATOR. The Knight, bewildered, turns
To leave, but stops
Upon the Hermit's question.

HERMIT. Go where?
There is nowhere to go.
Movement — ha! — it's all illusion.
From Jerusalem to Babylon to Rome —
You move, but always find
Your eyes above the same two feet.
The selfsame view, the selfsame you.
You can't escape yourself. Here, sit with me.

KNIGHT. I am tired — I'm suddenly very tired.

HERMIT. I know, I know, my friend. This life is hard.
Come, sit here.

KNIGHT. But —

HERMIT. Come, my friend, and sit. But for a moment,
If you please. I know your kind quite well.

KNIGHT. What do you know of me?

NARRATOR. The Hermit wryly smiles as he pokes the fire.

HERMIT. Of you, not much, but I don't need to know that much
To know you well. Are you not man?
The thinking ape? The fallen angel?
You're all the same. There isn't much to know.
Here.

NARRATOR. The Hermit waves toward the empty seat.
    The weary Knight returns his now-ponderous sword
    To its scabbard, and slumps beside the fire.
        (looking offstage)
    The great bird's restless eye abruptly stops — and there!
    Upon the mark he fixed his fatal stare.
KNIGHT. What do you know of men?
HERMIT. I know, for example, you are seekers.
KNIGHT. Yes, and our seeking makes us stronger, doesn't it?
    And from our journeys don't we learn and grow?
HERMIT. And shrink. As our knowledge grows,
    Don't we shrink? Once lords of this small garden,
    Didn't we walk like demigods with weight and purpose?
    But now we're less than dust
    Upon an endless, empty swirl of space and light.
    And as the ever-farther star is found, is not the universe
    Made emptier and we smaller?
    Less significant?
    Less meaningful?
    As the ocean grows, don't the ports recede and shrink,
    And doesn't our boat become smaller and smaller
    In the burgeoning vastness?
NARRATOR. The Knight starts as if shaken from a dream.
    Seeing his dead friend, he stands abruptly.
        (looking offstage)
    The brindled bird unfolds his wings
    And leans into the darkling winds.
KNIGHT. What spell is this?
HERMIT. No spell, but only truth.
KNIGHT. Damn your words! I've come for justice for my friend!
HERMIT. To this again, you foolish man? Why be so frantic
    To mete out doom? You cry for justice —
    We all demand the same — yes, even me!
    No one here's to blame for this man's death
    But his own tortured mind, find that!
    Bring to court his conscience, then condemn.
KNIGHT. But you didn't stop him!
    Instead you robbed him of his hope
    And in its place pushed toward him that rope.
NARRATOR. *(to the audience)*
    The Hermit stands and approaches the Knight.

HERMIT. He got the rope from me, it's true. It's true.
  But let me ask you this:
  Is it just to help one get what most he wants?
  To go where most he wills?
KNIGHT. Yes, I suppose.
HERMIT. Yes, you suppose. *(laughs lightly)*
  If a traveler who's suffered many plodding miles
  Should meet a flood that stays his passage home —
  Is it not grace to help him on his way?
  To free his feet caught in the mire?
  To ferry him across the swelling river
  That he may reach his much-desired station?
KNIGHT. Why certainly.
HERMIT. Why certainly. For it's an envious man that grieves
  At his neighbor's good, and finds his joy
  In his neighbor's thieves.
KNIGHT. That is sinful.
HERMIT. It is. So all I did was help the traveler home.
  Yes, I but feed the hungry stranger
  Who comes here starved of peace and rest.
  I give him the recipe, th'ingredients.
  And he now feasts upon eternal rest, at peace,
  At happy ease, ignorant of hunger or craving,
  Knowing no more the shrieks, the moans, the panics
  Of this our doleful life.
  What if the passage brings a little pain,
  What makes the frail flesh blanch at the bitter wave?
  We are born in pain, and so to leave it any other way
  Would be disproportionate. Besides,
  Is not a poignant pain well worth the numbing ease
  That lays the soul to dreamless sleep?
  Sleep after toil, port after stormy seas,
  Ease after war, so death after life. Peace.
KNIGHT. A coward's path.
HERMIT. Cowardly, yes, it's true,
  But do not be so hard upon yourself.
  The fear of death is natural.
KNIGHT. Me? I've felt the breath of everlasting dark
  Upon my face and stood unflinched.
  I tell you, demon, I don't fear my death.
HERMIT. Ha! You've the strangest way of showing it.

NARRATOR. *(pointing at the sky)*
    The great bird through the sky descends,
    From silent air in silence sent.
HERMIT. Just look at you!
    You threateningly roam the world
    Onion-layered with steel leaf and mail,
    Prickled with filed-sharp blades
    And larded with blunt-edged weapons.
    While I sit here naked, unarmed, unguarded.
    Now look at us:
    Who 'mongst us here reeks of the coward?
KNIGHT. Yes, but —
HERMIT. The caitiff? The fearful fool of fortune?
KNIGHT. Enough, black soul! So! Are we to lay our breath
    At life's first bitter turn, expose our throat
    To the first sharp tooth?
    Are we not to guard ourselves from plot and asp?
    Is the reply to every threat to die?
HERMIT. Is the answer to every threat to live? Why?
    Surely life's more complicated,
    And we are made to feel our way between the poles.
    We all know of extraordinary sufferings
    Where death would be preferred to life.
    Who would prolong the madman's torture?
KNIGHT. Although we may foreshorten life, we shouldn't.
    For it's god's role to determine the ribbon's length,
    And make the cut in time.
    The sentinel may not leave his post
    Until his captain gives the word.
HERMIT. Yes, but he who appoints the sentinel
    To his place gives him license to stand down
    Upon the morning drum.
KNIGHT. But surely that's not god's intent.
HERMIT. Oh, naïve man! What deed is ever done
    In heaven or this earth, that's not the will of god?
    What can we say without his nod?
    What deed without his word?
    What thought without his smile?
    Does he not script it all?
    Did he not make us? Give us life and reason?
    Grant us sense and eye?
    To think, to move, to act?
    Our times in his eternal book of fate

Are surely written, including our unyielding expiration.
Who then presumes to know his destiny
Or his scheduled end? None, so god's decreed.
So when the unwound hour is come,
Let none ask him whence, nor why. It's done.
NARRATOR. The Knight a'sudden feels a weight
    Oppress his soul.
KNIGHT. But — but aren't we meant to do great deeds
    So fame outlives our brittle lives?
HERMIT. My, how presumptuous you can be! Ha!
    You are as feckless as the rest. In but a couple score of years
    Your self-important pantomimes will molder
    Into dust as if you never lived.
    The man who slayed the lion and saved the town
    Upon the thousand years
    Is dust as is the town and all its people. To what difference?
    You control nothing, influence nothing, keep nothing.
    So throw your sails against the winds of fate
    And keep your precious, aimless life.
    But remember this —
    There's only one thing you can control:
    Your death. Relieve your soul!
KNIGHT. If everlasting fame eludes us,
    Then surely we are here to do some good:
    Shield the orphan, heal the sick,
    Protect the weak.
HERMIT. The good, ah yes. A prickly problem, that.
    We could spend a dozen desultory hours
    Debating what is good. Is mine the same as yours?
    But let's assume a man can do some good,
    Though small and futile it would be.
    Answer me this: Do not all men sin?
KNIGHT. They do.
HERMIT. Yes! And what virtue does any man stock
    That's not outweighed by a hundred unpacked sins,
    A thousand insults, a thousand thousand oversights,
    Omissions, errors and accidents?
NARRATOR. (looking offstage)
    It turns, the great owl, and downward leans,
    Through senseless night a shaft unseen.
KNIGHT. I — I —
HERMIT. Come, come sit with me. Sit here.
NARRATOR. The Hermit sits, followed by the Knight, head low.

HERMIT. For each good deed we do, can't we point
       To a thousand selfish acts? For each kind word,
       A dozen curses? With the water used to wash our hair,
       We could quench a hundred thirsts. With the clothes
       We cut to rags, we could warm five hundred shivering frames.
       With the crumbs we let fall from our fat chins
       We could save a thousand children from starvation.
       Right outside these doors, these doors here,
       Souls live in desperate agony,
       Deprived of shelter, wracked by hunger, torn
       By need's unyielding tooth. Right outside.
       Yet here we sit self-satisfied, don't we?
       Having plugged our ears to their hoarse cries
       We sleep the sleep of peace, untroubled,
       Our conscience rests unconcerned.
       My god — How do we look ourselves in the mirror?
KNIGHT. I don't know — I — I've thought the same.
       What should we do? What can we do?
HERMIT. I don't know the path of righteousness.
       Who does? But this I know:
       That he who stumbles from the path
       Goes farther astray the farther he goes.
       If you agree, then go no farther, but lie down here
       And take your rest; prevent the ills
       That you would do, and the myriad sins that stalk you.
       Oh, you sad and wretched man,
       If in true balance you weigh your state,
       The sinning death of your soul is near.
       Why, then, does a man of sin like yourself —
       In iniquity high heaped, spiteful in the eyes of others —
       Desire to draw to the last drop his villainy?
KNIGHT. But I try to do the best I can. My life —
       It isn't easy.
NARRATOR. Downward, downward breaks the owl!
HERMIT. Your life's not easy? Oh evil, self-deluded man!
       For each hang nail you bitterly curse,
       A thousand moan the loss of a hand!
       And even though your fate be unsteady,
       A thousand others fall upon the rocks,
       And eat life's sorrowing tears.
       What are your petty pains and pleas
       To the anguished cries of a thousand million?
       Are you deaf? If you've no ears, then borrow!

Don't talk to me of your sorrows —
Your shallow complaints are a selfish disease
That rots black your soul with cancerous ease.
Ah, you sinful, ignorant monster!

KNIGHT. I have — I've lived a mean and selfish life!

HERMIT. Yes! Now look at you — yes really look.
Know who you are and what you are.
Isn't it the law: All flesh must die?
Of what must be done, then isn't it better
To do it willingly, purposefully, intentionally,
Rather than linger, sipping at the virulent trough
Until the dregs of sin be emptied out? Is death so bad?
Think.
Death is the end of woes and the stay of sin.
Die soon, O fairy child. Give in!

NARRATOR. The owl, a sharp, unflinching stone.
(looking back to the audience)
The Knight in torment moans.

KNIGHT. Ah! Ah!
The light — the light — inclement glare!
Leave me! Blind these eyes!
Come moonless night, enfold my naked ugliness;
Conceal these hands, these eyes, this heart of wretchedness
So light no more reveals their festering sins!
What have I done? Not done? What is this life
That leaves no sin unfinished, no good fulfilled? Just strife.
Although we raise our cups to virtue's spring,
We drink the rancid wash, lick the poisonous sting.
Oh night, oh night, oh dreamless night,
Wrap me in your forgetful cloak from sight,
Until I am unseen,
Unknown.

NARRATOR. *(looking offstage)*
His fatal talons drawn come forth
And rip the shivering course.

HERMIT. Come, friend. Be done with it! Be done with all!

NARRATOR. *(to the audience)*
The Hermit's words pierce deep
The Knight's raw heart, knowing all were true.

HERMIT. Of the suffering and the sin, be done!
Of the pain and hurtfulness, be finished!
Seek out the peace of death. Seek death unerring, death
Unweighing, death, unknowing death.

NARRATOR. The Hermit takes the blade from the bag
    And holds it out.
HERMIT. Here take this dagger. Take it, sire!
    Your hand knows what your heart desires.
NARRATOR. As the Hermit presses the dagger
    Into the hands of the disconsolate Knight,
    Unseen, the wanderer's fellow knight enters the cave.

(The Fellow Knight enters the stage and stops.)

    She watches as the glistering blade quakes
    Within the Knight's once-stoney hand,
    Sees the blood recoil from his face
    As if to flee some terrible thought.
    Then the Knight raises up his chin, brings up the ravening blade,
    And his Fellow Knight, with sudden sense awakened,
    Leaps forward to stop the hand, to stop the blade,
    To stop —
              (looking offstage)
    The black bolt scores the grassy tops — rises!
              (to the audience)
    The Friend says to the Knight:
FELLOW KNIGHT. What's this, faint hearted knight? What siren calls
    You to this selfless act? You,
    Who has survived the battle's sharp-edged clatter,
    Who has disease and hunger thwarted,
    To end this way? In steely, unmerciful reason?
    Don't let the taunting logic fog your mind,
    Nor devilish truths corrode your spirit. Arise!
    Arise, brave Knight, arise, and leave
    This cursèd reverie.
KNIGHT. But why? But why continue?
    All the Hermit says is true. Is true.
FELLOW KNIGHT. Of course it's true, you fool!
    Why sift reasons to prolong
    When there's not reasons for the start?
    Only he who calculates the logic of our birth
    May ask a tally of the days before our death.
    Ah, look at life, at us! Alive.
    Although the world a thousand ways
    Would have us dead, here yet we breathe, we see, we feel.
    Look how rare and ephemeral we warm beings are
    Upon this cold and sterile plane.

Look at how unlikely is our existence here —
Upon this land, this planet, in this universe:
Those thoughts should lean on us
Until our forward movements cease
With matched unlikeliness, whenever that will be.
Just look!
KNIGHT. I — I —
FELLOW KNIGHT. If nothing else then balm your heart with this:
The Hermit's words are right and true,
But left unsounded is compassion's voice —
Compassion sung without reserve or warrant —
For others and for ourselves.
So drink till drunk life's bitter cup accursed,
And though you do your best forgive your worst.
The same holds true for every man.
Now quench your thirst on that, and stand!
NARRATOR. *(looking offstage)*
Hollow handed, the horned owl draws
And surges toward the deepening pall.
(to the audience)
And so the Knight on wobbling stilts is raised,
Supported by his friend's more grounded legs.
Then leaves the fading man toward sinking night,
Leaves the Knight toward morning's light.

(The Knight and Friend exit. The narrator looks offstage.)

The mottled bird beats its wings
And toward the deepening night he swings,

There, from aurora's blue-black skies,
To where fading stars match rav'ning eyes.

Powering wings
  Thrash the air —
Rising, rising,
  Toward its lair.

The bird draws out its plumed cape
And lights upon its perch to wait

Upon the rising dawn, the day,
To watch till darkling skies hold sway.

(to the audience and the Hermit)
Then he, beneath the great owl's sleepless eye,
Then he, the sunless Hermit, curls his lip.
He sighs upon the licking flame,
And spinning failure's thread upon his mind
Takes up the unstained blade.
He looks it over wistfully, twists the light
Upon its edge,
Then sighs another time
And thrusts it in his chest.
Then again.
And again. Into his breast
The steel is swallowed —
But alas, death has no flavor.
He drops the blade with scorn, and sighs once more,
Staring into the fire's lapping tongue.
And there he waits out time till time is ended,
Till the great bird's watch is suspended.

(The lights go down.)

FINIS

A MIRACLE TOO MANY

CHARACTERS

Abbot, head of the Grandmont Abbey
Woman 1, seamstress
Woman 2, servant
Monk at Grandmont Abbey

TIME / PLACE

Stephen's grave near Grandmont Abbey in the Auvergne

Circa. 1124 AD

(Scene: The graveyard of the monastery of Grandmont in the Auvergne, 1124. A woman, kneeling, works on the Abbot's formal robes while a monk watches.)

ABBOT. If you cannot fix it, madam, cover it.
WOMAN 2. Fear not, your grace, no one will discover it.
    It's just a small tear. Rest assured.

(Woman 1 enters excitedly.)

WOMAN 1. Abbot! Another miracle, your grace!
ABBOT. Another?
WOMAN 2. *(almost her herself)*
                  What's that? One, two —
ABBOT What this time?
WOMAN 1.   A lock of his hair has cured
    A woman's gout.
WOMAN 2.   That's three this week, what else will he do?
ABBOT. *(sarcastically)*
    Just gout? No lepered limbs restored?
    No dead men raised from grave-wrapped doom?
WOMAN 1. *(helping with the Abbot's garb)*
    No, just a cure of gout, your grace.
ABBOT. Well, that's progress I guess. Go write it
    In the book.
WOMAN 1.   With all the others?
WOMAN 2. Three miracles this week, with two last night.
ABBOT. Yes, with all his others have it written.
MONK 1. That's less than last week. What was that — ?
WOMAN 2. Seven miracles, brother, we counted!
WOMAN 1. Our ears buzz with amazing stories.
WOMAN 2. I've heard of demons routed,
    And ears that again hear sound,
    Bent backs now standing erect,
    Barren women now expect;
    Every kind of miracle sublime
    Is added to god's mysterious glories!
ABBOT. *(coolly)*
    A most miraculous time. Are they here?
MONK. *(looking out at the audience)*
    The people gather, hands entwined
    For Stephen to hear their pleas.

ABBOT. And so, dear brother, this spectacle must cease.
    Oh, hear us, god, and heed our prayers!

(The women finish their preparations of the Abbot and step to the side. The monk leads the Abbot to the front of the stage.)

MONK. *(clapping his hands to the audience)*
    Peace, peace! My people! Peace!

(The monk steps to the side and the Abbot steps forwards and addresses the audience.)

ABBOT. *(making the sign of the cross)*
                         In the name
    Of the father, the son and the holy spirit.
MONK & WOMEN. Amen.
ABBOT.   May the spirit of Jesus be with you.
MONK & WOMEN. And also with you.
ABBOT. My friends, in these struggling days,
    In this life of need, what can we do
    But pray that our fervid faith
    Will make us in heaven complete.
    And so we come today, in spirits meek,
    To call on one of god's favorite, his grace,
    Stephen of Thiers, of holiness famed,
    To our hearts close and to god's throne near.
    In his life, Stephen was a model for our race.
    He founded the Grandmont Abbey, and here
    He led the righteous in their observance
    Of gods' severe benevolence:
    Practicing self-castigation, extreme
    Poverty, fasting, silence, and abstinence.
    Yes, faith unknowable in god all powerful.
    No miracles did Stephen need, just faith.

(The women and Monk assent, quietly saying "yes" or "amen" and nodding throughout.)

    And since his ascent to heaven's blessings
    He's graced us with many miracles, taught
    Us of his greatness many lessons —
    Bringing light to dark, yea, song
    To silent, bringing air beneath the grounded.

His clavicle curing consumption,
His left knee leprosy, and his right hand
Removing rubella and gout. All this
And more, his faith has fev'rishly wrought!
His miracles multiply, and daily redound.
For Stephen is truly a saint reaching down
From heaven's dais to drive evil out.
   And so his fame floats upon the wind
And on every breathe his miracles sound,
On every tongue is raised a hopeful din.
And as the ear will hear, men will come —
From each direction, every town,
They come — to see the holy signs,
They come — dropping their plows and yokes
They come — they wend, they walk, they wind
To this penitent abbey and its quiet hands.
They come in miseries sorely laden,
With bodies broke and fading,
To touch the holy genius of Stephen,
To be cured by his relics, his tomb, his cloak,
His death-wizened flesh and brittle bones;
They come to witness the invisible god of heaven
Reap grain from this salted land.
   And so we pray today, heads bowed:
Dear Stephen, saintly Stephen, great
And holy Stephen, let you hear
The pleadings of this earthly prelate.
I beg of you, in the name of all that's dear,
To do what's good and true and right.
Have mercy on us Stephen, on us poor
And sinning children who come contrite.
   Oh Stephen, please close mercy's door
And stop these incessant miracles! Please!
   Give no more sight to the blind! Cure you
No more lepers! Stop giving voice to the mute!
Cease to impregnate the foolish young daughters!
Oh Stephen, Stephen, Stephen — see!
See, that with these multitudinous feats,
Faith wilts beneath the sun's carnal heat,
And people turn from faith unknowing
To what they'd smell and taste and see.
When a weedy promise for a better life
Overspreads the bitter, unwelcoming ground,

Then faith is starved of air — all's strife.
What need have men for this thing, hope?
To live's to suffer, it is our fate to cope.
Better blind faith in the unseen unknown,
Than warm expectation in the uncaring cold.
Yea, people, take this vessel hope and smash it
To a thousand pieces, into the dust press it
And wash it from your feet with your own tears.
Hear me, people, return to your abodes,
Take up your yokes, put down your hopes,
And seek not miracles in a crooked mirror.
Yea, close your eyes to this world's sinful suit!
If all our prayers were answered as told,
What use is faith when actions sneer her?
  So hear us, Stephen, humbly we sue
You to cease these faith benumbing feats!
Stop pushing men's hearts in retreat
With a multitude of promising miracles undue!
Hear us, Stephen, in our time of mourning,
But also pay heed to our solemn warning:
If these wonders do not stop falling from the air,
We'll gather your bones and throw them
Into the heart of the swift-turning river!
We warn you, holy one; yea, heed our prayers!

MONK & WOMEN. Amen!

ABBOT.   May almighty god bless you,
    The father, and the son, and the holy spirit.
    Go in the peace of Christ.

MONK & WOMEN.   Praise
    Be to god! Amen. Amen. Amen.

(The Abbot walks solemnly off the stage. The women follow.)

MONK. Return to your homes, my simple friends.
    Return! This age of miracles has come to an end.

(The Monk follows the women offstage.)

FINIS

THE DREAM OF THE SEED COLLECTOR

An imaginative account of the final years of the life of Russian biologist Dr. Nikolai Ivanovich Vavilov.

CHARACTERS

Dr. Nikolai Ivanovich Vavilov, the Soviet Union's leading agricultural
scientist
Khan, a local Afghan guide

Interrogator 1 and 2, Soviet investigators and torturers
Lysenko, a rival Soviet agriculturalist

Mauria, a friend of Vavilov and Lysenko (and a mountain nymph)

Singers/Dancers/Musician (optional)

TIME / PLACE

1935-1943

Lecture Hall
Saratov Prison Interrogation Room
Pamir Mountains
Soviet Agricultural Institute

For more information about the life and work of Dr. Vavilov, read
The Murder of Nikolai Vavilov by Peter Pringle.

SCENE 1

(Scene: The stage has an old straight back desk chair center-upstage facing away from the audience. Upstage and to the one side is a heavy, mid-20th century office desk facing center stage. It has a similar desk chair. The play opens with a spotlight appearing on Vavilov who is lying unconscious center stage.)

INTERROGATOR 1. *(offstage — echoing, getting more distant as he speaks)*
    Prisoner Vavilov?
    Prisoner Vavilov — can you hear me? Prisoner Vavilov!
    Do you hear me? Our interrogation isn't over!
    Prisoner Vavilov!

(Interrogator 1's words fade into voice of a woman.)

WOMAN'S VOICE. *(offstage)* …. Our keynote speaker, Dr. Nikolai Ivanovich Vavilov.

(Projected on the back screen are the words: 1936 INTERNATIONAL BIOLOGY SYMPOSIUM. The polite applause of academics at a conference awakens Vavilov who gets up wearily, but he's eager to speak.)

VAVILOV. *(to the audience)*
    Gentleman, distinguished scholars, fellow biologists:
    Thank you for inviting me tonight
    To ravel out the roots of human agriculture.
    To do so we must travel back in time —
    Ten thousand years, or maybe more —
    A time when early man — a restive and
    A hunter — literally put down roots
    And altered history's roving vine.
    Who first took seed to soil, took hoe to shoulder, and,
    In patience yet unseen in humankind —
    (Unknown in all the universe!)
    Waited hungry weeks and months
    For that blank stone to unfold its fruit?
    Who was that man? That woman
    Clutching at the promised ground?
    Stabbing at the fecund flesh?
    Who was it fed the millions who have followed? That,
    We'll never know — their name was writ in dust

Upon the vanquishing winds.
But by their legacy we are sustained:
We reap what they have sown. We may not know
The who, but we can search the what:
From what crude plants were seeds first plucked and plowed?
From what strange weeds did wheat and barley
Evolve beneath our ancients' care and careful breeding?

(*A light rises on Mauria sitting on the chair, she yawns loudly and turns from Vavilov.*)

MAURIA. Aah, fiddle faddle!
VAVILOV. Huh? What? (*sees Mauria and smiles*)
　　　Ah, yes, I see! It's you. Where was I?
　　　Yes, this pursuit, led by my institute and its biologists,
　　　Is placing Soviet agriculture and the socialist pennant
　　　At the forefront of new crop development.

(*Mauria shows a bit more interest, nodding her head. But as Vavilov continues, she becomes more bored, then becomes visibly agitated when he mentions Mendel.*)

　　　For by retracing our ancestors' steps,
　　　Sizing our feet within their prints
　　　And rediscovering the plants they used
　　　We are developing new breeds —
　　　Stronger, hardier, more productive, faster growing crops —
　　　New breeds to sate the world's aching bellies
　　　And flesh their walking skeletons.
　　　Yes, through the use of Mendel's genes,
　　　We can manipulate the blueprints
　　　Of the plants from which our modern crops were bred —

(*Mauria wads up the piece of paper and throws it at Vavilov. Vavilov responds good naturedly.*)

　　　What the—? You! Ha ha! Now let me be,
　　　I'm trying to explain my research
　　　To these distinguished guests.

MAURIA. (*chanting*)
　　　Mendel, blend all, pea pod stew —
　　　Flag leaf, clum node, spikelet, boo!

VAVILOV. Now, now! You've had your fun.

MAURIA. Come, talk about us: not about boring old genes
    And boring old Mendel!

(As Vavilov speaks, Mauria harrumphs and moans, forcing him to speed up his speech.)

VAVILOV. Not now, not now! This is important!
    To leverage the genetic prov'nance of these plants,
    My staff has systematically collected
    Seeds from across the globe, the cultivated and the wild,
    Traversing ice and sand to make
    Mankind's first living library: Yes, to make
    The world's most comprehensive catalog of seeds!
    From Asia Minor to Morocco, from Colombia
    To China, Chili to Afghanistan,
    We've collected more than twenty thousand specimens!

MAURIA. And Baikal Lake? Baikal Lake?

VAVILOV. Why yes, we went to Baikal Lake as well.

MAURIA. And what did you find there?

VAVILOV. Ah, Baikal Lake, the pearl of Siberia.
    A treasure, yes. The lake's a mile deep
    (The deepest in the world!) surrounded all
    By mountains. Their immuring ruggedness
    Makes it the home to several thousand species
    Unique in all the world — a lab for natural selection.
    And thus, we went to find peculiar strains
    Of rye and wheat, to catalog their seeds —

MAURIA. Ugh, seeds! No more seeds! What else?
    What other stories did you learn there?

VAVILOV. Um, Baikal Lake — a region sometimes known
    As Peristan, a magic place where nymphs
    From the corner winds convene
    To celebrate and dance.

MAURIA. *(pleased with this direction of the conversation)*
    Dance, yes, dance!

(Music starts playing softly. Mauria stands, turns her chair to face the audience, then dances around Vavilov and affectionately strokes his arm while he, distractedly, tries to finish his story. The rear screen, meanwhile, shows a beautiful mountain lake and fields of flowers.)

VAVILOV. By the glimm'ring fire's glow, the old men tell
    Of a nymph in raiment bright as snow
Who used her charms and rustic spells
To help men fall in love. (Although
    It's said the love she made
    Would often drive them mad.)

    Across the ice-capped peaks, wisped and white,
      Across the crystal shimm'ring lakes,
She skipped and fluttered free as light
Unknowing love's cruel twists and breaks
    Until one day she met a man,
    Until she met a man.

MAURIA. Come, come with me!

(Mauria takes Vavilov hand and leads him toward the chair.)

VAVILOV. Oh, I don't know. What about these —
                (gesturing to the audience)
MAURIA. *(stroking Vavilov's face)*
    No more talk! The moon — it's rising!
VAVILOV. *(a bit confused)*
    The moon? I thought it was the sun!
MAURIA. *(laughing)*
    The moon — it changes as my mind.
VAVILOV. But you are very beautiful! Just like the moon —
    Or sun — or whatever —

(Mauria kisses Vavilov and he swoons. The music starts to fade out. The rear screen goes blank.)

    I'm feeling very heavy — I can't — I can't —

(Vavilov slowly collapses next to the chair. Mauria laughs and exits.)

SCENE 2

(Scene: The stage lights expand to show the desk with two men: Interrogator 1 is seated and taking notes while Interrogator 2 reads from papers and leans on the desk. Prison bars and a stone wall are projected on the rear screen.)

INTERROGATOR 1. Vavilov! What's all this nonsense? Prisoner Vavilov! Get up! You waste our time talking about fairies!

VAVILOV. *(getting up weakly and sitting on the chair)* What? Huh? I'm sorry. I must have — I haven't slept three days — if I just had some sleep —

INTERROGATOR 1. You'll answer our questions then you'll sleep. But you don't answer them, do you? Instead you tell us about fairies and seeds!

VAVILOV. *(groggy)* I'm doing the best I can — I don't understand —

INTERROGATOR 2. Listen Prisoner Vavilov: We ask questions and you answer them. It's that simple.

VAVILOV. *(hanging his head)* I will, I will.

INTERROGATOR 1. We're at war and you're facing serious charges: being part of an anti-Soviet wreckage organization and a spy for a foreign intelligence service.

VAVILOV. That's not true!

INTERROGATOR 2. It's not? But you say you're working to end famine, but while you gather seeds, our people starve!

VAVILOV. No — no! It just takes time!

INTERROGATOR 1. We have evidence — sworn statements!

VAVILOV. What evidence?

INTERROGATOR 1. That's confidential.

VAVILOV. Then how am I to defend myself?

INTERROGATOR 2. With the truth!

VAVILOV. I'm telling you the truth! If — if I just had some sleep I could explain this better!

INTERROGATOR 2. Sign the confession — then you'll get some sleep.

VAVILOV. No! I won't — I won't!

INTERROGATOR 1. Augh! *(picking up a paper)* Look at all your travels, Prisoner Vavilov. Mexico, Afghanistan, England, the United States, Brazil, China — you're quite the world traveler. Why?

VAVILOV. *(increasingly sleepy)* I've been searching out the origins and varieties of crops in order to create new plants — stronger, more productive varieties.

INTERROGATOR 1. New plants? What's that even mean? Plants have always existed. They can't be created. Rather, they must be trained to be stronger, Prisoner Vavilov. They must learn — like our citizens — to achieve perfection. That's what Comrade Stalin says. That's what Dr. Lysenko says!

VAVILOV. *(more tiredly)* But plants don't work that way. They are the result of millions of years of evolution and gradual change over time. Their genes —

INTERROGATOR 1. Lies, Prisoner Vavilov! Lies! Genes imprison mankind in his body and cut off any hope of perfection! What is our life then but mechanical and pre-ordained? No!

VAVILOV. *(increasingly sleepy and unsteady)* But that's not the way — the seeds —

INTERROGATOR 1. Are you saying man is just his genes — like the fascists? Should we breed master race?

VAVILOV. No, men are not plants. Our variety makes us stronger —

INTERROGATOR 2. *(grabbing a paper from the desk and looking at it)* Tell us about your travels in the Pamir Mountains. That region is restricted, but you were given access. How was that? What did you want there?

VAVILOV. The Pamir Mountains? Uh ... Ah, yes. *(laughs lightly)* We traveled there because — because we thought their 14,000-foot peaks — towers of ice and sky — might have stronger, um, uh, varieties of — of wheat that, uh, grow quickly ... strongly ... feed more people — beautiful mountains ....

(Vavilov slumps back on the chair, asleep and unresponsive.)

INTERROGATOR 1. Does anything grow at that — Vavilov ... Vavilov! .... Vavilov!

INTERROGATOR 2. Vavilov!

(As Interrogator 2 speaks, both interrogators go dark and Vavilov suddenly awakes and begins speaking his next lines. A picture of high, forbidding mountain peaks is projected on the rear screen.)

SCENE 3

VAVILOV. *(standing, revived with energy)*
> The jagged peaks, churned up like river ice,
> Stared down upon the crumbling rims and vales.
> Ah, what desperate joy! It looked as if
> The sun were hanging from those haughty peaks!
> We trudged five weeks on broken paths; crossed
> Chasms deep, leapt fractured glaciers — hugged
> The narrow ledge a thousand feet
> Above the raging River Pyandzh. A place
> So hard, so cold you'd think that nothing lives,
> But you'd be wrong — so wrong! Amid the waste
> And wind of this unwelc'ming world, life thrives:
> The wild onion, hardy mountain grasses,
> The flat-horned goat, the beetle, molds and moss.
> Even here! Yes here amid the wind-cracked rock
> The existential urge to root and breathe
> Defeats the unmoved cold! And so each step
> Encouraged me, yes, knowing what awaits
> Might be the plant, the grain, the seedling germ
> That possibly could feed the world's hungry.
> Fortunately, we had brave Khan to guide us.
> Khan! Yes; his bright embroidered robe
> And insatiable appetite for life contrasted
> With the stark, grey mountain all around us.
> But he was an astute man, yes, a man
> With an inexhaustible curiosity
> To match his knowledge of the land.

(A heavy-set man about 50 years old enters wearing a central-Asian robe embroidered with colossal multicolored flowers and a silver belt.)

KHAN. *(nodding toward the place the two interrogators had stood)*
> Dr. Vavilov! Dr. Vavilov! Those men — this doesn't look so good.
VAVILOV. Khan! Root them from your thoughts!
> They're party eunuchs, bureaucratic weeds.
> Our work stands for itself,
> It rises 'bove the hacks and partisans.
> These are truths given for the eye and mind to see, to use.
> No matter the party in control.

KHAN. Yes, doctor, that is how you'd think it would be,
　　　But man's a passionate animal, aroused
　　　By prejudice and pride to acts unthinking and
　　　Unthinkable. And then the orchard gets the axe
　　　Because a single cherry's sour.
VAVILOV. (pulling wheat beards out of his pocket)
　　　Forget them, Khan. Here, look what I have found!
KHAN. What? Ah, wild wheat. For this you've haggled
　　　Bandits, bureaucrats, and icy storms?
　　　For this? For seeds? You are a funny man, Dr. Vavilov!
VAVILOV. Yes, yes, for this! For these blanks, these lines —
　　　Unread, unlived — and for the sheer unlikeliness
　　　Of all our lives! For life and its potential, yes!
　　　　　　　(holding up the weed)
　　　But this may hold a miracle, my learnéd one!
　　　This feral wheat will ripen twenty days
　　　Before our Russian wheat. And here it reaches
　　　More than four feet tall with rigid culms,
　　　Large ears and roots. It's not so rich in grain,
　　　But with the proper breeding, well, this plant
　　　Might spare the poor from hunger's twist.
KHAN. Ah, Dr. Vavilov, I don't know much about this "genetics"
　　　You talk about. I'll take it all on faith.

(While Vavilov speaks the lines below, music starts to play. At first, Vavilov doesn't notice it. Khan doesn't hear it at all.)

VAVILOV. It's science, Khan, not faith! Each seed contains
　　　A blueprint of its characteristics.
　　　We pluck some traits from this,
　　　And mix them with our Russian crops,
　　　Then we can breed a stronger, healthier plant,
　　　A more productive grain.
　　　But this takes time, yes, generations —
　　　Time we might not have.
　　　　　　　(pauses suddenly hearing the music)
　　　What's that?
KHAN. My friend, there's more to life than seeds —
　　　There is a world around you. (leaning close to Vavilov)
　　　And between us:
　　　It's not a very good one. You play along,
　　　You get along. Make nice, Dr. Vavilov:
　　　The wine is good, the women pretty.

VAVILOV. *(as if awaking from a dream)*
    I know, I know. But life is short,
    And I'm tired of the fleering smiles and sterile speeches
    Of the party brats and ignorant dogmatists —
    Like rust they wilt my work,
    Like aphids eat my precious time.
    It's too important! Look at Karpechenko, there —
         (looking offstage)
    My brightest student. Just last month,
    He packed his suitcase for America
    But I showed him what we're doing here
    And he could see the promise, he could see the prize!
    And now he's staying here to help. He knows,
    He sees it!
KHAN. Karpechenko, eh?
VAVILOV. Yes. He sees it — he wants to be a part of it!

(While Khan talks, Mauria and several dancers enter, lightly walking or dancing around the back of the stage.)

    But it's a struggle. They always find me.
KHAN. I have no doubt you'll feed the world —
    If giv'n the chance. But watch your step: The state
    Is like a giant — somewhat dim up here.
         (pointing to his head)
    Most times, obsessed by his own body,
    He's relatively friendly. But his mood can change
    In seconds and — without reason or intent —
    Destroy you. Yes, remember that, Dr. Vavilov.

(While Khan speaks, Vavilov's eyes follow Mauria and he speaks distractedly.)

VAVILOV. I will; everything's under control.
KHAN. You stay alert, doctor!
         (Vavilov does not respond)
    Oh, now you are a dreamer! Ha!
    You are a funny man!

(Khan laughs and exits while Vavilov and Mauria step forward.)

VAVILOV. Hello, my friendly sprite.
(Vavilov watches the dancers, fascinated.)

MAURIA. *(singing)*
>There
>>Where the water's grasses swayed
>She saw the stone-eyed mortal man
>As if of soil and mountain made,
>>And there she fell in love.

>There
>>By the water's quivering gleam
>He glimpsed the black-eyed nymph,
>The light and breeze glowed on her cheeks,
>>And there he fell in love.

>Aged and ageless,
>>Moon and sun,
>Flesh and sprite,
>>Together one.

>There,
>>Mortal man and light-haired nymph
>Turned back the bitter, stony soil
>And laid to bed the seeds of bliss,
>>And there they grew their love.

>Dream and matter,
>Flight and run,
>Water, light,
>>Together one.

(The music ends, the dancers exit. Mauria comes up to Vavilov.)

>Dear man, insatiable.
>You have endured it all:
>The shivering and the sweat,
>The springtime's winter thaw,
>The river's ripping coil.
>And more — and worse — and all
>For what? For seeds?

VAVILOV. For light, for science,
>For empty stomachs.

MAURIA. And party?

VAVILOV. Yes. For all, for all.

MAURIA. Ah, Dr. Vavilov,
>This gypsy's life in search of seeds — it does you harm.
>You're tired and frayed by this exposure.
>Nor does this ragged search for seeds comport
>With whom you are: the leading Soviet biologist.
>Your peers forget your handsome profile,
>Your seat at party meetings gathers dust.
>Come back to Moscow, come back home
>And take your place among your comrades, come.

VAVILOV. *(with a confident smile)*
>You'll see. You'll see. The world will see!

MAURIA. But it's been years! And whispers grow less hoarse:
>You know the party dimly views
>Your endless talk about genetics. Ah,
>Come, come. Your future chokes in weeds,
>And you've no fruit to show for all this search.

VAVILOV. I will. I will! It just takes time and patience.

MAURIA. And if you're wrong?

VAVILOV. I won't be wrong,
>But if I am? Then others will have learned
>From my mistakes.

MAURIA. I couldn't stand that doubt.

VAVILOV. Who knows what seed will grow and thrive? But time
>And trial will tell. Come cold, come heat, come dark,
>A thousand seeds will fail and die, but one,
>One lonely stem with just the right genetics
>And just the right environment, will break
>The soil and reach up toward the feeding sun!

MAURIA. Such waste! Such senseless waste!
>To say a thousand lives must die
>A random and unpurposed death so one,
>By luck and parentage, will live: That's horrible!

VAVILOV. But true. For plants, at least.

MAURIA. My dear, dear Dr. Vavilov —
>Lay down this strident world and come with me,
>Return to Moscow where we'll build a home —
>You and I — a new and better place —
>Sharing all, denying none.
>Come, let us weave that loving nest where we
>Can huddle undebased by poverty's stain,
>Unbowed by money's stone. Come, come with me!
>In love's white afternoons we'll feast the upon sun,
>The light and warmth, shared equally on all;

Blind to want or wanting. You and I
In a society anew, recast and reshaped!
At peace with self, with others and the soil.
Yes, come with me, my love — our home awaits!
VAVILOV. *(laughing lightly)*
It sounds so beautiful! But can human nature bend
In such impossible shapes?
MAURIA. This is a dream we're making real!

(Music starts as Vavilov speaks.)

VAVILOV. Dream. Is it possible for me, a man
Of science, me, a dusty, unrepentant
Skeptic to put down reason, to exchange
Facts for some well-wished hopes and live my life
In an impervious dream?
MAURIA. Why yes, all men and women live in dreams —
And some in nightmares.
VAVILOV. *(disconcerted)*
In nightmares?

(Mauria takes Vavilov's hand and they start dancing to the music. He goes along with her, but pre-occupied in thought. They dance into the shadows, offstage, and the music fades out. The rear screen goes dark.)

SCENE 4

(Scene: Dark stage. A spotlight rises on Lysenko and Interrogator 1 by the desk. There is no rear projection.)

LYSENKO. Why hasn't he confessed? Can't something be done? Can't more — more forceful methods be used?

INTERROGATOR 1. Comrade Lysenko, are you questioning our abilities?

LYSENKO. No — I just — I —

INTERROGATOR 1. We've interviewed him dozens of times. Sometimes up to nine hours. With some persuasion *(looking at paperwork)* he's finally admitted to not carrying out orders, paying insufficient attention to details, being hampered by a bourgeois outlook on life, not paying enough attention to Marxist theory and practice, and not choosing good people for his staff.

LYSENKO. Ah, those are nothing!

INTERROGATOR 1. Nothing? Perhaps you'd like a taste of our methods?

LYSENKO. *(frightened, stuttering)* No — I — I — It's just —

INTERROGATOR 1. What do you have against the prisoner, Comrade Lysenko? What's he done to you? To anyone? Is he so dangerous? He's built 400 research institutes — he employs 20,000 people. He's published dozens of books and articles. He spends all his time talking about seeds. Seeds! He hardly seems dangerous!

LYSENKO. He's the most dangerous kind of traitor to our system — the elitist! Vavilov has his university degrees, his foreign languages, his world travel and his bourgeois manners. He and his elitist friends. What are we to them? What am I? What, but the son of a peasant? His kind doesn't want to make room for men with thick, hard hands like mine, hands toughed and broke upon the hoe. I don't study the hairy legs of flies!

INTERROGATOR 1. But he has praised your work numerous times. He even brought you into his institute.

(As Lysenko speaks the following lines, the lights go down on Lysenko and Interrogator 1, and rise on Vavilov examining a wheat stalk. Manicured fields of wheat are projected on the rear screen.)

LYSENKO. He has — because he needs me and he fears me.
  Oh, he lathers me with shallow praise,
  With vouchsafed smiles, fleering kindness.
  But all to paint the fool of me — to pin me to the board —
  I'm to be seen, to approve — but not to speak!
  Yes, he disdains me but he needs my good review.
  Yes, he'd convert me to his new ideas,
  Oh, if he could — but never! No, no, no,
  My will is steel, my heart is stone!
VAVILOV. Comrade Lysenko!

(Startled, Lysenko walks toward Vavilov.)

LYSENKO. *(suddenly nervous, insecure)*
  What? Oh, Dr. Vavilov.
VAVILOV. You looked around? You've had a chance to see,
  To touch, to question? Yes? You saw the labs?
  So what d'you think? Our bean farm is remarkable, eh?
  The flowers, pink and white, display the three-to-one ratio
  Just as Mendel's laws predicted!
  Amazing, yes?
LYSENKO. Ah, well. That —
  Uh, that anomaly, yes, it clearly is a freak.
  Just blind man's luck, bald numbers and math tricks.
VAVILOV. Oh, no, no! We've affirmed it many times right here.
  I'll send you the reports.
LYSENKO. Don't bother —
VAVILOV. Our tests confirm the genetic base for plant
  Development and change — the twinned
  Genetic information from both the parents,
  With dominant and recessive traits.
LYSENKO. You've sown your seeds among the thorns, doctor.
  Yes, drop this heresy! I've found that plants
  Can be trained to change their traits. We're not
  Forsworn by slaving fate or mechanized
  Genetics. No. Why, I've had winter wheat —
  Through simple tweaks in moisture and in temperature —
  Become spring wheat!
VAVILOV. So you say, you say. I'm just unsure of its
  Broad application, *(to himself)* if any.
  (to Lysenko) I'm anxiously awaiting the data from your work,
  But you never send it.

LYSENKO. The study has — has been put — put on hold.
　　We've many new experiments in progress —
VAVILOV. *(to himself)*
　　The results have no mirror. Ha!
LYSENKO. What's that, Dr. Vavilov?
VAVILOV. I said "good news!"
　　Together, we'll make our nation strong.

(Mauria enters.)

MAURIA. Dr. Vavilov! Professor Lysenko!
　　Together! This is all so nice! Very nice!

(She leans on Lysenko. A sun appears on the screen behind them. Lysenko is very excited to see her, while Vavilov is visibly upset.)

LYSENKO. Mauria! My dear! More beautiful than ever!

(Lysenko kisses her on the cheek. Vavilov withdraws a bit.)

MAURIA. *(to Vavilov)* Why so glum chum?
VAVILOV. It's nothing.
LYSENKO. He has no time for us. You know how he is.
MAURIA. *(still focused on Vavilov)* Hmm, that's too bad. Let's all go for a
　　walk — a walk in the park always cheers me up!
VAVILOV. Hmm, I'm not in the mood. I must go.
LYSENKO. See how he is!
MAURIA. Come!
VAVILOV. No, I have … work to do.

(Mauria tries to take Vavilov's hand, but he turns from her. She frowns angrily.)

MAURIA. You're being naughty! *(taking Lysenko's hand)* Then we will
　　walk!
LYSENKO. Delightful!

(The lights go down on Lysenko and Mauria as they walk offstage. Lysenko speaks the following lines in the dark, as the moon appears on the background. Music plays softly.)

LYSENKO. You'd better watch your step, Dr. Vavilov.
　　You have your gilt diplomas, your data and

Experiments, your institute beside
The Fontanka. Yes, you have your Mendel
And your Darwin, too. But I have friends
I've friends inside the Politburo. Yes.
Yes. I know Comrade Stalin! He listens to me!

(Lysenko and Mauria exit.)

VAVILOV. What use are scientists when shamans rule?
　　　　Don't like the face of nature? Call the conjurers!
　　　　Yes, phone the alchemists! Why need we eyes
　　　　Or hands to see, to feel? Why need we minds
　　　　To think? To wrestle reason on the mat
　　　　Of this stark universe? Yes, when the answer's crowned,
　　　　We're left to seek the proof among the entrails.
　　　　Ah, what a waste! Yes, let the politicians give
　　　　Us voice, the priests our thoughts,
　　　　　　　　(motioning toward the place Lysenko exited)
　　　　　　　　　　　　the Kozlov Gardner
　　　　Our nourishment. We're ground to meal beneath
　　　　The blunting stone of willful ignorance.
　　　　Dubohzkey — Stanislaw — to dust!
　　　　Kazlosfy — Berken — Listz — All gobbled up!
　　　　Yes, one by one, the buzzing swarm's devour'd them,
　　　　Never to be seen again while we — while I —
　　　　A feckless scarecrow, has lost his voice. And why?
　　　　Because the facts are deleterious —
　　　　The truth is poison, knowledge treason, ignorance
　　　　Wisdom. What strange, strange weeds this soil's produced!
　　　　Now, one by one the sepals peel away,
　　　　Until the flower — fragile — wilts and shivers.
　　　　And like those withering petals I shudder, alone.
　　　　My god, what is this world? Yes, what am I?
　　　　　　　　(looking at the moon)
　　　　Ah, Kate, is that the sun or moon?
　　　　The moon — or else my mad mistaking.

(The creaking and slamming shut of a prison door. Sudden blackout. The music stops.)

SCENE 5

(The lights come up. Vavilov stands centerstage unsteadily. he looks haggard and exhausted. Interrogator 1 sits at the desk, his feet propped up, as if taking a break. He takes out a cigarette as he speaks. The rear screen remains blank.)

INTERROGATOR 1. How long you been standing there, Prisoner
    Vavilov? Getting tired I bet, eh? Why fight it?
VAVILOV. *(delirious)* Too tired — too tired — I won't —

(Vavilov almost falls over.)

INTERROGATOR 1. Whoa! You almost fell! Ha! You'd better stiffen up.
    We have many hours more. *(lighting a cigarette)* Everyone
    confesses, Prisoner Vavilov. Eventually. The generals, the
    politicians, the doctors and their pretty wives, the musicians, the
    farmers, the framers and the firstborns, they all sign the
    confession. No matter what words we've written. So don't take it
    so hard. Personally, I like you, Prisoner Vavilov. You're just a
    little too cerebral, a little bowed down by too many books. You
    mean well, I really believe that you do. But when we decide we
    want a confession you will confess. *(slight pause as he stares into
    space and smokes)* You know — *(starts laughing)* Do you know who
    you remind me of?
VAVILOV. *(delirious)* The rush-candle's light?
INTERROGATOR 1. *(laughing)* No, that's not quite right, but I like it.
    No, you remind me of Jack … of beanstalk fame! *(laughs)* I'm
    going to call you Jack. You and your magic seeds! *(laughs)*
VAVILOV. *(dreamily)* God be blessed, it is the blesséd sun.
INTEROGATOR 1. Jack and the beanstalk. You remember: Once upon a
    time —

(Music plays as Mauria enters.)

MAURIA. Jack — Jack! We've not money enough to buy a bit of bread
    for another day. You've sold the old cow. Give me the money or
    the nation must starve!
VAVILOV. *(showing her the beans — sounds a bit dopey)* I — I don't have
    any money — but I've got magic seeds!
MAURIA. *(desperately)* Magic seeds?

(Vavilov hands Mauria the seeds.)

VAVILOV. Yes, mother! They're carefully bred to be resistant to disease
    and poor weather.
MAURIA. *(angrily look at the seeds)* What?
VAVILOV. They mix a high-altitude breed with its shortened season
    with a breed known for its fullness and yield. And if we plant
    them overnight, we can have two growing seasons in one year!
MAURIA. *(weeping)* You traded our cow for seeds? The nation will
    starve! Oh, Dr. Vavilov! How could you be such an idiot? Such a
    traitor? The nation is ruined! We'll starve to death, you terrible
    boy!
                (striking Vavilov like he's a child)
    Take that! And that! You terrible child!
VAVILOV. *(shielding himself from the blows)* No! No, mother! Ah! Stop it!
MAURIA. And as for your precious beans — they go in the trash!

(Mauria throws them offstage.)

VAVILOV. No, mother, no — not in the trash!
MAURIA. Now off with you to bed. Not a sip shall you drink, and not a
    bit shall you swallow this very night. You've always been a
    disappointment to me!

(Mauria exits angrily)

VAVILOV. No, mother, no!

(The music stops.)

INTERROGATOR 1. — a terrible disappointment to the nation and to
    Comrade Stalin. Do you understand, Jack?
VAVILOV. But mother — I smell the blood ...
INTERROGATOR 1. *(annoyed by Vavilov's answer)* All I'm saying is the
    facts don't really matter, because we'll tell you what the facts are.
    So forget that lying sun.
VAVILOV. What wrinkled maid, what withered bud?

(Vavilov collapses on the floor. Interrogator 1 gets up and walks to Vavilov.)

INTERROGATOR 1. Jack! Jack! Vavilov! Now you've done it. I have to get Gregor Ivanovich. Gregor! Bring in the instruments!

(Interrogator 1 exits. The lights dim.)

SCENE 6

(The lights come up. The rear screen shows a dark, thick forest at night, lit by a moon low to the horizon. Vavilov lays in the same spot on the stage. Nighttime sounds — crickets, etc. — can be heard. Khan enters cautiously and quietly.)

KHAN. Dr. Vavilov? That you? Ah yes!
VAVILOV. *(awakening from a deep sleep)*
    Hmm. Huh? Hmm. Who's there? Khan?
KHAN. *(hissing)*
    It's Khan, Dr. Vavilov! Wake up!
VAVILOV. Let me sleep! So tired!

(The night sounds start to fade.)

KHAN. Hmm, sleep is death, my friend. You must get up!
VAVILOV. But why?
KHAN. The world, it has become a baleful field
    For th'weary skeptic's eye, the measured word,
    The unclipped coin. The chorus wields the stick
    And dire the lukewarm sung "amen." This world —
    It is a squirming vipers' den. This light,
    A frowning sun.
VAVILOV. That's nothing new.
KHAN. That's true. But these are dangerous times for one
    Named Dr. Vavilov.
VAVILOV. What do you mean?
KHAN. I mean they've taken Karpechenko.
VAVILOV. *(getting up)*
    No, I don't believe it.
KHAN. Believe it. Yes, they've taken Karpechenko.
    And next they come for you. For you!
VAVILOV. *(more fully awake)*
    Karpechenko. It doesn't make any sense.
    He hasn't done anything —
KHAN. Doctor, doctor, doctor —
    Still — you try to make some kind of sense
    Of angry axmen in the orchard? Well,
    Stop both'ring. And be glad the blade's fall'n not
    On you — not yet. Now, you must flee.
VAVILOV. From what? From whom?

KHAN. *(looking around nervously)*
    Hurry, it's the sun.
VAVILOV. I thought that was the moon.
KHAN. Come! It's the sun, it's the moon.
    I've forgotten what they call it now. We'd better go!
VAVILOV. What?

(Khan tries to pull Vavilov with him, but Vavilov resists.)

KHAN. This life is an amazing thing, a gift
    One doesn't simply toss away
    On principles or theories. No!
    Live and enjoy the spark
    Of dew upon the winter wheat.
VAVILOV. I —I don't understand!
KHAN. Save yourself, Dr. Vavilov! Just save yourself!
VAVILOV. Why — why do I need to save myself?
KHAN. Because the truth can't save you, because love
    Can't save you, because hope can't save you — god
    Can't save you, Dr. Vavilov. You must save yourself!
VAVILOV. But where? Where will I go?
KHAN. Anywhere. It's a big world. But you must leave
    The Soviet Union. Now. Forever.
VAVILOV. Forever?
KHAN. Forever. It's too dangerous here.
VAVILOV. All this is madness. Madness. All my years
    Of work here — what about my work? I need
    To save my work.
KHAN. You need to save yourself.

(Mauria enters and stands on the side of the stage. Vavilov stands.)

MAURIA. *(in a strange dream-like monotone)*
    Save yourself, Dr. Vavilov.
KHAN. Ah! They've found us!
MAURIA. Save yourself, Dr. Vavilov. Save your nation.
VAVILOV. From what?
MAURIA. Save your nation, save yourself, Dr. Vavilov!
VAVILOV. I don't understand, I am a scientist,
    I'm not a politician. I just want
    To do my work.
MAURIA. Your work is your nation. The nation is your work. You
    Are the nation.

VAVILOV. I only want to grow better crops, to feed our people.
MAURIA. The people are the nation, the nation is the party.
    Save your nation, save your party, save your people.
    Save yourself.
VAVILOV. What are these riddles? What do you mean?
MAURIA. Save your party, save your nation!
VAVILOV. I can't don a robe and murmur prayers
    Upon the faithful. I don't believe in utopias,
    I don't care about the means of production.
MAURIA. Have faith! Save the party, save the nation, save yourself!
VAVILOV. I can't shut my eyes — I cannot simply
    Dream it and believe.
LYSENKO. *(in a strange dream-like monotone)*
    Save yourself, Dr. Vavilov! Save the nation!
    Save the truth! You value the truth, you dig for it,
    Claw the bitter loam to uncover it, you scrape
    And scratch the earth to unroot it. You'll even climb
    The icy heights to glimpse it, but now you must save it.
VAVILOV. What do you mean? I can do nothing about the truth.
LYSENKO. Stop chasing heartless dreams and ghosts. Give not
    Your soul for cold reason. Give not a sky
    Of love for an ounce of seed. See with your heart!
VAVILOV. You're talking nonsense! What does that mean?
MAURIA. Save your nation!
LYSENKO. This natural selection, this Darwin, this Mendel — ah,
    Beware the vanity of man, all is vanity.
MAURIA. Save your party!
VAVILOV. Is it vanity to feed the hungry? Perhaps!
    But it is surely vanity to press
    Our hopes against nature's mold, to bribe
    Her art, to expect her to serve the handmaid of our will.
    She laughs at such presumption. And I laugh too.
LYSENKO. Then you laugh at the hopes of men, at all men.
MAURIA. Save yourself!
VAVILOV. Only at the willfully ignorant man
    Who walks with his eyes closed and trips
    Into the sewer. At him I laugh.
LYSENKO. Laugh lightly, Dr. Vavilov. For though he fall
    In the sewer he may accrue more of this world's blessings
    Than the unblinking wise man.
MAURIA. Save the nation, save the party, Save yourself!
VAVILOV. I will not dress myself a wise man, but neither
    Will I strip the fool.

MAURIA & LYSENKO. Then you will not be saved —
    Will not be saved!
VAVILOV. If being saved is living blind, I don't want it!

(Music starts to play.)

MAURIA. Daydream playthings catch our eyes —
    A distant glimmer, lover's sigh.
    A wishful may, a wishful might
    Lead our hearts on dreamy nights.
      Though it may also bring a fright.

    Toward the middle, push the pot
    Put faith in faith, put luck in lot.
    What we'd wish to be will be
    Regardless their asymmetry.
      Does it matter what we'd see?

LYSENKO. Falling down the tears we cry,
    The spilling wine, the bloody tie,
    Glass-made houses all will fall
    Yet our heart-broke voices call
      To bring them back and make them whole.

    See! Th' horizon's shivering break!
    Eventually every man must shake,
    And see the cold light's certain edge
    And learn stiff facts, forget their hedge,
      And meek, surrender to the ledge.

MAURIA. Save your nation.
LYSENKO. Save your Party.
MAURIA. Save your people.
LYSENKO. Save the truth.
KHAN. Save yourself, Dr. Vavilov. Run! Run!
VAVILOV. No! I'm — I'm too tired to run.

(Mauria and Lysenko laugh as the exit, the music fades to silence.)

KHAN. Then good luck, Dr. Vavilov! Good luck, my friend!
    I'm sorry but I cannot stay.

(Khan runs offstage looking over his shoulder to see if anyone is following him. The rear screen changes to a window looking out at the night.)

VAVILOV. Good luck to you, my learnéd one!
　　　I have more work to do here. So much work.

(Interrogator 1 and 2 enter and stand at the edge of the stage.)

INTERROGATOR 1. Dr. Vavilov?
VAVILOV. What?
INTERROGATOR 1. You are wanted in Moscow.
VAVILOV. *(coolly)* About what? It's late and I am busy.
INTERROGATOR 2. We were not told. But you must come right away.
VAVILOV. Let me get my papers and my bag —

(Interrogator 1 and 2 approach Vavilov.)

INTERROGATOR 1. There's no need. Someone will collect your things.
　　　Please come with us now.
VAVILOV. Will I be back?
INTERROGATOR 1. Please come with us.
VAVILOV. It is the moon! The moon, I say!

(Interrogator 1 and 2 escort Vavilov offstage. music starts and Mauria enters with two or three dancers, as if looking for Vavilov.)

MAURIA. *(each verse represents an increasing desperation and anger)*
　　　Where are you, love? Come out! Come out
　　　Of hiding! Please come out!
　　　　This game is poorly played,
　　　　You've had your fun, now let's away.
　　　Come now, end our loveless drought!

(pauses look around)

　　　What's happened, love? What? Why ignore
　　　My lonesome cries? My moans heart sore!
　　　　My words are thrown upon the skies,
　　　　My songs unwound upon the tides —
　　　But still your silence roars.

(pauses look around)

Enough, I say! The clock's run down —
Enough of love's reluctant vows.
   My generous heart you've careless spurned —
   It's set aflame — now seethes, it burns!
Beware, pale man, and woes redound
   On him who wears my scorching frown.

(Mauria and the others exit. the music stops. The lights go down. The rear screen goes black.)

SCENE 7

(Scene: Dark stage. A spotlight comes up on Vavilov — showing signs of being beaten and starved — sitting on a chair in front of his interrogators. Interrogator 1 stands; Interrogator 2 takes notes at the desk. Prison bars are again projected on the rear screen this time with the moon seen beyond the bars.)

INTERROGATOR 1. We're finally making progress, Prisoner Vavilov. You admit to being a member of the counter-revolutionary Peasant Labor Party.

VAVILOV. Whatever you say.

INTERROGATOR 1. Is that a yes?

VAVILOV. Yes.

INTERROGATOR 1. You also admit to building an anti-Soviet ring at the Institute that included Govorov, Karpechenko, and Flyaksberg.

VAVILOV. Yes. *(to himself)* Such men — what might have been!

INTERROGATOR 2. What was that? Speak up, Prisoner Vavilov.

VAVILOV. Yes.

INTERROGATOR 2. Yes, you'll speak up? Or yes you admit to building an anti-Soviet ring.

VAVILOV. Yes — to both.

INTERROGATOR 1. Now tell me, Prisoner Vavilov, did you ever spy for the United States or Nazi Germany?

VAVILOV. No!

INTERROGATOR 1. Come now. We can talk all day and all night — you know we can. *(A pause — Vavilov is unresponsive)* Okay. *(looks at some papers from the desk)* These collaborators you've given us, Prisoner Vavilov, they're all known traitors. Come, you know more. Tell me again about Yakovlev. It was Yakovlev, you said, who recruited you into the anti-Soviet group. Why? What were his reasons?

VAVILOV. *(robotically, as if rehearsed)* He came to learn of my anti-Soviet attitudes and my high esteem for American and Western European agriculture practices. Like him, I favored developing strong peasant-owned farms.

INTERROGATOR 1. The development of kulaks?

VAVILOV. Yes.

INTERROGATOR 2. Prisoner Vavilov, you must speak up! How am I to write down what you say if I can't hear you?

VAVILOV. Yes.

INTERROGATOR 1. What have your sabotage activities consisted of?

VAVILOV. *(as if by rote)* Mostly pointless scientific work, and ignoring
　　the developmental and experimental work of other Soviet *(coughs)*
　　scientists.
INTERROGATOR 1. Who did you protect from the investigation? *(long
　　silence)* Prisoner Vavilov, do we need to step out again?
VAVILOV. Leonid Govorov, Georgy Karpechenko, Constantin
　　Flyaksberg, and Andre Karpeclic. I chose these men because of
　　their anti-Soviet views.
INTERROGATOR 1. You said Karpechenko?
VAVILOV. Yes. I convinced him not to go to America.
INTERROGATOR 1. But now you turn him in, eh? *(Vavilov is silent)*
　　We'll he's made accusations against you as well. What do you
　　think of that?
VAVILOV. A man does what he must. Life trumps all.
INTERROGATOR 1. What kind of foolishness is that? *(Vavilov is silent)*
　　Well, you don't have to worry about him anymore. He was
　　executed this morning.
　　　　　　　(Vavilov starts laughing bitterly.)
　　Be quiet! Stop it! This is getting us nowhere! *(Vavilov is impassive —
　　to Interrogator 2)* Ah, this is pointless, Gregor. *(to Vavilov)* We'll be
　　back!

*(Vavilov is unmoved. Interrogators 1 and 2 leave. Mauria enters. The moon
appears larger on the rear screen.)*

MAURIA. There you are!
VAVILOV. Here I am.
MAURIA. You left me.
VAVILOV. I'm just a man.
MAURIA. You can't leave me!
　　I don't think you understand.
VAVILOV. For one with wings the sky's
　　A boundless, wondrous thing.
　　But men are made with heavy feet
　　To carve the dust of our own seed.

　　Us mortals, we are born to grieve,
　　To gnaw at time's acerbic leaves.
　　Oh, we dream a full repast but then
　　Must shun our dream at last.

Our love, this love's a playful dream,
But folly, yes, a dangerous scheme.
It's but a feverish chimera plied
To sate the penitent's wistful eye.

Your love — unreal, unworldly, cursed —
It only makes our hung'ring worse.
Far crueler, though, it is for mortal beasts,
To force their failings 'cross their teeth.

MAURIA. (*growing increasingly angry*)
How dare you, Dr. Vavilov! You are a fool!
I hoped for more from you; yes, so much more.
I thought you of the newer gods!
Ah, but my love was poorly spent.
VAVILOV. Far better is god's pity that his love.
MAURIA. You'd spurn my love? Leave it wait?
Who rents my heart earns my hate!

If squalid, mortal life you want, so be it!
If the light eternal burns your eyes, then leave it!

If death your heart affirms, then claim it!
No more I'll love one who so defames it!

Don't blame me, but your timid heart
For when your riven part from part!

(*Mauria starts to exit.*)

VAVILOV. (*calmly*)
Is it day or night?
MAURIA. The sun is shining bright, open your eyes!
It's shines across the Soviet paradise.

(*Mauria exits.*)

VAVILOV. Ah. (*pause*)
It is the moon. I knew it was the moon.

(The lights go down. On the rear screen, the following words appear: DR. NIKOLAI VAVILOV DIED OF MALNUTRITION AND DISEASE IN THE SARATOV PRISON IN JANUARY 1943. The music fades to silence.)

FINIS

A GHOST FROM THE ASHES

"I tell you, the dead are killing the living."
— Aeschylus, The Libation Bearers, Translated by James C. Hogan

☐

CHARACTERS

Fidel, Carlos lieutenant, in his mid 20s
Ysmael, gang leader, Carlos second in command, early-to-mid 30s
Tomasa, Carlos gang leader, in her late 20s

Miguel, Carlos gang leader, early 30s
Orlando, Carlos gang leader, early 30s

Tino, Ysmael lieutenant, late to mid 20s
Alvarez, Ysmael lieutenant, early 20s
Vincente, Tomasa lieutenant, early 20s

Manny, local aligned with guerillas, early 20s
Ramon, local aligned with guerillas, early 20s

General Hernandez, leader of the militia, late 40s or older
Colonel Fuentes, general's aide, 30-40 years old

Sophia, hotelkeeper, friend of Fidel, 70 years old

Stranger, young man, late teens or early 20s

Various Local Residents, Police and Soldiers

SCENES

Various Street Scenes
Ysmael's Office
Apartment
Hotel Lobby
Militia Leader Headquarters

LOCATION/TIME/DATE

A Small City in Colombia
June 1985

ACT I SCENE 1

(The scene: A nighttime alley leading to a street corner, stage right. Trash bags lay in a pile in the alley. A road construction marker flashes drowsily at the corner. A gunshot is heard in the distance. Some indistinct shouting is heard offstage. Then a couple more shots, this time closer. The sound of running feet. Voices are heard off stage.)

TINO. *(offstage)* Drop it, Manny, or I'll unpack your brains!
MANNY. *(offstage)* All right! All right! Don't shoot!
TINO. *(offstage)* We got him here, Fidel!
FIDEL. *(offstage)* Good — good. Bring him in the alley.

(Fidel, Tino and Alvarez enter with Manny. Tino and Alvarez push Manny onto the pile of trash bags then put their guns away. Fidel, who doesn't have a gun, stands back while Tino and Alvarez hover over Manny.)

TINO. *(panting and wiping his brow)* A broiler! Oven! Ah — a furnace! Ugh! And you, you fucker — making me run! I'll cook you good, you scampering cockroach!

(Tino motions as if to strike Manny, but doesn't. Manny cowers.)

FIDEL. Okay, okay. What's with you popping at us, Manny? You could've plugged someone.
MANNY. Fidel! I just — I just seen three young wolves with guns coming all crazy — I didn't know it was you, Fidel. Straight up!

(Manny tries to get up but Tino pushes him back down roughly.)

TINO. Just look at me! Shit! I'm oiled up for the roaster. Damn this heat! *(to Alvarez)* Here, feel my shirt! It's soaked. Feel it!
ALVAREZ. No way, that's gross!
TINO. Damn this heat! And damn you, Manny — forcing me to run like some broiled devil! Well, now Hell's door is opened — let's start the party!

(Tino kicks Manny.)

MANNY. Hey! What'd I hurt? Come on! Come on! I said your faces were a blur. I panicked! Straight up! I said I'm sorry! Sorry!

FIDEL. Well, now we need to talk, my friend.

MANNY. Sure, anything, Fidel. 'Bout what? You know I'm cool.

FIDEL. I know. That's why we're talking now instead of cracking open your nut right here.

MANNY. *(fearfully)* What? What? I didn't do nothing!

FIDEL. The missing leaf — where is it?

MANNY. What leaf? What?

FIDEL. *(turning away angrily, to Tino and Alvarez)* Wrap him up.

(Tino an Alvarez tie Manny's hands behind his back, then throw him back down on the pile trash bags.)

MANNY. No, I'm not sure! What leaf d'you mean? *(to Tino)* Come on, I'll talk. You got to clue me in! Come on, I'll talk! I'll talk!

FIDEL. It seems some leaf has, well, it's left the nest and no one knows where it is. I just want to bring it home.

MANNY. Come on, Fidel — Fidel! Hey, you know me. I'm just the middleman, a body in a suit, a name and feet, that's all. You know — just doing what I'm told. I don't know a thing. Shit, I'm stupid, you know that.

FIDEL. You need to smarten up and fast. Pick him up — he can talk to Carlos.

(Manny becomes increasingly hysterical — resisting Tino's and Alvarez's attempts to pick him up.)

MANNY. Car-Carlos! No, man, no! Not Carlos! Please! *(bawling almost indistinguishably)* No, don't take me to Carlos. Whatever you want! Whatever! Please, oh, please don't take me to Carlos! God no! No, no, no! Ah fuck! God no!

(Tino and Alvarez give up trying to pick up Manny and smile at each other. Manny continues blubbering while Fidel, Tino and Alvarez talk.)

FIDEL. You're getting smarter, Manny. Yes, you are.

TINO. Hey, if Carlos likes you, he'll just slit your fucking throat and pull your tongue out through the hole. But if he doesn't like you, well, things won't go so good.

ALVAREZ. *(pinching Manny's cheek)* But I think he'll like your pretty eyes. He collects'em, you know.

TINO. Oh yeah!

(Alvarez and Tino laugh. Manny starts blubbering louder but indistinguishably.)

FIDEL. My god, Manny! Steel up! Death comes to all of us and all you got's your word — and any shred of dignity left to you. Now, before we say goodnight, just tell me about the leaf. You got the brown but we, we didn't get no green. What happened to it?

MANNY. I gave — I gave the stash to Rico and he — he said I should get scarce a while. Said that he was tired of Carlos. Said he didn't believe in Carlos anymore. He said — he said Carlos should come get it himself.

FIDEL. Rico said that, eh? I didn't know he had the brass.

MANNY. Oh, Rico — man, he didn't look so good. All nervous twitchy and kind'a crazy eyed. I think the business's fucked up his head. Anyway, he told me to hide out a couple weeks.

FIDEL. How's that? You weren't gone a couple days.

MANNY. I tried — I tried — But it's too damn boring living in the hills, with nothing there but wind and crickets — and then the women there, the women — all angry and bony. Ugh, I hate them all!

FIDEL. *(smiling)* Shot you down, eh? Ha! They're smarter than you thought.

MANNY. *(throwing his body toward Fidel's feet)* Don't take me to Carlos, please! Don't take me, please!

FIDEL. *(while Manny is talking)* Shut up! Shut up and show some self-respect — Jesus!

(Tino grabs Manny by the shirt and roughly tosses him back on the trash bags.)

It's good that you came back, my cricket, that made it very easy for us — very easy. Just scent the hounds with cash and girls, and here you are. Yes, very easy. Now if you'd made me search the hills and far, well, that just might have pissed me off. But no, you made it easy. And you're chirping right along just like good cricket should.

MANNY. *(mumbling)* Sorry, sorry, sorry —

FIDEL. You are sorry. Now what'd he pay you?

MANNY. What?

(Fidel kicks Manny.)

FIDEL. Don't give me fucking "what" — We'll cut you neck to nuts right here! We will!

MANNY. *(moaning)* A hundred dollars — all American!

FIDEL. Clean his pockets.

(Alvarez rifles through his pockets producing some cash.)

162

ALVAREZ. 'Bout fifty bucks U.S.

FIDEL. *(to Alvarez)* Hold on to it. *(to Manny)* I'm surprised you've still got fifty dollars. Slowing down there, Manny?

MANNY. I just got into town this morning.

FIDEL. It looks like you still owe us fifty more. But I'll tell you what: I'm going to get the cash, but not from you, I'm getting it from Rico's hide — plus all the other money that he owes us.

MANNY. Do I — do I still have to go see Carlos?

FIDEL. *(after a short pause)* No, Carlos needn't break a sweat on you. Lions don't catch flies.

MANNY. Oh, thank you! Thank you! You're a good man!

FIDEL. Tino, he needs cut.

(Fidel makes a motion by his ear with his hand.)

MANNY. What? What? *(to Tino)* What's he mean?

(As Fidel speaks the following lines, Tino pulls out a knife.)

FIDEL. We got to mark you, Manny.

TINO. Come, I'm just going to clip your wings, my little cricket!

FIDEL. This way we know you won't be blubbering to Rico 'fore we track him down. Because if he sees the mark of Carlos, then he'll know you talked, and he'll take out the garbage for us. It's for your own good.

(With Alvarez holding down Manny, Tino cuts off the top of Manny's ear. Manny is screaming hysterically. A policeman enters anxiously.)

POLICEMAN. What the — ? Ah, Fidel. *(pausing to look at the situation, he relaxes)* Is everything okay?

FIDEL. It's fine.

POLICEMAN. *(taking off his hat and wiping his brow)* Oh boy, this heat wave — it just won't break.

FIDEL. *(unable to hear over Manny's screaming)* Say what?

POLICEMAN. *(loudly)* I say, this is some heat. You need some help here?

FIDEL. Nope. We're good. But thanks.

POLICEMAN. Well okay. Just, uh, be sure to clean up your mess. Goodnight.

(Manny stops screaming. The policeman exits. Tino and Alvarez untie Manny and step back.)

FIDEL. *(to Manny, after he stops screaming)* There, was that so bad? Now get out of here.

(Manny, untied, gets up, holding his ear with blood dripping down his neck and shirt.)

MANNY. *(looking down at the ground)* Thanks, Fidel.

(Manny exits quickly.)

FIDEL. *(as Manny is scurrying off)* You stay low now, Manny. Just a day or so. It won't take long for us to smoke out Rico. *(To Tino and Alvarez)* Let's go. You can update Ysmael.
TINO. Wait a sec. I need to cool my grill.

(Tino pulls out a flask and drinks from it. He then hands it to Alvarez, who swigs. They sit down on some old crates.)

ALVAREZ. This fever — it won't break until we're broke. When will it rain?
TINO. Rain? What's rain? If my flesh weren't melting to a stew, I swear, I'd crumble to a pile of tinder!
FIDEL. You won't blow away too soon, you ox.
TINO. Ah me, not soon. But look — just look around. Everything's turned brown.
FIDEL. Yeah? How are we to fix it?
ALVAREZ. You'd think that Carlos —
FIDEL. *(laughing)* What the —? How can Carlos fix the weather?
ALVAREZ. I don't know, but you remember the Cueto brothers out of Cali. Remember them? Well, this was — what now — eight years past? They lorded over all this region. And Carlos, he was just ambition then. Well, one thundering night, Carlos sat with them to make his claim for more control. But they just laughed. A big mistake — a big mistake! Carlos stood, and smiling darkly said the brothers wouldn't live to feel the new day's sun. That night, while driving to their villa near the Cauca River, their car broke down and they were struck by lightning waiting for a ride. Both dead before the dawn. Just as Carlos said.
TINO. I heard that it was six men killed by three lightning bolts.
ALVAREZ. No, Fazio was there — he told me honest.
TINO. No! Faz couldn't have been there — he joined with Carlos just four years ago.

ALVAREZ. What the fuck! I'm just saying: If Carlos can control the lightning he can make it rain.

(A young man with a small mustache enters. He is awkward looking, wearing a hat and ill-fitted, ill-matched clothes — giving the impression of a clown. He is unusually cheerful and full of energy — rather manic. Tino and Alvarez generally avoid looking at him out of contempt.)

STRANGER. Hello, my friends. I see your practicing catch and release. But how's the fisherman of souls to satisfy his appetite when you just let them go?

TINO. We throw the small ones back.

STRANGER. *(laughing)* You're after bigger game! That's good! That's very noble! Ambition crowns us gods among the apes. Your friend, though, you've made quite a mess of him before you threw him back.

TINO. He wasn't our friend.

ALVAREZ. If you don't want the same, get lost.

STRANGER. No sooner said than done, for I've been shipwrecked on the reef of time — shelterless and trying to keep myself afloat. Some change would help to current me home.

(The Stranger goes to Alvarez and then to Tino with his hand out.)

A bill? A coin? A smile?

ALVAREZ. Fuck you. Get out of here!

TINO. Move on or get a thrashing!

STRANGER. They turned down Jesus, too.

TINO. Yeah? You don't look like him.

STRANGER. We share the face of god on us, or so the story's told, and by this logic we can assume he wears our mug; which, come to think of it, explains the world's muddled affairs where good is masked as evil, and lies charade as truth. *(walking to Fidel)* D'you know what day it is?

FIDEL. It's Wednesday.

STRANGER. Ah. For the English it's the day of Woden, the shepherd of the dead. He leads the wandering souls to their after-home, you know. It's true. Say, help a dead-tired man to find his home?

(The Stranger holds out his hand. Fidel pulls a bill from his pocket and gives it to him.)

I knew this town wasn't without a heart.

FIDEL. Okay, you've had your preach and filled the plate. Now move along.

STRANGER. I like it here — this town is nice. Very quiet but for the screams of men getting their ears trimmed.

TINO. Look here, patches, move it! Perhaps you'd like to meet with Carlos!

ALVAREZ. *(laughing)* Yeah, Carlos!

STRANGER. Carlos? Sure. I like all kinds of people! Yes, every man's his own song.

TINO. He'd teach a tramp like you to sing — his whip will help you to reach the higher notes. There used to be a slacker — Ricardo, was it? It doesn't matter, but this guy, he mooched and mooched off everyone like some damned flea. Well, he never did a bit of work — not good or bad. He was like a cobweb that left the itch on you. Well, one day Carlos found him lifting money from the community center fund. So Carlos locked him inside a barrel, stuck it full of four-inch nails, then rolled it down the hill and in the river. Oh! You should've heard the fucking song that weasel sang!

(Tino and Alvarez laugh.)

STRANGER. Ah, very quaint. A barrel of fun. But what's this man to me, this "Carly"?

ALVAREZ. Carlos! You've never heard of Carlos? Carlos Marquez? Carlos the Lion?

STRANGER. Hmm, I know a Pedro Marquez — and a Carlos DeLeone (who owes me money). And I know Reynard, my old butcher's cat. But I don't know any lion.

ALVAREZ. What the fuck? No, Carlos Marquez. Carlos controls the entire region — from here to Puerto Berrio. The leftists, the militias, the gangs — they all jump when he calls.

FIDEL. Look — Carlos keeps the peace here. He's brought order to this place, opened community centers, built football fields, helped widows.

STRANGER. A philanthropic murderer? Sounds fascinating. I'd love to meet him.

TINO. Ha! I don't think you'd like it very much.

STRANGER. Really, he sounds amazing. I'd love to talk to him of man and god.

TINO. You won't be offering up such airy thoughts when he boils you in
    oil. Ha!

STRANGER.   A dangerous man — I love it. God doesn't give the lion
    claws for their aesthetics. No! Why, all day long I see the same old
    sheep and cows. You have to take me to him — I've got to meet this
    man-lion — right now!

TINO. Look you — uh ....

STRANGER. Let's go! What? He doesn't have to be afraid of me.

ALVAREZ. *(approaching the Stranger angrily)* All right! All right — you're
    going to see him! *(pausing and getting a puzzled look)* But — but ....

TINO. But not right now. He's — he's out of town.

STRANGER. Then he'll be back soon.

ALVAREZ. I don't know...

STRANGER. Well, when did he leave?

TINO. It's — uh — been a little while.

STRANGER. A little while? How long's a little while? A week?

ALVAREZ. *(looking at Tino)* I don't know. It's been, what — six months?

TINO. I think it's almost eight months.

STRANGER. Eight months! Well, surely you've talked to him.

TINO. Me? Well, no.

ALVAREZ. No one has, but Ysmael.

STRANGER. Well friends, it might be time to check his vital signs. Eight
    months? To the sky bear, that's but a shrug. And yet the marigold
    is unwound from seed to flower to death. But for a man, well, the
    eight-month sleeper wakes to no trumpet.

TINO. *(angrily)* What's that you're saying?

STRANGER. I'm saying that if your nose detects a stench, you'd best be
    checking on your tenant.

TINO. Watch your fucking mouth.

STRANGER. Wait — you've never even thought of it? The lion, Carlos,
    might be dead?

ALVAREZ. Don't even say it!

STRANGER. Silence has no meaning, friends, yet words add little
    weight upon the blacksmith's blow.

    To speak foolishness is to own it.

    To speak silence is to break it.

    To speak truth is to uphold it.

ALVAREZ. We told you to shut your yap!

FIDEL. Enough now, gypsy, you've heard the growl, don't draw the
    teeth.

STRANGER. So, you're as thin-skinned as the rest? It makes you
nervous, eh? Though it may dress in patches, bells and pointed
shoes, the truth's the truth — and yet it's treated as a ragged
beggar. *(to Tino)* You wanted a song? Now listen!

(the Stranger sings the following)

> A bell, a bell, rung night to day,
> Heigh ho, heigh hey, the rain,
> It shakes the air, it quakes the bed,
> But cannot wake the dead.

TINO. *(grabbing at the Stranger)* Come here you fucking bastard!
STRANGER. *(eluding Tino)* Ah, yesterday moves slower than today, the
truth 'lights on a nimbler foot!
TINO. Come here!
STRANGER. What? You don't like my song?
ALVAREZ. Carlos isn't dead!
STRANGER. Perhaps he died not for our sins but of their weight — was
laid upon the counting table counting our omissions — here a
blackbird, there a pie. Yes, laid upon the kingly scales and found a
man of fire and feathers.

> The sky swirls and we creep.
> The wheel turns and we sleep.

> Goodnight!

(The Stranger starts to leave.)

TINO. Come here you damned mosquito!

(Tino and Alvarez walk toward the stranger to apprehend him.)

STRANGER. *(as he runs offstage)*
> He's dead, he's dead,
> And all the king's men
> They will not see him —
> Not ever again!

TINO & ALVAREZ. Hey! Hey! Stop!

(Tino and Alvarez chase the Stranger offstage. The Stranger's laughter can be heard offstage. Fidel follows to the edge of the stage but stops and watches. He is alone for a few moments. But soon, Tino and Alvarez reappear and they walk back sharing drinks from the flask.)

TINO. *(reaching out to Alvarez)* Give it here. *(taking the flask and sitting down again)* A bird can't fly on just one wing.
FIDEL. What? No luck netting that mosquito, eh?
TINO. It's like he slit the air and vanished in it.
ALVAREZ. Poof! And he was fucking nothing.

(Tino and Alvarez sit down again.)

FIDEL. A queer kid. Very strange.
TINO. Yes, really! Carlos dead. Ha!
ALVAREZ. It's unbelievable!
TINO. Unthinkable!
ALVAREZ. Yeah, really! Fuck.
TINO. Sure, no one's seen him in almost a year.
ALVAREZ. That's not that long.
TINO. A year, it's —
ALVAREZ. A year — that has been weird.
TINO. What if — ?
ALVAREZ. What if he's — ?
FIDEL. All right, enough.
TINO. But that stranger — he made some good points. He knew about the trip to Bogota.
FIDEL. He never said a word of Bogota!
TINO. Then tell us what you think, Fidel.
FIDEL. Carlos just tells me what to do, I see it's done, and I tell him it's done. That's what I think.
ALVAREZ. Dependable Fidel, always on the job. Well, what you going to do if Carlos —
FIDEL. Come on, enough! If Carlos heard us talk he'd hang us by our thumbs. Why let that gadfly stoke these fires in your skulls?
ALVAREZ. I guess so. But ...
FIDEL. But what?

TINO. But nothing. *(getting up)* Let's get back to Ysmael. Come on Al.

(Tino takes a drink from the flask.)

I'm still fucking roasting.

(Alvarez gets up and exits with Tino, talking quietly among themselves. Fidel pauses for a moment in thought, then exits. The lights go down.)

ACT I SCENE 2

(Scene: A private room above a nightclub which serves as Ysmael's office. There's only one window visible to the left behind a desk. There is also a small bar in the rear next to a door, center rear. A sofa and couple soft chairs — one nicer than the other — sit in the center in a small semi-circle around a coffee table. Tomasa, Orlando and Miguel sit on the sofa and one chair. The nicest chair, Ysmael's, is empty as he walks to the bar. Fidel stands by Ysmael's chair, Vincente stands at the edge of the room by the door. Ysmael sniffles and twitches nervously throughout the scene from recently using cocaine.)

YSMAEL. *(pouring himself a drink at the bar)* What do you take me for? A rube? A dope? Bah! It's all just feverish thoughts leaping from the infected mouths of dreamers to the thirsty ears of fools. Why, I'm surprised, Fidel, you'd even give a voice to this.

FIDEL. I give nothing but a report, Ysmael.

TOMASA. Carlos dead — fascinating.

YSMAEL. *(pacing around)* "Carlos dead" — Just saying it's absurd! The words can barely pass the lips without embarrassment. Who'd dare cross knives with Carlos? I remember Carlos coming here, right here in this very room, to talk about the mules. We were sitting here at the table, Julio Rivera to my left, when Carlos, he comes in and 'fore he even takes a seat, he pulls his gun and boom boom boom! Blasts Rivera three times in the head: Juan's brains and blood all over me! I was a god damned mess! We then find out later that Juan was rat for the CIA and Carlos knew, just fucking knew. No one told him, he just fucking knew!

FIDEL. *(darkly)* The stranger didn't say that he was killed.

YSMAEL. *(sneering)* So Carlos maybe drowned in the tub? Ha!

TOMASA. Carlos dead — fascinating!

YSMAEL. *(angrily)* What the —! What's so fucking fascinating about it? Why do you keep mumbling that? It ain't fascinating. It's bullshit! This silly, god-damned rumor just might make people do some silly, god-damned things!

(Ysmael goes to his chair and sits down. Fidel walks a bit farther to the rear.)

TOMASA. If people did no silly, stupid things then beans are all we'd eat.

YSMAEL. What is that supposed to mean?

TOMASA. The hungry tiger must be smarter than his meal.

YSMAEL. I — oh screw it. *(to the rest)* Anyway, I talked to Carlos
yesterday on the phone.

TOMASA. *(bored)* Again?

YSMAEL. Don't mess with me, Tomasa. Not now. *(sits down and
addresses the rest)* You know how Carlos — is. I don't know why he
won't come back in person. He's always had the fire in his brain.

ORLANDO. Like the time he'd only eat chorizo — ha!

YSMAEL. Yeah! Living in that pequeña casa eating chorizo every meal,
chorizo every day, chorizo for a month — and we just rolled our
eyes. But from that freaking mind comes brilliant fucking ideas —
like his plan to bring together the guerillas and the militias —
genius! And we've had peace for two years — and that's been great
for business.

MIGUEL. What'd Carlos want this time, Ysmael?

YSMAEL. He talked about the meeting Wednesday.

MIGUEL. Yeah, about that meeting, man. I don't know. This has me
staring at the ceiling at nights. The militia and guerilla leaders
meeting here the first time in two years and Carlos won't be there
to keep the peace. I'd sleep a whole lot better knowing Carlos was
going to be there.

ORLANDO. Shit. Me, too.

YSMAEL. Why? Aren't our beards grown thick enough? Carlos has faith
in us, why don't you?

MIGUEL. It ain't that simple, Ysmael. Carlos — Carlos knows things —

YSMAEL. And I don't?

MIGUEL. No, no, I mean, well, yes — well, none of us are fucking
Carlos. Don't you see?

ORLANDO. Miguel is right. You can't unleash two wildcats in a room
and not expect a scrap. But Carlos brings the hammer, and with it
the threat he'll fucking use it. All of us combined can't swing that
weight.

YSMAEL. Oh, they'll feel Carlos' heel on their necks, don't you doubt it.
They'll know he's very close and very closely watching them. If
there's a double cross, Carlos will grind their bones to fucking
meal.

MIGUEL. Yeah, but —

YSMAEL. It's time to make our businesses legit. I understand your
worries, I do. They're all well placed; this ain't a smash and grab.
But let's put these fears to use in our preparations. Carlos believes
in us. Tomorrow I'll talk to Garcia and we'll set up the meeting
with his commander. Then we'll take the steps to make sure it goes
smooth as my lady's ass.

MIGUEL. Okay.

YSMAEL. Good. We know the script. Now let's make sure that every line's performed on the mark. *(to Tomasa)* Tomasa, I want your people plain in sight — there can't be any foolishness. Garcia is beloved here. We couldn't keep the peace without him.

(Everyone nods.)

TOMASA. We'll be as plain as day and wide as the sky, with beaming smiles and loaded guns. It would take a fool to try us — but not a fool for long.

YSMAEL. *(getting up moving toward the door)* That's good, that's good. But now I've got to go. Fidel, I want you to find that Rico and I want that fucker dead. You got it?

FIDEL. I got it.

YSMAEL. You sure? I worry about you being too lenient with these bums.

FIDEL. Don't you worry, I'll take care of it.

YSMAEL. Good, good. *(starts to leave but stops, looks at everyone)* About this rumor: Keep it quiet. I don't want it breathed outside this room. You hear? You hear? That's good.

(Everyone exits except Tomasa and Vincente.)

TOMASA. Carlos dead? Those two words are as poisonous to the ear as the mouth. They're like a walking fire — it's sure to put a blaze beneath some men's hopes! But from that fire perhaps we can smoke out the lion, our missing Carlos. He'll have no choice but to rise up from his resting place. Vince!

VINCENTE. Yes, ma'am?

TOMASA. You heard the rumor here?

VINCENTE. I did.

TOMASA. I want this thistle sown, yes, planted in the ear of every man and woman in the city. I want it winding on every tongue.

VINCENTE. But what of Ysmael's order?

TOMASA. What of it? You sow, I'll reap. Besides, the best way to prove a falsehood is to repeat many times. Didn't you know that? Now you do. Just do what I tell you.

VINCENTE. Yes, ma'am.

TOMASA. Good, then go. We'll set aside the stones — instead we'll let the weight of words lean on their bones.

(The lights go down.)

ACT II SCENE 1

(Scene: Late afternoon. A clean but old city hotel lobby. The lobby is a large, fairly open room with the street entrance to the right. The lobby contains a small counter left-center stage, and several pieces of old furniture and perhaps a TV in a waiting area to the right, inside the door. To the left of the counter are stairs going to the rooms. Beneath and behind the stairs is a door to the back alley. A woman in her late sixties, Sophia, sits at the counter, desultorily reading a magazine, fanning herself with a piece of paper. Fidel enters followed closely by a man and woman.)

FIDEL. Forget about it. Don't bring it up — don't even think about it!

WOMAN. But you won't tell us if it's true!

MAN. We met him once — Carlos — just one time. I'll never forget it! It was opening of his community center on El Poblado Avenue.

WOMAN. Yes, yes.

MAN. Carlos cut the ribbon then started handing out American twenty-dollar bills — oh! The children danced. Such a happy scene!

FIDEL. I remember that.

WOMAN. Yeah, it was some time back. I think that building is a pawn shop now.

FIDEL. What? Where'd all the money —

MAN. Yes, that's right. But to our question.

WOMAN. Is it true?

FIDEL. Look — I'm not debating madmen, devils or ghosts. I asked if you knew where Rico was. That's all I want to know. And you followed me in here with a bunch of fool questions. But you never answered mine, did you? Where's Rico?

MAN. Rico? What? What do you want him for? We've haven't seen him since his sister died.

FIDEL. Just recently?

WOMAN. Not long ago. A month — or maybe less.

FIDEL. She live 'round here?

WOMAN. No, she was out of town. I'm not sure where.

FIDEL. Do you think he went to her old place?

MAN. I doubt it. He didn't even go to her funeral.

WOMAN. What kind of monster doesn't go to his sister's funeral?

FIDEL. You sure he didn't go?

WOMAN. Positive.

FIDEL. If you find out where she lived, you let me know.

WOMAN. Sure, sure. But — you didn't answer our question.

(Fidel frowns.)

MAN. *(looking around furtively, then speaking in a whisper)* Is Carlos dead?
FIDEL. Augh! Get out of here! Save your whispers for the altar shadows, and when you're ready to speak to the light of day, you come see me.
WOMAN. You see, he never answers our question!
MAN. It must be bad. Yes, very bad.
WOMAN. Worse than we feared!
MAN. That's bad.
FIDEL. Oh, for Christ's sake — Carlos isn't dead. Now move along!

(Fidel guides them narrowly to the door.)

There you go.

(The man and woman leave while talking quietly to each other.)

SOPHIA. A curious pair of birds!
FIDEL. *(coming over to the counter)* Curious but not rare. Like wrens, they light on me everywhere I go. "Oh, the stranger! What'd he look like? What'd he do? What'd he say? Do you believe him?" The rumor has inflamed their brains.
SOPHIA. It's all I hear.
FIDEL. Hmm.
SOPHIA. Most people think that Ysmael killed Carlos. What do you think?
FIDEL. Thinking's overrated.
SOPHIA. *(smiling)* Some people think the Governor did him in, and others say the DEA, some even think that Jesus reached down from heaven and scooped him up. Who do you think killed Carlos?
FIDEL. I'm just Carlos' errand boy searching for Rico. I'm not here to think.

(Sophia laughs and comes around the counter and puts her arm around Fidel.)

SOPHIA. My boy, my boy! If you don't want to tell me, that's fine. But such a lie! *(she laughs, then stands back, seriously)* This rumor — it's like a splinter — no one can stop the fussing till it's out.
FIDEL. What's said, though, can't be plucked from the air and — unspoken and unheard.
SOPHIA. The answer won't put out the rumors?

FIDEL. I'm not so sure now. Questions like that — they create a void. Everything rushes into that gap and soon nothing's able to stop the undertow — not even the truth.

SOPHIA. What of Ysmael?

FIDEL. What of him?

SOPHIA. He claims he's spoken to Carlos.

FIDEL. So?

SOPHIA. D'you think he's lying?

FIDEL. I never said —

(Tomasa walks in with Vincente. She walks over and stands next to Fidel. Sophia does not move.)

TOMASA. Ah, Fidel, my loyal friend! Another scorching day out there — I love it! Hot and hotter! Best and better! It gives the city a crisp feel, and lends a hardness to the stone. But how are you both doing?

FIDEL. Good, I guess. This is a surprise.

TOMASA. What? Can't I visit?

SOPHIA. You've never come before.

TOMASA. Then I guess I'm overdue and I owe you both an apology — the fault is mine to let habit bar me from your door.

FIDEL. Well, what can we do for you?

TOMASA. Ha! You and I, we're all about the business, eh? Nose to the trail, so to speak, eh? But me — I like to talk, and you, you like to listen and absorb — soak it in like a sponge. Ha! Now, though, I need your full absorption — alone if you don't mind.

(Fidel looks over to Sophia, who walks away.)

FIDEL. Okay. What's up?

TOMASA. I have a tip on Rico for you. *(pulling out a slip of paper and handing it to Fidel)* He was seen at this address a while back. No guarantee he's there right now, but maybe you can find his scent there.

FIDEL. *(looking at the sheet)* Thanks. I know that place. I heard his sister died recently. I wonder if that had anything to do with his grab.

TOMASA. His sister dead? Hmm, that's too bad. I heard that he was propping her up. Sending her money.

FIDEL. That's odd.

TOMASA. What's so odd about that?

FIDEL. He didn't go to her funeral. *(putting the paper in this pocket)* But never mind that. Thanks for the tip.

TOMASA. You're welcome. That's one mystery.

FIDEL. There's another?

TOMASA. *(smiling at his question)* Another? Why it's the mystery of all mysteries! Don't be coy. You can play the stoic, but not the fool. Ha! *(suddenly become severe and serious)* These rumors of Carlos' death — they smolder in the people's ears. I had some questions about the stranger.

FIDEL. You and everybody else. I told you all I know.

TOMASA. You did, but it was sketched in hasty strokes. You didn't know the stranger? He didn't look familiar?

FIDEL. No, not at all.

TOMASA. *(staring deeply at him)* You didn't recognize his face? You looked him in the eye?

FIDEL. He stood as close to me as you.

TOMASA. *(stroking her chin)* And nothing looked familiar, hmm? What did he wear?

FIDEL. Um, a buttoned shirt, in blue and white, uh, a tight blue cap. Looked nineteen to twenty-five — a small mustache. Quite hyped up, maybe on drugs.

TOMASA. A tight blue cap? *(pauses in thoughtfulness)* No accent? No clues to where he was from?

FIDEL. Oh yeah, he spoke with an accent — crazy north-north-west, but that land has no borders.

TOMASA. *(she pauses, then laughs out loud)* Ah, that's true, that's true! *(then becoming serious again)* But Carlos — dead? D'you think it's possible?

FIDEL. I've heard of a German cat that lives in a box. It's said to be both alive and dead — at the same time. No one knows until they open the box and look at it.

TOMASA. *(laughs again)* You're full of strange wisdom, yes, you are! But if we open the box — ?

FIDEL. I'd hardly base my thoughts upon the ravings of a gypsy.

TOMASA. But Carlos dead? It seems impossible.

FIDEL. Then it must be impossible.

TOMASA. *(smiles broadly)* You're right: The simplicity is obvious! I remember, oh, some years back, before you joined — he had a meeting with suppliers from the north. Those were the seed days — the planting of the Carlos legend. His men said he should take some backup to the meeting in case of trouble or a double cross — these dealers were notorious cheats and killers. But Carlos wouldn't hear of it. Instead, he wanted me and Pablo — just me and Pablo — to drive him there. When we met he handed me the keys. (For some strange reason Carlos had me drive. I doubt he

even knew my name — he just waved at me and said "You
drive.") Well, we get there and I recall as he walked in the house,
he turned to us and smirked, then through the door he went. We
sat there quite a while, when suddenly the air cracked with gunfire
— screams and curses, shattering glass, and more gunfire! Pablo,
white as a ghost, screamed "Let's go — get the fuck out of here!"
But I was froze with fear. I didn't have enough of sense to leave.
Ha ha! I thought for sure that Carlos was dead and they'd come
out to finish us — but I couldn't move. Then, who comes out, but
Carlos, and he smiles, perhaps surprised to see us waiting for him.
Well, he gets in the car and never says a word. I shook so bad that I
could hardly drive. Ha! I never doubted Carlos after that.

FIDEL. And there's no reason to start now. Why, almost every week he's
calling Ysmael.

TOMASA. Yes, that's true. If those calls ....

FIDEL. What?

TOMASA. Oh, it's just silliness, I guess. Ysmael has no reason to deceive
us, does he? He'd have nothing to gain by it. But even if he did,
he'd never do such a thing, would he?

FIDEL. I can't speak for Ysmael's motives.

TOMASA. Yes, yes. Who can? Each man's heart's a cipher. But he was
livid about the rumors, wasn't he?

FIDEL. He was, but I imagine he has lots of reasons. Next week's
meeting for a start.

TOMASA. (glancing out the window) Yes, yes. The meeting. Yes, that's
true. Well, I've another reason for my visit.

FIDEL. (with a curious smile) There's more? Please tell.

TOMASA. You've always been Carlos' personal soldier. If he wants
something done, and done right, he knows you'll make sure it
happens.

FIDEL. (unsure where this is going) Yeah.

TOMASA. Whether it's money, women or drugs, he trusts you without
limit, and without doubt. So he's let you freelance without a
membership in any of the gangs. That's a laurel — a credit to your
loyalty and honesty.

FIDEL. Thanks, I guess.

TOMASA. And while I'm sure you like the freedom it affords you, be
aware that there's danger in this freelancing. You're standing all
alone, exposed with no one to watch your back.

FIDEL. But Carlos.

TOMASA. Yes, yes, I suppose. But that's rather abstract protection from
a bullet in the spine. I've come to offer you a place inside my
organization. Not much will change — you'll still serve Carlos as

you always have, with your accustomed freedoms, but I'd like to have you in our family — to stay with us. You'll be safer there. And we could use a person of your talents and judgment.

FIDEL. Well, Tomasa, I'm not quite sure what to say. I'm flattered, of course. I appreciate the offer, but I'm happy with the way things are.

TOMASA. The way things are don't always stay the way they are. From the butterfly's wing come hurricanes.

FIDEL. I know. And I appreciate your concern but I think I'll stay where I am.

TOMASA. I like you, Fidel. You're not living out some coked-up Hollywood fantasy. You don't care about the drugs, or the money or the sex — in that way you're much like Carlos. Very Spartan. Bored with the trappings. Yes, you've got feet, you're grounded, you know the earth — just make sure you jump when it starts moving. (pauses) So you won't come? Well, I can't say I'm surprised. The hole you burrow will always be your own. I'll have my people keep an eye on you — we'll be your guardian angels.

FIDEL. Thanks, but there's no need for that.

TOMASA. Of course, of course. The offer stands, though, if you feel a change in the weather coming. Oh — what time is it?

FIDEL. It's about six fifty-five.

TOMASA. Ah, I must leave. That leftist, Garcia, will be here any moment. You can avoid these social niceties, but I, sadly, can't. The man's got free hands you know. But then you wouldn't know. Such is a woman's fate in a man's world. Yes, what they see, they feel compelled to touch, and what they touch, to own. But they forget to ask the price, and it's a price they can't afford. They never understand. Well, thank you for the chat.

FIDEL. Sure. Stop by any time.

TOMASA. Really? That means a lot to me.

(Tomasa waves goodbye to Sophia and leaves with Vincente. Sophia comes over.)

SOPHIA. Now that was weird. What'd she want?

FIDEL. She had a tip on Rico.

SOPHIA. Just business. Hmm.

FIDEL. And asked if I would join her organization.

SOPHIA. She asked you what?

FIDEL. To join her gang. She said it was too dangerous to be separated from the herd.

SOPHIA. Well, I can't say I disagree with that reasoning. But joining up with her, oh my! Why, she's the shopping cart that has the crazy wheel. Her gang?

FIDEL. She said her men would keep an eye on me. Is that supposed to be a comfort or a threat?

SOPHIA. I don't like it — not one bit.

FIDEL. It's very strange.

SOPHIA. It is. That woman's strange!

FIDEL. Her crazy honesty is disarming.

SOPHIA. I'm not sure how crazy or how honest she is.

FIDEL. In just six months, she's risen from nothing to leading Pablo's gang. That's pretty amazing.

SOPHIA. I'd never believed it if I hadn't seen it. She's so odd!

FIDEL. She raised a lot of questions about Ysmael, too — about his motives.

SOPHIA. Does she think that Ysmael —

FIDEL. I don't know. She dressed his motives poorly. And yet her words were veiled and indirect. I'm not quite sure what she was telling me, so I remained as vague as possible myself.

SOPHIA. That was a good idea.

(A crashing noise comes from outside. Then a rapid series of gunshots, then a machine gun. There is screaming and more shots fired. Then more confused shouts, gunfire and noise. Sophia and Fidel duck to the floor.)

Dear lord Jesus! What's that?

(Fidel cautiously scampers to the window. Offstage someone shouts, "Where did he go?" Suddenly a man with a small machine guns rushes in the door and grabs Sophia as a hostage.)

INTRUDER. Back off everyone! Hands up!

(Fidel raises his hands but walks toward the intruder.)

Where's the back door? Stop right there!

FIDEL. Let her go.

INTRUDER. Shut up, fucker, or I'll cut you in half. Where's the god damned door!

FIDEL. Back there — behind the steps.

(The intruder starts moving toward the back door with Sophia past Fidel. Tomasa enters quickly carrying a pistol, enters. The Intruder spins and seems surprised to see Tomasa. Fidel knocks away the intruder's gun, and throws him to the floor. Sophia is thrown to the opposite way.)

TOMASA. *(raising her gun at the intruder)* Ah, there you are —
FIDEL. Don't —
INTRUDER. *(hisses something that sounds like "Trap!")*

(Tomasa fires multiple shots into the intruder. Everyone pauses for moment. Fidel helps Sophia get up, Tomasa walks toward the dead man.)

FIDEL. Are you all right?
SOPHIA. *(nodding her head weakly)* I think so.
FIDEL. What happened? Why'd you kill him?
TOMASA. *(searching the dead man's pockets)* He killed Garcia — shot him
    down in the street.
FIDEL. Jesus Christ! That's going to pour gas all over the fire.
TOMASA. You bet.
FIDEL. Were there others?

(Vincente comes in.)

TOMASA. *(laughs quietly to herself, puts her gun away while standing)* Yes,
    all dead. *(to Vincente)* I took care of the last one.

(The lights go down.)

ACT III SCENE 1

(Fidel, Tino and Alvarez enter an apartment. The afternoon daylight peaks around the edges of the tightly drawn curtains, but otherwise the room is dark. Bottles and trash and clothes lay on the floor, along with several sleeping people. Tino wipes his brow.)

TINO. What the hell — it's burning up in here! It's like a firecracker lit
    on both ends — fuck! It's hot!
ALVAREZ. The heat! The heat! Shut up about the fucking heat — it only
    makes it worse. What's up with you? "I'm so hot! I'm burning up!"
    You going through menopause or something?

(Fidel and Alvarez laugh.)

TINO. Menopause? Fuck. At least I'm done with puberty. I got hair all
    over my body, little boy. Someday, if you're balls fall down, you
    might too.
ALVAREZ. Yeah, maybe you should shave your fucking back, you
    fucking ape.
FIDEL. *(walking to the center of the room)* Okay, now. Stay alert. Let's
    wake up these orphans.

(Tino and Alvarez go through the room and kick the people sleeping until they start to get up. Fidel bends down and nudges them.)

    Any of them him?
TINO. *(to one of the people)* Any of you him? You, are you him? Is he you?
    Them, are you him? No, you're her, not him. *(to Fidel)* I don't see
    anyone of him or her in them. Eiee! This is giving me a headache.

(While Tino talks, unseen by Fidel, Tino or Alvarez, a man furtively stands up from a pile of old clothes behind Fidel. He hides behind the door.)

FIDEL. Folks — has anyone seen Rico? Rico Duarte? We're told that he
    was here not long ago. *(to a middle-aged woman sitting on the floor
    near him)* You — have you seen him?
WOMAN. Who — what? Rico? No —

(The man behind Fidel pulls a knife and lunges toward him. Fidel sees him just in time to escape the knife. They struggle, then Tino strikes the man on the head and he goes down unconscious. Alvarez picks up the knife.)

TINO. Jesus — you almost got slit open.

(Alvarez looks over the body.)

FIDEL. *(loudly and angrily)* Damn it! Is that the punk Rico?
ALVAREZ. *(turning over the body)* No. I don't know who that is. He must
    have been hopped out of his mind.
FIDEL. *(to the woman)* Who's that? Who is it!
WOMAN. I don't know! I don't live here. I just passed out here last
    night.
FIDEL. Just passed out here? Who'd want to sleep in this fucking dump?
    Eat and breathe this filth? You people got no fucking pride? No
    dignity? *(he starts kicking stuff around)* Rotten food and trash. Look,
    dirty needles. A disgrace!
TINO. What do you expect of a pig but a grunt?
FIDEL. *(to one of the others)* Who the hell lives here? Who? No one wants
    to talk?

(No one responds. Fidel pulls open the curtain revealing the bright afternoon light. The people cower and groan.)

    Here — let's pour some disinfectant in the room — some honest
    light. You see? The truth hurts. Don't shield your eyes and groan —
    look at yourselves! Twisting your faces from your nakedness! Look
    at the gutter you're crawling through, people! Open up your eyes,
    god damn it, look! Counting out the minutes till you escape again
    down the shadowy pipe of junk and cheap rum. There's nowhere
    else to run, my friends! This is the bottom. Give up trying to forget
    your face, and embrace the light's hard and unforgiving glare. Ah,
    you're hopeless! All of you!
TINO. Look at them — drug moths and good-time trippers — scum! We
    should throw them all outside with the trash. They're just needle-
    whores — all of 'em. *(pulls out a flask and taking a drink)* Look at
    them.
FIDEL. *(drops his head and pauses, then quietly)* They're people.

(Fidel deliberately walks over and re-closes the curtain. Turns to the woman and kneels down to talk to her face to face.)

FIDEL. You — do you know anything about Rico? Where can I find him?
WOMAN. Maybe a couple weeks ago — I seen him come and go.
FIDEL. But not lately.
WOMAN. No, not in a while. At least a week.
FIDEL. What was his play? Drugs?
WOMAN. No, Rico never touched the stuff. He was clean. He hated it.
    Every time I saw him he'd rant about it.
FIDEL. Then what's the story? A couple people said they saw him here.
WOMAN. They didn't tell you why? He came here for Mrs. Rodriguez'
    daughter, Fatima. He promised to bring her home, to get her help.
FIDEL. Mmm.
WOMAN. I heard it got a little messy. He was dragging the girl out and
    she was screaming. Then Raul pulled out his gun and started
    shouting. Well, Rico didn't never carry a gun.
FIDEL. Really?
WOMAN. He didn't like them. But he stared down Raul and left with
    Fatima under his arm.
FIDEL. Oh. Okay. Call me if you hear something.

(Fidel hands her some cash.)

    Buy yourself something to eat — no drugs.
WOMAN. Thanks.

(Fidel stands up.)

    I did hear — I heard —
FIDEL. What?
WOMAN. *(not sure if she should say something)* I — I —
FIDEL. What is it. *(kneeling down again)*
WOMAN. I heard — that Carlos — that Carlos — is dead. Is that true?

(Tino and Alvarez snicker. Fidel stands, visibly trying to control his anger.)

FIDEL. Where'd you hear that garbage?
WOMAN. The people talk. I hear things.
FIDEL. You're hearing things, all right. I'm looking for Rico. That's all.
WOMAN. Well — is he?
FIDEL. What?
WOMAN. Dead.
FIDEL. Yeah, but he don't know it yet.
WOMAN. Not Rico — Carlos.
FIDEL. You'd best wean off that stuff. You're hearing the unicorns sing.

WOMAN. But is he — is the rumor true?

FIDEL. You dreamed it. You didn't hear it. That's the story. Now let it go. All of you.

(Fidel turns to leave but stops when the woman continues.)

WOMAN. You know I met Carlos, once. He handed me a shiny bronze medal.

FIDEL. He did?

WOMAN. Yes, my son was killed at — at the river ambush four years back, along with others.

FIDEL. Oh yeah, the tussle with the Pisa Cartel. I remember that fight. I'm sorry to hear 'bout your loss. Carlos took care of you, didn't he?

WOMAN. Carlos gave all the mothers of the dead a beautiful bronze medallion. It was emblazoned with a picture of a lion and a wolf and an eagle. And all were looking up toward a light — the sun, the future, perhaps to Carlos. And it had leaves entwined around the edges — and a shiny blue ribbon!

FIDEL. Where's yours at?

WOMAN. *(looking ashamed)* I — I had to sell it. With his father dead, I didn't have a job or any money. I was living in the alleys — and then the drugs. But it would shine — that thing would really shine! I used to stare into it and I would see another world.

(Fidel pulls out some more cash and gives it to her.)

FIDEL. The medallion sounds very beautiful. Here — do right with this. *(to Tino and Alvarez)* Let's get out of here.

TINO. The sooner the better. I'm fucking dying here.

(They start to leave, Fidel first.)

ALVAREZ. Tino's starting to get the vapors. Ha!

TINO. Yeah. Fuck you.

(Fidel, Tino and Alvarez exit. The lights go down.)

ACT III SCENE 2

(Scene: Ysmael's office. Ysmael, Tomasa, Miguel, Orlando and Fidel sit around the coffee table. Ysmael restlessly twitches.)

YSMAEL. What've you learn about those goons so far?

FIDEL. Four of them, from Ecuador. None local. Their connection we're trying to trace, but there's not much thread.

YSMAEL. That's it? That's it — Nothing? We're left here clutching at smoke?

FIDEL. They knew every tick of our operation — the date, the hour, the place. And came well armed: explosives, automatic weapons, vests. If Tomasa's men were less than lightning quick, it would have been much worse.

YSMAEL. *(agitated)* Worse? Worse!

(Ysmael gets up an angrily throws his glass against the wall where it shatters. He stalks around the room while ranting.)

How could such a fucked up fiery mess be worse! That I'd like to hear! Our hands are stained with failure! The government's coming. A war's a'brew! And yet — and yet it could have been fucking worse?

TOMASA. *(coolly)* Such a tantrum, Ysmael. It solves nothing. I'm disappointed.

YSMAEL. Yes. Disappointment seem the flavor of the day! I hope you like the bitter wash of it 'cause our mouths will soon be filled with it. And you — don't talk to me of tantrums! We'd know the masters if you hadn't cut the puppets' strings!

TOMASA. They answered life for life, breath for breath. My way — and Carlos' too. You getting soft?

YSMAEL. Now listen —

MIGUEL. Look, it's obvious — not? This has the general's fingerprints all over it — perhaps with help from someone inside Garcia's camp.

YSMAEL. *(stalking around the room)* Perhaps — I just don't — I suppose. It could have been a freelance job, or power struggle in Garcia's gang. It could — ah! It doesn't matter! It doesn't matter now if General Hernandez went down in broad daylight and pumped

Garcia full of lead — you see? 'Cause now Garcia's dead and we're all wearing his blood. The people are up in arms and, worse, this could lead to a war. And that's bad for business.

ORLANDO. Agreed. And that's why now — yes more than ever — we need Carlos — need him here — right now. He's the only one who can knock some sense into everyone.

TOMASA. Orlando's right. If the cons and the Marxists want a war, then Carlos is the only man to stop it.

YSMAEL. *(sitting down)* Carlos, Carlos! Always Carlos! Well, I heard from him. He torched me for forty minutes.

MIGUEL. He's coming back?

YSMAEL. Carlos? I don't know — don't know.

MIGUEL & ORLANDO. *(exasperated)* Augh!

MIGUEL. If not now, then when? Must flames swallow everything we've built before he's smoked out?

YSMAEL. Can anyone predict what Carlos will do? *(to Miguel)* Can you? *(to Tomasa)* Or you? Hell, maybe this *is* his plan! Who knows?

TOMASA. The rumor's spreading fast — his frown would solve that pretty quick.

YSMAEL. And that — on top of everything! If I catch anyone who's spewing that crap, they're dead — god damn it — fucking dead! *(to Fidel)* Has it been you?

FIDEL. *(sitting up and staring at Ysmael)* No, god damn it! It's been buzzing all around me, but I've said nothing!

TOMASA. *(to Ysmael)* All the little birds are whispering and they agree on this: You killed Carlos.

YSMAEL. What?

TOMASA. They say you had most to gain.

YSMAEL. Fucking gibberish!

FIDEL. It's true. That's the talk.

TOMASA. But tongues will wag, the ears will flap, and all the men and women have their say. What's a girl to do to stop it?

YSMAEL. Their twittering will stop in day or two — for some, perhaps forever. Tell them Carlos is returning.

ORLANDO. I thought you said he wasn't coming.

YSMAEL. Yes — he wanted it a secret. But now everyone needs to know.

ORLANDO. That's the best news I've heard all week!

YSMAEL. What are we? Babies? We can't take a dump without Carlos to help us?

MIGUEL. Come on. This town — it's Carlos', it's his creation, no? He made it in his image. Each man wears Carlos' mark branded on his neck, and on this obligation every head hangs. Only Carlos can pull the leash.

YSMAEL. Augh! Carlos has more faith in us than you!

TOMASA. It doesn't matter now, does it? Carlos will be here and later we can learn to tie our shoes.

ORLANDO. Amen, amen.

MIGUEL. So, when's he coming?

YSMAEL. A couple days, maybe three.

ORLANDO. That's good. Man, I feel better already.

TOMASA. *(standing up)* Well, I gotta go. We'll meet again tomorrow afternoon?

YSMAEL. I'll call.

MIGUEL. I have to go, too. I'll see you all tomorrow.

(Tomasa and Miguel exit.)

FIDEL. I guess I'll —

YSMAEL. Fidel — wait. What's new with Rico?

FIDEL. Still looking. He's just a couple steps ahead of me. But the gap is narrowing. We'll get him.

YSMAEL. Good, good. It's just too bad though. He was always so reliable. Finished all his jobs. I guess he got greedy. Now he'll have to pay.

FIDEL. Hmm.

YSMAEL. What else are you hearing out there?

FIDEL. 'Bout what?

YSMAEL. The rumors.

FIDEL. Stop trying to lay that all on me!

YSMAEL. I'm sorry. Really. You're not the one. I know you aren't. I was just fucking upset. But you can help: I want the word put out: Anyone who even mentions Carlos' death will get cut up. We'll fucking douse them!

FIDEL. Our threats will only clarify their suspicions — that you killed Carlos.

ORLANDO. That makes a lot of sense. If we keep blowing on the sparks we'll only make more flames.

FIDEL. You know what's going to stop the rumors? Carlos walking 'cross that street, picking up his paper, waving to the kids, and coming in that door. That will choke the air from those lies.

YSMAEL. Hmm. I don't like it. I don't like it! No. But I guess you're right. Okay then. Let me be.

(All leave but Tino. Ysmael sits down next to the phone staring at it. Tino stands off to the side.)

YSMAEL. The phone's a curious thing, my friend. From far away, from beyond the sloping horizon, there comes a call — a sudden shout: You jump, you run to answer its persistent, needy cry — and all for a bodiless voice, a faceless sound, a fleshless tongue descending in your ear and touching the quivering nerve. A haunting voice that's here, but isn't here — the vibrating end of a quavering conversation.

(Ysmael silently stares.)

TINO. You wanted to talk? About a plan?
YSMAEL. The plan?
TINO. The plan you wanted to me to hear.
YSMAEL. Ah, yes! Yes! I lost myself.

(Ysmael pauses to push the phone away.)

Yes, Tino, I've given them a voice, but they have no the ears; shown the way, but they've no eyes. They prefer to trudge the well-worn circles in the grass. Perhaps my plans are too fantastic. No? Well, Miguel, Orlando and Tomasa — they'd make the world of stone, but actually it's made of matchsticks. And if they want to burn, so be it. But I won't be consumed with them. Tino, my friend, I have a job for you — a job that cannot fail, or else it is our certain death; a job that's as tasteless as it is necessary: I want Miguel, Orlando and Tomasa dead within two days.
TINO. All of them, dead?
YSMAEL. That's right. I don't care how. But dead. If they won't move, then their dried-up stalks must be plowed beneath the soil to feed the brand-new seed. But what a waste.
TINO. What about Fidel? You didn't mention him.
YSMAEL. Ah, Fidel — yes, he's a wild card. I can't predict his mood. So he must die. *(pause)* Take charge of this yourself. Use Alvarez, Jose, Roberto and Salazar. And only them. It must be swift and clean — yes, fast and lethal. We'll have one chance. Whatever you need, you let me know. You got it?
TINO. I got it.
YSMAEL. Soon things 'round here will take a virgin shine, and there will be a place for you.

(Tino nods and starts to leave, then stops.)

TINO. I almost forgot. What's Carlos say?

YSMAEL. Carlos? How could we forget about Carlos? *(he laughs lightly)* Don't you worry. I'll take care of Carlos.

TINO. *(skeptically)* You will?

YSMAEL. It's done. Don't give it a second thought. *(looks toward the phone)* Yes, this is Carlos' idea, you know.

TINO. It is? Oh, okay.

YSMAEL. *(pulling the phone back to him)* It is. He called me. On this very phone and told me what he wanted. And now you know…. What Carlos wants.

(Tino nods and exits. The lights go down.)

ACT III SCENE 3

(Scene: Evening. A street in the city near the hotel. Manny and Ramon enter drunkenly. Ramon broods darkly.)

MANNY *(singing/reciting)*

> Dear Consuelo, sweet Consuelo,
> M'darling kitten eyes,
>   She laughs all the jokes I tell
> And winks at all my lies.

RAMON. That was terrible.
MANNY. Well love's a terrible thing.

(Manny laughs drunkenly as Sophia enters from the opposite side carrying a small bag of groceries.)

MANNY. *(blocking her way)* Ah, my sweet Consuelo! *(laughs)*
SOPHIA. Consuelo? You need to get to bed and sleep it off!
MANNY. That's what I just singing 'bout! Ha!
RAMON. We've been sleeping for years, old woman, but now we wake. We see!
SOPHIA. See what?
MANNY. The sun — right there! Bold and growing. Can't you see it? *(laughs)*
RAMON. For years, we've bent our eyes and hid our tongues from our own thoughts. But now we look, we see, we speak!
SOPHIA. You drink.
RAMON. *(morosely)* The militia killed him — yes, right here in the street like a dog! Poor Garcia. Now our time is come!
SOPHIA. Don't be doing anything rash.
RAMON. Is it rash to breath? We call it living!
SOPHIA. Just remember what the town was like before.
RAMON. We've paid enough for that peace — a dead man's peace: born casket dumb and penny blind. What life is this — this bare hole? This cold-coffin lie.
SOPHIA. Yes, but don't be stupid.
MANNY. *(laughing)* What's stopping us?
SOPHIA. A man named Carlos.

191

RAMON. A man named Carlos, eh? Carlos is dead, you know! That's
what they say.
SOPHIA. Want to bet your life on that?
RAMON. I wouldn't get two bits for this watery soup of a life!
SOPHIA. Better an empty life than a dead certainty. Here at least we
know our troubles.
RAMON. That's all we know!
SOPHIA. But Carlos —
RAMON. But Carlos nothing! I used to fear the name of Carlos — but
today I asked, "Afraid of what?" Afraid to lose this field slave's
life? My star was never going to rise in Carlos' sky.
SOPHIA. You'd better watch your mouth.
RAMON. Why? I'm no longer scared. I found the boogie man, and he
was hiding right here.

(Ramon pulls out his knife presses the point to his heart.)

> I cut him out. Now Carlos doesn't scare me anymore! D'you want
> to see what I would do to Carlos if I found him here?

(Fidel enters from behind Ramon.)

FIDEL. I'd love to.
RAMON. *(turns his knife toward Fidel)* Maybe I'll show you.

(Fidel pulls a gun out of his jacket and aims it at Ramon.)

FIDEL. Maybe I'll take off the top half of your head. Not that you'd miss
it.
SOPHIA. He's not worth it.
RAMON. *(suddenly smiling, more friendly as he puts away the knife)* Why do
we fight, Fidel? Shit. We got no beef between us, right? Manny and
me — we were only messing 'round.
SOPHIA. Let him go.
FIDEL. *(taking down his gun and putting it away while staring at Ramon)* I
should cut you ear to fucking ear. How about it, Manny? It would
be shame to mess up that pretty mug.
RAMON. I got no argument with you, Fidel. We all like you. Really.
You're okay. If you find yourself outside without a key, though,
you call. Me, Manny — Castaneda — we'll let you in.
FIDEL. Castaneda? Ha! Forget about that school boy and keep your
noses clean, or they might get cut off.
RAMON. Don't you worry. You remember what I said.

(Ramon and Manny start to leave.)

FIDEL. Hey Manny — hear anything from Rico?
MANNY. Nothing, Fidel, I swear. Like he disappeared. There's not a
    peep in the street.
FIDEL. You tell me if the birdies start to sing.
MANNY. Sure thing.

(Manny and Ramon exit.)

SOPHIA. You — carrying a gun? Now I've seen it all.
FIDEL. Yeah, well, the neighborhood's gone to hell since the Pannies
    moved in. What are you doing out after dark anyway?
SOPHIA. Just picking up a couple things.
FIDEL. Yeah? You'd better get on home. It isn't safe here at night
    anymore. Things are getting a little weird 'round here.
SOPHIA. Yes, there are guys with guns roaming around.
FIDEL. Goodnight.
SOPHIA. Don't stay out all night.
FIDEL. But that's when the mice come out to play.
SOPHIA. *(shaking her head as she leaves)* Okay.

(Sophia exits. A shadowy figure is seen entering from the opposite side.)

FIDEL. *(turning toward the figure while reaching for his gun)* Who's there?

(The Stranger approaches him, hands up, smiling.)

STRANGER. Don't shoot, Marshall! It's just the Gypsy Kid. Relax that
    itchy finger. You'll simply waste a bullet trying to get me.
FIDEL. Don't worry, Gypsy Kid. I won't try to catch you. I wouldn't
    know what I had if I did.
STRANGER. You would and you wouldn't.
FIDEL. What's your business here? What do you want?
STRANGER. Want? Me? Nothing. But many men have many wants and
    every need. I'm content to trip the shadows and streetlamp pools.
    What has you up tonight?
FIDEL. You've caused some restless nights.
STRANGER. I have? Lil' ole me? It's said the truth has strange effects.
FIDEL. The truth? It's more the lies that keep men awake.
STRANGER. Whose lies? That's the question.
FIDEL. What do you know of Carlos?
STRANGER. Carlos is the sound of a man's name. I told you all I know.

FIDEL. Then I've got news for you.

STRANGER. Oh?

FIDEL. Yeah. Carlos will be back in just a couple days. Reports of his untimely end appear to be just smoke.

STRANGER. With smoke there's fire. But that's fine — I have no problem being proven wrong. But how am I to prove that something doesn't exist? There's my quandary. Little Mama Hubbard searched her shelf for nothing, but finding only something. Poor little dog!

FIDEL. What makes you smarter than the rest of us?

STRANGER. I'm not smarter, no. It's just that I see better with my eyes than with my hopes.

FIDEL. Have you seen something?

STRANGER. It's not what I've seen but what I haven't seen. But who knows for sure? Perhaps he is alive, perhaps he's dead. Perhaps I killed him.

FIDEL. *(laughing)* You? Not likely! I've seen a lot of men try to kill Carlos — they've all suffered for their shortcomings. All of them.

STRANGER. Perhaps it was no man that killed the mighty beast.

FIDEL. What? A tiger came in town to eat him? Ha!

STRANGER. Perhaps — perhaps he never existed. But I'm playing the fool. I have a gift for you.

FIDEL. You do?

STRANGER. But I won't give it to you now — later — you're not ready for it yet.

FIDEL. How very mysterious.

STRANGER. I hear your looking for a man named Rico — I know where you will find him.

FIDEL. Okay. So why the wait? Or aren't you sure of that either?

STRANGER. Of this, I'm dead certain. But it doesn't feel quite right to tell you now. You need to keep on looking. Keep snooping around. But I'll have another tip for you tomorrow — a tip on something else you'll want to see. But you'll have to have eyes or you won't see anything.

FIDEL. Oh yeah? Sounds intriguing!

STRANGER. Oh, and one other thing you should know. Rico's sister — she OD'd a couple weeks ago.

FIDEL. She did? That's too bad. Don't wait too long to tell me where to find him. I don't want him to get away.

STRANGER. Trust me, he's not going anywhere. He's waiting for you.

FIDEL. For me? Very interesting. *(pause)* You know, I think I might be leaving here.

STRANGER. You might?

FIDEL. I haven't told a soul. I don't know why I'm telling you.
STRANGER. Perhaps because I have no soul.
FIDEL. Maybe so. But I need to tie up some loose ends. Like Rico.
STRANGER. And what else?
FIDEL. I think you know.
STRANGER. I think I do. I think I do. *(slight pause)* But it is late, and the
    night is young.

    The sky swirls and we creep,
    The wheel turns and we sleep.

    Good night!

(Fidel watches the Stranger exit, then exits the opposite direction.)

ACT IV SCENE 1

(A city street in the afternoon. A dead man lays on the street covered with a sheet. Policemen move back and forth across the stage. Off to the side of the stage, Fidel watches. Ysmael enters.)

YSMAEL. Who is it?

FIDEL. Escobar and two militia men — dead in the car.

YSMAEL. You found'em?

FIDEL. Yeah, I got a tip.

YSMAEL. A tip? Really, from who?

FIDEL. It was — anonymous. I don't know.

YSMAEL. That's one hell of a tipster. How long's the car been here?

FIDEL. Folks say the car was parked here a couple hours ago.

YSMAEL. In broad daylight?

FIDEL. Yep. They were bound and tortured, too. It's pretty gruesome stuff. You think it's a blood killing — for Garcia?

YSMAEL. I wouldn't be surprised if Carlos — revenge, yeah, that's what it looks like. And here, dumped downtown, that's bold. Too bold. Revenge with exclamation point. They think we're weak.

(Miguel enters.)

MIGUEL. Ah, you're here. Did Fidel fill you in.

YSMAEL. Yeah.

MIGUEL. What do you want us to do?

YSMAEL. Work with Tomasa on this. I want these killers — found by dusk and dead by dawn.

MIGUEL. They shouldn't be hard too hard to track with all these witnesses, no? They'll go down with the sun.

YSMAEL. Good. Maybe Louie's men can help. He's close to the LRT.

MIGUEL. You didn't hear?

YSMAEL. Hear what?

MIGUEL. That Louie left. He joined with Castaneda.

YSMAEL. Castaneda? That worthless pickpocket? Hmm. Then the day is farther 'long than I feared. The rats are leaving.

MIGUEL. Okay. I'm going to see what I can find on Escobar. *(to Fidel)* If you see any breadcrumbs, let me or Tomasa know.

(Fidel nods. Miguel exits.)

YSMAEL. A mess. This ain't good — ain't good at all. A fire's taken hold and only blood — and lots of it — will douse the flames.

FIDEL. Ysmael, is Carlos really coming soon?

YSMAEL. What did you hear? Are you calling me a liar?

FIDEL. No, but I need to know. You're sure he's coming in a day or so?

YSMAEL. As sure as sure can be. Now look, Carlos will be Carlos: He moves on winds that only he can feel. You know the way he is. He says he'll come — well, you never know.

FIDEL. Uh huh.

YSMAEL. What's this all about?

FIDEL. There's something else — there's something that I need to tell him.

YSMAEL. Really?

FIDEL. Yeah.

YSMAEL. But you're not going to tell me?

FIDEL. You'll know, and soon. Just personal stuff. Well, I better go.

YSMAEL. Okay. I'll let you know as soon as Carlos comes.

FIDEL. Thanks.

(Fidel exits. Lights go down.)

ACT IV SCENE 2

(Scene: Afternoon hotel lobby. Sophia is at the counter reading a magazine. Tomasa enters alone.)

TOMASA. Sophia — what a lovely day!

SOPHIA. But it's so hot and dry! We haven't had a rain since — since I can't remember!

TOMASA. Ah, but I like it — hot and piercing dry. The sun seeps in your pores and burns down to the wick of your soul.

SOPHIA. Some might say that's a description of hell. But even in hell, they enjoy a bit of rain — for the diversity, if nothing else.

TOMASA. Diversity is nice. It's the valleys make us wonder at the spires.

SOPHIA. And here you are again. What's this? Twice this week!

TOMASA. I know! It's awkward that first time, but then it gets easier the more you do it!

SOPHIA. Yes. So we'll expect more visits?

TOMASA. Certainly! Why not? I like to be with people — I really do. All kinds and shapes. People are more interesting than books. I like to read the stories of their lives. Like yours.

SOPHIA. Like mine?

TOMASA. Of course, here you are, a sister running a successful business on your own. We're a lot alike.

SOPHIA. I don't know about that.

TOMASA. Really. We're strangers in a foreign land. Eve's ghost in the weeds — wandering a world we neither made nor fit, yet defying the odds: You running a hotel — and me, well, doing what I do.

SOPHIA. But you, you've got a lot more nerve than me — You play with the big boys. I give you a lot of credit.

TOMASA. Don't slight your own achievements — you run an honest business in a most dishonest town. A man would bankrupt this place in a month trying to do better by doing worse. But you make it work.

SOPHIA. Why — I don't know what to say. Thank you! *(pause)* Were you looking for Fidel?

TOMASA. He's not around?

SOPHIA. He isn't now.

TOMASA. Well, it's not important. I just thought that I'd stop by. But I must go. Enjoy the day!

(Tomasa exits.)

SOPHIA. *(to herself)* Strange woman, she is.

(Fidel enters from the back door.)

SOPHIA. You just missed Tomasa — you might be —
FIDEL. Let her go. I don't feel like talking to her.

(He sits down on one of the chairs in the lobby. Sophia comes around the front of the counter.)

FIDEL. We found Escobar in the street — sliced to ribbons.
SOPHIA. Escobar — the militia captain?
FIDEL. Yeah.
SOPHIA. That's doesn't sound good.
FIDEL. It's not. I don't know what's going to happen next.
SOPHIA. None of us knows what tomorrow brings.
FIDEL. Yeah, but — strangely — I'm just as puzzled by the past.
    Everything I did, and everything I didn't do, all my work for
    Carlos. It's as if lightning has struck and suddenly re-colored
    everything I thought I knew. It's all changed.
SOPHIA. Are you talking about —
FIDEL. Did I ever tell you about my mother?
SOPHIA. I don't recall.
FIDEL. She was a grifter, a bunco. Ah, she enjoyed the game; the lies, the
    plot, the clever performance. Whatever it took, whatever the role,
    she'd lay down every card until the pot was bare. And me, there at
    her side, I'm sure I was an inconvenience. But I was sometimes in
    the game and played my part. When I was nine or ten, she started
    leaving me in hotel rooms alone for days. And then she'd show up,
    with cash or a bag and we'd beat a hasty exit from that town. One
    time, she introduced me to a man she said was my dad, but I
    assumed it was all part of some scam. I don't know if she ever told
    me an honest word — I'm not sure she knew any! Ha!
SOPHIA. Now that's no way to speak —
FIDEL. I don't think she'd tell you any different. That's the life she
    loved, the life she chose. But it wasn't mine. When I turned fifteen,
    I let that hotel door close behind me and I never looked back.
SOPHIA. I remember when you walked right through that very door
    and asked about a room.

FIDEL. That seems so long ago, like a different life. I was 20 by that time. When I met Carlos …. Yes. Well, Carlos is supposed return here tomorrow or the day after. And then — and then I'm telling him I'm out.

SOPHIA. You're out?

FIDEL. I'm leaving town. Moving on.

SOPHIA. *(brief pause — then she forces a smile)* Well good for you! Now haven't I been saying that for months? Haven't I been praying that you'd leave this horrid place?

FIDEL. You have.

SOPHIA. And now's a good time. I've got a bad feeling about the future here. This town, it reeks of death — it always has. Even Carlo couldn't blow the stench from out of the streets. *(pause)* But what if Carlos isn't —? What if — ?

FIDEL. Carlos isn't back? I don't know. I'm not sure if I can just leave — if I can simply walk away unsure.

SOPHIA. Walk away from what? Unsure of what?

FIDEL. Unsure if Carlos — if he's dead.

SOPHIA. What's that to you? Who cares?

FIDEL. I care. I can't blind myself to all the years with him and leave here unsure if he's alive or dead. And if he's murdered, then something must be done.

SOPHIA. Something? Avenge him? Oh! That's crazy talk! Avenge a man like Carlos? Since when did Carlos need vengeful angel hovering over him?

FIDEL. I owe it to him. And to me.

SOPHIA. You paid your debts to him eleven times over. You owe him nothing. Even he would say that.

FIDEL. But if he's murdered, and no one does a thing —

SOPHIA. That's an occupational hazard he accepted.

FIDEL. It's a personal thing.

SOPHIA. What's this? Honor among thieves?

FIDEL. Maybe something like that.

SOPHIA. Carlos and honor? He treated you well, but don't confuse honor with self-interest. You served his purpose well, and had you not, he'd have had no problems plugging you in the back of the head.

FIDEL. It's not his honor I'm talking about, it's my honor and my promises! To think that someone — someone close to him —

SOPHIA. Is there any innocent blood in this town? Besides, maybe he died in an accident. Or the DEA swept him up.

FIDEL. Could be. But I don't know if I can leave without knowing.

SOPHIA. Ugh! More crazy talk! You leave this town and leave it soon —
if Carlos comes or not. Honor! Dear lord!
FIDEL. *(getting up)* Well, first I've got to find someone.
SOPHIA. Do you think you'll find him?
FIDEL. I'm sure I will.
SOPHIA. I'm sure you will. Be careful.

(Fidel starts to leave and Sophia walks to the hotel counter.)

What's this? Fidel — wait! Here's a note addressed to you. I didn't
see who dropped it off. I don't know how it got there.

(Fidel takes the note and opens it.)

FIDEL. You didn't see who dropped it off?
SOPHIA. No.
FIDEL. It's a message from my gypsy friend.
SOPHIA. Oh really?
FIDEL. This might be just what I was looking for. It's getting dark. I'll
see you in a couple hours.
SOPHIA. Be careful! I don't trust that gypsy — not a bit.

(Fidel exits through the front door. The lights go down.)

ACT IV SCENE 3

(Scene: The militia leader's headquarters at night. General Hernandez sits on a comfortable chair smoking a cigar and looking over papers. His aide, Colonel Fuentes, enters.)

HERNANDEZ. Is tomorrow's transportation taken care of?

FUENTES. Yes, sir. The car and security team are prepared. We'll leave at eleven hundred hours.

HERNANDEZ. Very good, very good. Things are, shall we say, a bit unstable there these past couple days.

FUENTES. *(smiling)* With our help.

HERNANDEZ. Yes — ha! I've heard some rumors of Carlos' death. Have you?

FUENTES. *(sits down)* The rumors have a thousand legs.

HERNANDEZ. Ah, but quantity doesn't make for quality. Are they true? Are they true?

FUENTES. As far as we can tell, Carlos hasn't been seen for about a year. It seems the very peak of oddity, but Carlos, well, he's very odd.

HERNANDEZ. Could it be some ploy? A trick?

FUENTES. Who knows with Carlos. Two years ago, he suggested to everyone he was dying of cancer.

HERNANDEZ. *(smiling)* That was fucking brilliant. While everyone was jostling to take over his position, he bagged them all. An ingenious plot! Ha! It may not matter if he's dead — the rumors by themselves have weakened him. And now we have Tomasa on our side. Her murder of Garcia was very cleverly done, and she'll help us with Ysmael.

FUENTES. That crazy woman's very helpful.

HERNANDEZ. Yes, yes. Our partnership with Carlos has been nice — we've done quite well — but those guerillas still await us. At some point, one of us must rise up and destroy the other.

FUENTES. With Carlos and his thugs removed from the city, we'll have a clear path to destroy the leftists.

HERNANDEZ. Tomorrow, I'll be coy and non-committal — all light and promises, all smiles and tomorrows. But then, next month, we'll put in place our plans and eradicate Carlos' infection from our lands — and with him the Marxists.

(The lights go down.)

ACT IV SCENE 4

(An alley beside of an old, decrepit apartment building in the city. There is a door near the back of the building. Fidel and Tino walk around from the front.)

FIDEL. He's got to be here somewhere.

TINO. We looked in every room, from the basement to the attic. He's not here.

FIDEL. I know he's here.

TINO. How do you know he's here?

FIDEL. I got a tip.

TINO. From who? Someone reliable.

FIDEL. I — I don't know. Yes, he's reliable.

TINO. Who was it?

FIDEL. I can't say. He said, though, that Rico's sister OD'd last month.

TINO. *(drinking from a flask)* Ah, more drug trash.

FIDEL. He might be upset, so be prepared. I'm told he's waiting for us. And I don't want him hurt.

TINO. What the fuck?

FIDEL. If you don't have to, don't hurt him. Let's give him a chance return the money.

TINO. You've gone soft — or crazy.

(Alvarez comes from the other direction.)

ALVAREZ. Nothing in the back. He's not here

FIDEL. He's here. He must be here.

ALVAREZ. Then he's a magician.

TINO. Or a ghost!

ALVAREZ. *(seeing the door)* Wait. Where's this door go?

TINO. The basement, no?

FIDEL. *(walking to the door)* I don't remember seeing this door in the basement.

(Fidel tries the door it opens a little. He takes a step back.)

It's open. It might be a mechanical room. Be ready — this could get hot.

(They all pull out their guns.)

TINO. Let us go in first. This is our specialty.
(*Tino slowly opens the door. It's dark inside. He pulls out a small flashlight and starts to peer in. Suddenly he kicks his head back.*)

Oh my god — the smell! Jesus!

(*Tino covers his face with a cloth and goes inside followed by Alvarez. They are in there a few second. They come out gasping for air.*)

ALVAREZ. I think I'm going to be sick! It singed my nose!
FIDEL. What is it? What!
TINO. (*coughing*) Dead —
FIDEL. Who's dead?
ALVAREZ. Rico — maybe a week.
TINO. In all this heat — it's not a pretty sight and an uglier smell.
    Hanging by the neck from the joists.
FIDEL. (*to himself*) He did know.
TINO. What did Rico know?
FIDEL. Nothing. It looks like we're done here. Rico's taken care of the
    problem himself. Give Paulo five hundred pesos to clean this up.

(*Fidel starts to walk towards the front of the apartment building.*)

TINO. (*holding out a piece of paper for Fidel*) Wait — we found this. A note.

(*Fidel takes it and reads it over slowly.*)

TINO. Well, what's say?
FIDEL. (*after a brief pause, reading*)
    "Carlos, where are you? I've been waiting for you. But you don't
    come.
        But then, it's all your world — isn't it? You're everywhere — in
    everything — in our eyes, our mouths, in our clothes and on our
    beds, clawing at our conscience and crawling on our skin! Like a
    disease — a mad infection — burning us up from within!
        You didn't know my sister, but she knew you — shot you into
    her veins, felt your torrid rush, your crackling sizzle, your manic
    fever. But then, like all of us, she died of your excess.
        It's time to end this mad song. This brief light's made
    tiresomely long with misery. So one more time I raise my hand for
    you.
        You did this Carlos! You did this!"

TINO. *(to Alvarez)* If Carlos did this, he must be alive.

FIDEL. Rico didn't mean it literally, moron.

TINO. Huh?

FIDEL. He didn't mean that Carlos actually strung him up. He meant that Carlos drove him to kill himself.

TINO. Oh, that's too bad.

FIDEL. Yeah, that's a tough break for Rico.

TINO. I meant about Carlos.

FIDEL. What? Oh. Yeah. Carlos.

ALVAREZ. Damn, this is way too weird.

TINO. Way too weird.

FIDEL. *(starting to walk offstage)* Go find Paulo. Have Rico's body fixed up and returned to his family — if he has any left. Don't tell them about the note, or him hanging himself. We just found him dead.

TINO. You have gone soft.

FIDEL. Just do it.

TINO. Got it.

(Fidel puts the note in his pocket. They all exit. The lights go down.)

ACT V SCENE 1

(Scene: Evening in Ysmael's office. Ysmael and Tino push around a man tied up. The man is beaten badly and barely conscious.)

YSMAEL. So you killed Escobar, you dog! Eh? And now your turn has come, bitch. Life's used you up, and now it's time to throw out the wrapper.

TINO. He says it was a Castaneda operation.

YSMAEL. That hollow bum? I should have guessed. He has no class, no imagination. "Dump'em in the street!" That's very clever! *(to the tied-up man)* What? You thought you'd get away with it? Did you really think the wolves wouldn't catch you? In Carlos' city? Ah, but don't you worry 'bout the loneliness of eternity, 'cause Castaneda will be joining you shortly. *(to Tino)* Where are the others?

TINO. All dead. This is the only one Tomasa could take alive.

YSMAEL. *(to tied up man)* A coward too? You left your friends. Tsk tsk. *(to Tino)* I'll miss Tomasa's lethal efficiency.

TINO. Yes.

YSMAEL. *(to tied up man)* I'm saving you, my monkey, for General Hernandez — your death will be our evening's entertainment. So don't make any other plans —

(Alvarez storms in. The sound of sirens is audible when the door opens.)

ALVAREZ. Ysmael!

YSMAEL. *(surprised)* What the shit?

ALVAREZ. *(breathlessly)* The sirens!

YSMAEL. It's a fire — so what?

ALVAREZ. There's a fire in the furniture store.

YSMAEL. Yeah, and?

ALVAREZ. At the furniture store!

YSMAEL. So make sure the fire crews get there.

ALVAREZ. The furniture store — next to the lab.

YSMAEL. The lab? God damn it! Could Carlos — no, no, no! Get Jose and everyone you can find — save as much as possible. *(to Tino)* Watch for General Hernandez, and let me know when he gets near.

TINO. Will do.

YSMAEL. Go, go!

ALVAREZ. Got it.

(Alvarez and Tino leave as Fidel comes in.)

FIDEL. Did you hear?
YSMAEL. Yes, yes, god damn the timing! Jose is going to save as much
    of the product as he can. Take charge out there — I'm expecting
    General Hernandez any second now. And take whoever else you
    need. And Fidel — see if you can find the source.
FIDEL. Will do.

(Fidel leaves.)

YSMAEL. Fidel! Fidel!

(Fidel re-enters.)

FIDEL. Yes?
YSMAEL. Have you seen Tomasa?
FIDEL. No, I came here straight from my place.
YSMAEL. Damn it. She should be here. We need her. Have someone
    find her.
FIDEL. Will do.

(Fidel exits. Tino comes in.)

TINO. We saw the General turning on the block.
YSMAEL. Good, good. I want the Dictador — same that Carlos drank. I
    want this room to reek of Carlos. I want the general knowing who
    I'm speaking for. Carlos won't be here, but he'll be felt.
TINO. You said to put those things away.
YSMAEL. I know I did, but now I'm saying get them out. *(smiling)* I'm
    calling on a higher power.
TINO. We'll pull them out and —

*(A huge explosion outside shakes the room. Ysmael and Tino are almost knocked
to the floor. They stagger cursing, confused. The explosion is followed by a
flurry of gunfire and shouts offstage that continue through the remainder of the
scene. Alvarez rushes in the room. Smoke pours in from the opened door.)*

ALVAREZ. Bomb — a car bomb out front — death — everywhere!
YSMAEL. The General?
ALVAREZ. Dead!

YSMAEL. Jesus Christ! Well — find out what's the gunfire all about.
ALVAREZ. Okay!

(Alvarez exits.)

YSMAEL. Tino — get the guns. I'll try to call Jose. We need some backup
     here! Damn the fire!
TINO. *(running out)* Got it.

*(Tino exits. Ysmael picks up the phone and starts dialing while he gets out his
pistol and checks it.)*

YSMAEL. Mother fucker. Hello? Hello?

*(Ysmael throws the phone on the floor. Tino comes in with several automatic
weapons. He hands one of them to Ysmael along with a satchel of ammunition.)*

TINO. Here's the guns. The phones are dead.
YSMAEL. I know, I know! What's with all the shooting? It sounds like
     a fucking war out there —

*(The gunfire starts to sound louder and closer. Inaudible shouts are heard.
Alvarez rushes in.)*

ALVAREZ. *(panicked)* They're coming here — this way! This way!
YSMAEL. Who, you idiot?
ALVAREZ. Fifteen — twenty soldiers, heavily armed. They stormed out
     after the explosion — and they're coming here! They're coming
     here!
YSMAEL. Clear out, you stupid ape!

*(Ysmael pushes Alvarez out of this way walks toward the door, but just as he
gets close, bullets start flying into the room. Ysmael fires back, and Tino and
Alvarez join him. They slowly retreat to behind the desk. The opposing gunfire
slows down a bit.)*

ALVAREZ. We're trapped! Trapped!
YSMAEL. Shut up! Shut up! We've stopped them for a second.

*(Ysmael quickly, but calmly, looks around. The tied-up man gets up to leave.
Two men enter the room, guns blazing. They kill the tied-up man, but Tino and
Alvarez kill those two. While the gunfire outside continues unabated, there is a
temporary lull in the gunfire inside.)*

YSMAEL. The window is the only way out.
TINO. To the roof. There, we can leap onto the store and make our way
    escape from the building next door.
YSMAEL. Yes! Yes! Let's go!

*(Ysmael opens and gets through the window first. Two gunmen, wearing
camouflage and masks, enter the doorway and start shooting. Alvarez, hurrying
to the window, is hit and he falls on the desk. Tino crawls out the window while
shooting. A moment after the gunfire stops, the gunmen cautiously enter. The
lights go down.)*

ACT V SCENE 2

(Scene: Hotel lobby at night. There are no lights on — the stage is lit by the flickering orange glow of the city fires. Occasional bursts of gunfire, sirens and shouting are heard outside but in the distance. In that shimmering light, Fidel cautiously watches out the front window of the hotel while Sophia paces around the room, occasionally stopping to look at Fidel. As Sophia nears Fidel, two gunshots are heard in the distance.)

SOPHIA. Death's at the door. Do you hear him knock?

(Fidel nods but keeps a watch outside the window. Three more gunshots are heard, this time much closer.)

FIDEL. He's getting louder and more insistent.
SOPHIA. But death will wait — he'll wait the welcomed hand that
    unlocks the door and pulls him in. He'll wait.
FIDEL. He will? I never knew the pale horseman to be so well
    mannered.
SOPHIA. He must be when the moths swarm the flame. The light is so
    irresistible that they clog the slaughterhouse gates. Then Death
    needs their help to file them through the door in an orderly
    fashion. That's why he knocks and says his "Please" and "Thank
    you" as he herds in the angry husks of men to their fulfillment.
FIDEL. What happens when he visits men in their beds?
SOPHIA. Then Death just barges in unbid, no manners whatsoever.
FIDEL. Then we'll hope to meet a ruder Death.
SOPHIA. *(turning to look out the window)* Amen. What's going on? It's too
    dark for my old eyes to see.
FIDEL. The fire's spreading to other buildings, but the wind is blowing
    it the other way, so we're safe for now. I don't know about Ysmael
    or Tomasa. Ysmael's office was destroyed by the explosion — I
    couldn't find them anywhere in town. The soldiers started getting
    too thick to continue looking.
SOPHIA. Tomasa? Ysmael? Who gives a bean for them? You'd better
    think about yourself — it isn't safe here for you.
FIDEL. No one has a grudge with me.
SOPHIA. A grudge? Carlos' enemies are searching out his friends, and
    Carlos has fewer friends every second.
FIDEL. *(looking out the window)* I suppose.

SOPHIA. Yes, I'd suppose. You act so brave, but see you're keeping
 your hand close to that gun.
FIDEL. *(after a short pause)* You know I've heard in Santa Marta a man
 can find some decent work.
SOPHIA. I've heard the same; it sounds so nice there: the sun and the
 beach — the ocean sky. It would do you good.
FIDEL. Might do you some good.
SOPHIA. *(laughing)* Me? Oh no, oh no! Santa Marta's a great place to
 start a life — but this town is the place to end a life. Yes, my old
 grey head's too full of mud, my back too stiff, my blood too thick.
 Right here's where I should bide the days until my end, or till the
 end of time. Whichever's first.
FIDEL. *(looking out the window)* Well, we should be okay here for a while,
 if not until the end of time. *(Fidel laughs lightly)*

(A scuffling sound is heard from the back of the hotel. Fidel signals to Sophia to keep quiet, pulls his gun out and walks to the one side. A figure stumbles in and Fidel raises his gun. It's Ysmael.)

FIDEL. Hold it right there!
YSMAEL. Fidel? Fidel — wait! It's me! It's Ysmael!
FIDEL. *(lowering his gun)* Ysmael? I wasn't even sure if you were still
 alive —

(Ysmael throws himself in a chair.)

YSMAEL. *(panting)* By a breath, brother, a breath — militia boxed in the
 office — set the place on fire — I escaped — escaped — getting on
 the roof — jumping to the next building —
FIDEL. Where's Tino and Alvarez?
YSMAEL. *(regaining composure)* Both dead, all dead. Alvarez — he died
 in the office. Tino and me — we were surprised in the alley by the
 bank. I stumbled free, but Tino — Tino didn't make it.
SOPHIA. *(to herself but making sure it's loud enough for all to hear)* It's
 funny how that worked.
FIDEL. What brings you here?
YSMAEL. I came to find you. I need your help, and you need mine.
 They're looking for us both, and we need to stick together if we're
 going to get out of here alive.
SOPHIA. *(to Fidel)* Leave, but let his feverish carcass here. He carries the
 plague on him.

YSMAEL. *(getting up from the chair very agitated toward Sophia)* Shut up, old woman! Death won't even touch your bloodless carcass! Those are not men out there, but piranhas — devouring every man in sight. They took Miguel and stabbed him in the eye, and Orlando, he was disemboweled alive — the horror on his face — I saw it! I saw it!

FIDEL. *(while the other two are talking)* Wait —

SOPHIA. *(to Ysmael)* Whose fault was that? Why'd they die?

FIDEL. *(while the other two are talking)* Both of you —

YSMAEL. And then I saw two soldiers whipping a man to death — peeling long strips of flesh from his body while he screamed. I saw it!

SOPHIA. Then — then you've made devils — devils of them all!

FIDEL. *(suddenly agitated)* Both of you be quiet! There is — I need — I need — *(to Ysmael)* There's something I need to know.

YSMAEL. What? What is it?

FIDEL. I need to know that this wasn't just a big lie.

YSMAEL. Come on, Fidel. You've known me for years. Haven't I been straight with you?

FIDEL. *(struggling with the words)* I — I need to know. I need to know if this was all just a game, a scam, a ruse. Did it all make any difference?

YSMAEL. I don't understand.

SOPHIA. What do you mean?

FIDEL. I mean, was Carlos just the next lord of the flies to rise up from the swamp? Just to be replaced by another?

YSMAEL. What? We don't have time for this? We need to go!

(Ysmael starts pacing around.)

FIDEL. Were you really speaking to Carlos?

YSMAEL. Now? Now you want to talk about that — with the city burning down around us?

FIDEL. I need to know. I need to know now! My loyalty was to Carlos. My promise —

YSMAEL. You're not making any fucking sense. I'm not asking you to save my life, damn it! I'm asking you to save your own skin.

FIDEL. Then just answer me this: Is Carlos dead? Did you kill him?

YSMAEL. Kill Carlos? Me? My god man! We're standing on a barrel of gas in a fireworks show.

FIDEL. I need to know. Right now. I think that — I don't know what's right or what to do —

YSMAEL. Then I'll tell you what to do: Leave here and save yourself —

SOPHIA. Let him talk!
YSMAEL. And then his next words may be last —

(Unseen by the others, Tomasa walks in quietly from the back of the hotel — coming in the same way as Ysmael. She raises her gun.)

TOMASA. His last? Not yet.

(The others are surprised by her voice and turn, silent.)

> Now put them down. The guns — there, put them down! You too, Fidel. I know you have one now. Ah, Sophia. Three times this week! I said I wasn't going to be a stranger.

(Ysmael and Fidel put their guns on the floor.)

YSMAEL. Tomasa it's us. It's me — Ysmael.
TOMASA. I know your face — too well. Back away from the guns.
YSMAEL. Thank god you're here. Fidel has lost his mind. Let me get my gun and we can blow this place before the morning puts a target on our backs.

(Ysmael starts to move toward her and his gun.)

TOMASA. Stop right there!
YSMAEL. What the fuck? Have the fumes gone to everybody's head 'round here? Look folks: If we don't get out now, we're dead. Come on, Tomasa! Like the good old days.

(Tomasa signals for them to step back, then she kicks both guns away, keeping a wary eye on Ysmael and Fidel.)

TOMASA. Hmm. Let's not talk about the good old days. They weren't that good.
YSMAEL. I don't understand —
TOMASA. Don't try. Who does? The sunsets cycle beneath our feet as we careen toward some precipice we'd rather not consider: That's all you need to know. This inferno, though, suits us well. But what I want to know — and what Fidel here wants to know — and what everyone wants to know — is Carlos, only Carlos. Carlos! Always — anything — Carlos! And so I ask: These past few months, have you been speaking to him? Really?
YSMAEL. You too! Has everyone gone fucking insane?

TOMASA. Insane? There was a time that would have cut me to the quick, but now, it's only a line drawn in ashes.

YSMAEL. What's happened to you?

TOMASA. *(flatly)* I ask: Is Carlos alive?

YSMAEL. The city's an inferno! There's time for all of this, but far away from here. Now let's get out before we're choked on our own blood!

TOMASA. *(louder, angrier — walking toward Ysmael)* Have you talked to Carlos?

YSMAEL. This is absurd! I'm bailing on this suicide squad. Good luck to both of you — you'll need it!

(As Ysmael starts to leave, Tomasa raises her gun.)

FIDEL. No, Tomasa!

(Tomasa shoots Ysmael in the leg and he collapses to the floor.)

YSMAEL. *(wailing)* Ah! You crazy bitch! You shot me! Ah! Shit! Ah! God damn it! Are you fucking nuts?

SOPHIA. Tomasa — !

FIDEL. This is not the way —

TOMASA. *(even louder, aiming the gun at Ysmael's head)* Is Carlos alive?

YSMAEL. *(sobbing and shielding himself with his hands)* I don't know! I don't! I don't think so. But I'm not sure. Ah!

TOMASA. Have you been talking to him?

YSMAEL. Ah, my leg! My leg — the blood! I'm bleeding —

TOMASA. Have you talked to Carlos?

(Tomasa shoots two times next to Ysmael.)

YSMAEL. I made it up! I made it up to keep the peace! Oh, fuck, my leg! To keep the peace! I didn't know. I thought that he'd be back, any day, any day. Then people started getting nervous — things started coming apart. I said it the first time — almost by accident — the first time out of desperation and everybody settled down, stayed calm. It was the only way I could keep everything together. Now — now look around — you see what's happened — once people thought that he was dead — Jesus Christ! I'm bleeding to god-damned death here!

FIDEL. You haven't talked to him! Then you — you must have —

YSMAEL. No I didn't kill him — I swear — I didn't kill him! Damn it, ah! Someone help me! I didn't kill him. I didn't kill him!

SOPHIA. I was wrong —

YSMAEL. I didn't kill him!

TOMASA. *(laughing)* Of course, you mouse-brown thing, of course you didn't kill him. You don't have the stones. Why, you don't even have the mind to envision such a thing. *(shouting)* None of you! Carlos was like a god! Who dares the jawbone? Wrestles the thunderbolt? Not you! Or you! None of you!

YSMAEL. *(whispering)* Get me some help, please. The blood —

(Sophia steps toward Ysmael to help him.)

TOMASA. *(waving her gun)* Whoa, stay back, sister.

SOPHIA. He's bleeding to death — just let me —

TOMASA. No, damn it! No! Step back or I'll spray your brains all over the fucking wall. *(to Ysmael)* No, you didn't kill Carlos. You're like the rest of the leopards, feeding on the weakest of the herd.

YSMAEL. God! Please help me!

TOMASA. Shut up! Who hunts the strongest, fastest, or deadliest? Who takes that beast who in a second can take you? Who kills a god? There, wondering if he'll read your thoughts. Or feel your panting breath. Or hear your thundering heart. You cannot hide from god — then how are you to kill him? I'll tell you.

(Tomasa moves toward Ysmael while he mutters "No, no, no" and winces.)

FIDEL. Tomasa, no.

TOMASA. *(moving toward Ysmael)* You move closer —

FIDEL. No!

TOMASA. You clear your head of thoughts so even you are blind to your intent —

SOPHIA. *(moaning)* No, no, no!

TOMASA. And then, when you're feeling nothing — nothing — you suffocate the fear, you gag the reason, you choke the shrill voice within you till there's nothing — then — then you pull the trigger.

YSMAEL. No!

(Tomasa fires the gun, killing Ysmael.)

SOPHIA. Oh my god — my god! You've lost your mind!

FIDEL. Tomasa — that's enough.

TOMASA. *(as is snapping out of a trance)* It's not enough! It's not! Get back! Both of you!

(After a slight pause, she turns to Fidel.)

Is Carlos dead? Yes, dead and gone? Or dead and coming back? Can he come back? Is that impossible? For Carlos? You don't know? Just like the rest but more loyal. *(She laughs.)*

FIDEL. Do you know something? Where is Carlos?

TOMASA. Can a dead man harm me? Can he from death's grave reach out to haunt my dreams? To shadow my steps? To cloud my mirrors? Especially if I know he's dead. Especially if I killed him?

FIDEL & SOPHIA. You —

TOMASA. Yes, I killed the god! At least I think I did — I thought I killed him. Ha! It's so confusing now. Surprised? No? Yes? I guess it doesn't matter, does it? Who gives a rat for other people's thoughts?

About a year ago, the lion came to our apartment — Pablo wasn't there — on business or whoring, I don't recall. But there was Carlos — Carlos at my door! I let him in of course, he said he'd wait for Pablo. Well, we had a drink and he regaled me with his stories — oh, you know his stories. He was quite the charmer. I was, of course, fascinated. Then, he leaned across and kissed me, softly. And I thought, "Carlos is kissing me!" But then he grew insistent, kissed me harder, crushed my wrists within his hands. It happened so fast and I just wanted him to stop, but he wouldn't, he wouldn't stop, in my own home he struck me, threw me on the floor, doing what he pleased. I couldn't do a thing — I was afraid and stunned and bloody — and he was much too strong.

As he was walking out, he laughed at me — me, bloodied and bruised, crushed on the floor. He laughed at me as if I were a joke. He laughed!

After that, his laugh echoed in my ears. It haunted me, I heard it everywhere. And over the next few weeks, I found a strength — a strength I never knew I had, an angry strength that boiled up in me. Revenge played on my mind, and nothing else. The more I heard that laugh, the stronger I got.

So one wet night I followed him into an alley with a kitchen knife. I followed him, snuck up behind him. Could he hear my pounding heart? My panting breath? What would I do if he turned and saw me? But he didn't turn, and I stabbed him in the back — I thrust that beautiful blade between his shoulders — thrust hard! He angrily turned around, and seemed surprised to see me there — unsure what he should do. And then he kind of gurgled, and collapsed. He laid a bit there, drowning in his blood. And I crouched far away and watched. I thought I'd laugh at him when it was done, laugh in his face, but I was too afraid — yes, too afraid that he'd get up. Ah, can a knife kill a god? *(she laughs)* I wasn't sure! Finally he stopped his twitching and gurgling, then I got him in my car and dumped his body in the river.

SOPHIA. My god!

TOMASA. Then I waited — waited for the world to find me out. To find out their god was dead. But no one said a thing. His body didn't show up and no one seemed surprised that he was gone. Days passed, then weeks, then a month, then two, and then Ysmael said he talked to Carlos. He talked to Carlos! I must have only wounded him, I thought. I'm dead, I thought. And then I waited. I waited Carlos' revenge. I knew what he did to informants — what awful tortures he put them through.

But nothing happened. Days went by, and weeks, but Carlos never came, he never showed his face. He spoke to Ysmael, but Ysmael did nothing, said nothing.

Perhaps Carlos needed to recover from the wound, I thought. Perhaps he's only playing with me. Letting me dangle. Maybe he would send someone else to kill me. Oh, I couldn't a trust soul — but I wasn't going to cower or run or beg. He deserved what I had given. So I waited. That's when I killed Pablo —

SOPHIA. Pablo? I thought the government —

TOMASA. No, no. I killed him, too, and made it look like the army did it. Pablo treated me like his pet monkey. One night he ranted how he owned me, waved a knife around my face — I pulled out my gun and killed him right there. I'd fought a god — that worm meant nothing!

And then I started seeing Carlos in my dreams, in the shadows, in the windows. "Can a god just die?" I wondered. Can you keep him underneath the ground? Yes, I killed him a hundred times, but he always came back, came back.

And then I decided to resolve the doubts — about everything. I was going to force Carlos to show himself. So I started working with the militia and the guerillas — stoking their fires. *(motioning toward the windows)* My plan worked quite well, don't you think?

But now I learn that it was all a game, a game Ysmael played with us to keep his heel on our necks — a game that tortured me for months. Well, Ysmael deserved this fate. I had to kill Carlos a hundred times! But Ysmael just once.

FIDEL. It's over now, Tomasa. Carlos is dead and washed down the river somewhere. He's not coming back.

TOMASA. Is he dead? Really? Is it over? Is it? Ever? Can you say for sure that Carlos won't come back? You can't, can you! *(she laughs)*

217

SOPHIA. There's nothing left to —
TOMASA.
> The sky swirls and we creep,
> The wheel turns and we sleep.

FIDEL. You — you — the gypsy!
TOMASA. Your eyes have finally opened? This late? I had such hopes
for you, Fidel. We were both looking for the same thing.

(The sound of voices offstage.)

What's that?

*(Tomasa goes to the various windows and cautiously looks out. She stops at one
and stares. Then rubs her eyes with the back of her free hand)*

Is it — ? Could it — ? Carlos? Carlos! You came -- let's finish it! *(she
starts shooting out the window while shouting)* You bloodless fiend!
I'll send you back to hell! A thousand times if needed!

*(A flurry of automatic gunfire is returned from outside. Tomasa is hit and falls
dead. Two men rush in wearing ski masks, but pause cautiously in the shadows
by the door. Sophia and Fidel fearfully retreat to the back of the lobby.)*

SOPHIA. *(almost a whisper)* Is it him?
FIDEL. *(stepping toward the figures)* Carlos? Carlos?

*(The two figures, surprised by the presence of someone else in the room, spin
around and shoot, killing Fidel instantly, wounding Sophia. The intruders pull
up their masks revealing Ramon and Manny, dressed in makeshift army
uniforms. They warily walk from body to body looking at
them — but always alert.)*

RAMON. What the hell! Is anybody else in here? *(standing over Tomasa's
body)* Hmm, it's Tomasa. Dead. Goodnight, you witch. *(seeing
Ysmael)* And there, Manny, there's the serpent's head itself — it's
Ysmael. Is he dead, too?
MANNY. *(kicking Ysmael's body)* He's dead, Ramon. We got him!
RAMON. Good thing, the snake. *(to Ysmael)* Take your poisons with
you! *(walking toward Fidel)* And who is this? Ah, Christ, Fidel. For
you, my faithful friend, I feel bad. These others, I hope they rot in
hell, but you deserved a better fate. But if you hang with snakes,
don't be surprised if you get beaten with them. *(to Sophia)* And

who is this? Sophia — and she's still alive. *(he goes to her)* It doesn't look too bad, old woman, but I should shoot you anyway. You're old, what life is left in you?

MANNY. Why're you going to kill that old woman? What's wrong with you?

SOPHIA. *(weakly)* Fidel — ?

RAMON. Fidel is dead.

SOPHIA. *(through the pain of her wound)* Carlos — You're not Carlos. We thought that you were Carlos.

RAMON. Ha! Carlos? Me? No. There's no more Carlos. There never was. Now it's Castaneda! Castaneda and the people's army! Now it's our world.

SOPHIA. Then Carlos — he is dead —

RAMON. *(standing up and walking away from her)* Don't worry none on Carlos — he's the stuff of memories now! You just learn to say "Castaneda." Castaneda — yes, that's all you need to know. To Castaneda the whole fucking city bows. *(fires a couple rounds in the ceiling)* Long live Castaneda! It's our turn now! Long live Castaneda!

(Manny and Ramon laugh and exit. The lights go down.)

FINIS

ONCE UPON A MOONLIT WOOD

A Fairy Tale

CHARACTERS

Robin, a young adult fairy
Blossom, a young adult fairy and Robin's girlfriend
Bottom, a young adult fairy and Robin's clownish friend

Deb, a tall, attractive, domineering woman in her mid thirties
Clark, a tall, somewhat sheepish-looking man in his mid thirties, and Deb's brother in law

Various fairies (non-speaking parts, but depending on the production they may sing and dance)

TIME / PLACE

Contemporary U.S.A.

SCENE 1

(Scene: The stage is dark except for a full moon shining above and pools of light on the stage where moon shines down through the forest canopy. As music begins playing, fairies can be seen dancing or lightly running around the pools of light. The fairies then take turns stepping into the various pools of light and reciting/singing one or more lines of the song.)

FAIRIES. *(singing)*
    Where goes the moon, we fairies go,
    The sun our compass opposite.
      We gambol on the drooping light
    And take sole charge of all of it.

    Where rise the stars, we wake, we wake,
    In evening's altitude.
      We flit from linden leaves aloft
    That made our sleepy hood.

    Come night
    Come cool
      Come moonlit seed
    Alight
      On shimm'ring
      Bellied leaves
    The evening is the hour for games
    For pranks and plays and flirting lays.

    Where flash the firefly, we soar,
    Upon the dulcet airs,
      And with the whip-poor-will we traipse
    From limb to lock to lair.

    Where swirls the dark, we spin, we spin,
    And hedgerows leap and limn.
      In inky night we entertain,
    Beneath the stars we swim.

Come night
Come cool
  Come moonlit seed
Alight
  On shimm'ring
  Bellied leaves
The evening is the hour for games
For pranks and plays and flirting lays.

Where flash the firefly, we soar,
Upon the dulcet airs,
  And with the whip-poor-will we traipse
From limb to lock to lair.

BOTTOM. Enough! Enough!
  Let's have the human come!
  Raise the lights —
  Be off! Take flight!

(The fairies laughingly scatter into the shadows and hide. Blossom, Robin and Bottom hide upstage. The lights come up as if a patio light were turned on, revealing a few pieces of high-end patio furniture — two chairs and a table — with the woods in the background looking sleepy and peaceful. Deb enters carrying a drink. She does not see or hear the fairies.)

ROBIN. *(to Bottom)*
  Bottom, Bottom, look:
  See how the man-ape plods and scrapes the earth?
  See how it scratches, scratches, scratches?
  Ha ha! Dumb blinkered beast,
  She's alive to nothing but the furrow she dull plows,
  Staring down the bitter, ancient dust until,
  Unable to defeat it,
  She becomes it.
BOTTOM. Ah, Robin, you are right.
  From earth stitch bound
  To bound by the earth,
  From wealth and wile
    To want and dearth.
  Swish swish!

(Robin and Bottom laugh.)

BLOSSOM. Puff hard and long, my dandy lions —
    Laugh while you can, go on! Go on!
    But a smaller sail befits the storm you're in.
    Here, tra la, your labors are enjoined, your office pinned,
    Until the hours and your deeds atone your sins.
ROBIN. Atone our sins, dear Blossom? As if what's ill written
    Could be erased by good. Can it be so?
    Better it would be to rip apart the page, forgetting it,
    Than crib and crab the writing more.
BLOSSOM. More marred is not more possible, dear Rob.
    The fairy council has decreed you'll work
    The human swatch tonight.
ROBIN. Ah, work near humans!
    Briars and burdocks! I simply will not do it!
    Never, no, nil — nay, not, nix!
    I can't abide the human stench,
    Their squawking reeds and leaden gaits,
    Their bumbling impostures and oafish oofs.
    Why they're ugly louts
    That positively must be done without.
BLOSSOM. What? Why so red faced, Robin?
    Whose hand drew out this scene, but yours and Bottom's?
    Who was it gulped the riotous nectar to its lees?
    Who was it then uncaged confusion on the woods?
ROBIN. It was the hummingbirds, those flutt'ring sots!
    These deeds are best ascribed in their book, not ours.
BLOSSOM. Oh, they are? Please tell.
ROBIN. They are! They are! There, by the moonflow'r's bloom,
    I and Bottom did our chores in lively cheer —
BLOSSOM. Your tale already strikes false note.
BOTTOM. Oh, it would be too cruel to hit a truer one —
ROBIN. — When the hummingbirds approached.
    "Why toil so," they hummed. "You work too hard.
    Sit here with us and share a bracing drink,
    And then resume your chores with new-found vigor."
    And in politeness we agreed.
BLOSSOM. Your manners are renowned.
ROBIN. At first the hummings were all light and laughs,
    And many elbows we raised in conviviality.
    But then their humor took a prickly turn
    And fairies wore their barbs. Oh, such lies
    And falsehoods spoke, yes, such licentious acts
    They tacked on all the fairies — even you, dear Blossom!

BLOSSOM. They did?
BOTTOM. They did?
ROBIN. They did! Such vile things I will not echo.
BLOSSOM. Ah.
ROBIN. So we, of course, set shield to our shared virtue.
BLOSSOM. You did?
BOTTOM. You did?
ROBIN. We did! Then Englebert, that loud-mouthed lout,
     He challenged us to turn our glasses up.
     What could we do? "Are you afraid?" he buzzed.
     "Can't hold your drinks?" he hemmed.
     What then? Should we have so abased ourselves
     And all the fairies?
BLOSSOM. For us all, you should have done much less.
BOTTOM. Yet for the least, much more is always done.
ROBIN. You'd rather that we shriveled our reply and squeaked,
     "We cannot do it?" Demurred and stuttered, "N-no,"
     Dropped our chins and sulked away?
     Why? So these sad cloying sots could say
     They were our betters? So we could wear the collar
     Of their snickering whispers, their laughing looks,
     Their idiotic buzzing in our ears?
     You see our quandary. What could we do
     But what we did?
BLOSSOM. It's better asked: What didn't you do?
     Draped in the fraying nectar, you unraveled here
     A spiraling string of creased and rude calamities:
     You knotted up the vines, and tangled all the weeds,
     You dewed the moistened brook,
     And you unwound the clinging ivy. All that and more —
     The worst of which I blush to say.
ROBIN. Blossom, why should I button the blame
     When clearly I was not myself. These stunts
     I don't remember nor were they intended.
     They were not willed nor wanted, planned nor wished.
     Yes, by my flesh they were performed,
     But absent my consenting spirit.
BLOSSOM. Good point, my Rob, good point. Since that's the case,
     Your spirit's free to fly, discharged of guilt — fa la!
     But your flesh is here constrained to expiate its sins.

ROBIN. By Adam's leaf, the punishment is too severe!
  These hairless monkeys are insufferable!
  They're brained just like a leopard with no legs:
  All revs and lines; they are as clean
  As rain-swollen streams yet not so dirty
  As to be the least bit titillating.
  They grate the ears and sting the eyes, they foul
  The nose and burn the skin, then dull the brain.
  In sum: They are vile and sullied nuisance
  And their clumsy footfalls I can't abide.
BLOSSOM. Your words, dear Rob, are baseless cheats.

(Blossom walks toward Deb, followed by Robin and Bottom. They are invisible to Deb.)

  Just look: I think these pond'rous waifs
  Are rather cute. See how their eyes show depth
  And feeling — sadness, hope and love?
  Look how their lumb'ring legs and arms aspire
  To light empyreal, and see how full enrapt they are
  With any glint or glim hung before their eyes.
  Why, in the way they laugh and sing
  They're almost fairy like at times.
ROBIN. Oh, that's a crooked judgment on us all,
  You foolish thing —
BLOSSOM. You're calling me a fool?
ROBIN. More foolish than a fool, but yes!
  These meadow apes, oh, they reach liked gods
  But the prize exceeds their grasp,
  They think themselves of spirits light
  But crawl like worms upon this flesh of earth.
  Oh yes, they roil and belt, bawl and bellow
  As if to conjure all the leaves to dance,
  But yet their voice is but a pip.
BOTTOM. Pip pip!
ROBIN. But it's their pyrite pride that rubs me raw,
  The self-congratulating airs they blow,
  Their arms disjointed with patting themselves on the back.
BLOSSOM. What are we, then Robin, the roses to their thorns?
ROBIN. Why obviously!
BLOSSOM. Yet both grow fast entwined.

ROBIN. *(aside to Blossom)*
    What say you we depart this public spot
    And find a leafy nest in which to twine
    Ourselves in passionate sport? Eh?
BLOSSOM. You've nerve to ask that when calling me a fool!
    A mouth that coos aspersions sings its passions solo —
    Or with Bottom will duet.
BOTTOM. What?

    If I were a girl
    Yes, I'd be most fastidious
    And be at my wittiest in choosing my mate.

    For a girl must be careful
    And always so wareful
    That the man she has picked is first rate.

    Thus, given the choice,
    I would kiss all the boys
    And taste the warm charms that they offer.

    For how else is a girl
    To judge or begrudge
    What a lad has got stored in his coffers?

ROBIN. Ah, thistles on you both!
BLOSSOM. Oh oh! Persist and you'll not pleasure in a week!
    Enough: I'm gone before your prickly tongue
    Deflates the month! Tra la!

(Blossom leaves.)

BOTTOM. What a pleasure it'd be
    If I had a lass —
      That is if she wasn't
    A pain in my knee.
ROBIN. Wear your rimes less loudly or I'll dress
    Your hole more modestly! But that reminds me —

(Robin pulls a ring out of his pocket and holds it up to Bottom.)

BOTTOM. What's that? Oh, it's Blossom's favorite ring.
    How'd it fall into your pocket?

ROBIN. A midnight trick, I assure you, Bottom.
    But for now I merely borrow it, to return it when
    It pleases me.
BOTTOM. Its vanishment will sorely vex her.
ROBIN. Therein we're entertained, dear Bott. Her want
    Matched by her lack
    Should stage a scene we'll all enjoy.
    That's her redress for lording over us.
BOTTOM. You'll need some dressing when she finds you out.
ROBIN. Then, my bells, I guess she won't find out!
    She'll pace the woods in fruitless search until
    I'm satisfied, and then the ring will reappear
    And she won't be the wiser.

(Robin hums a short melody, putting the ring down on the patio table to admire it.)

    Besides, why should I care if she finds out?
    She doles more sweetened breaths
    Upon these moon calves than on me. Just look:
    What favor does she see in them?

(Robin walks around Deb, closely observing her. She continues to be unaware of them both.)

    See how their skin hangs heavy on their frames
    Like wet clothes wrinkling over a sagging branch?
    And look how their unwieldy bodies chop
    The nighttime currents into tangled rough.
    Their eyes reveal a soft, fog-muddled mind,
    An unplayful spirit, and a blunted wit.
    They sate the hours heaving brooding sighs
    And with'ring shrugs to one another, till,
    At last, some baubled mischief kindles
    Their desire and they become all enterprise and motion,
    All elbows and impatience, running to
    And back and from and up and down and forth
    (To no particular end that I can see)
    And then relapse into a sullen, grudging rest.
    What, Bottom, are these brutes compared to us?
BOTTOM. No more then less at everything, I'd say.

ROBIN. Exactly. Head by head, they show no art,
    Display no skill, and promise nothing.
    And by themselves they are most-common beasts —
    Not as well adapted to survive as most.
    Where are their crimsons and their claws?
    Their razor teeth, their wings, their speed?
    They have no size or heft, nor brawn or weight;
    They even lack the basic magic arts.
    Alone, they are a weaklinged thing,
    Deficient in most every living skill;
    But then, they rarely leave their hives alone
    And in a swarm they thrash about the world.
    Perhaps it takes another of their kind
    To manifest their higher qualities.

(Robin and Bottom resume their hiding place. Several fairies coax Clark onstage, then exit. Hearing someone behind her, Deb turns.)

DEB. What? Ah, look who comes. Dear Clark, swell Clark, brave Clark,
    Dear brother of my husband late. Tell me, my partner, what bold
    frontier in accounting have you conquered?
CLARK. Deb, must your mouth hang open to let out all your faults?
DEB. A closed door, like a closed mouth, never stopped a fool — he
    always finds a way to admit himself.
ROBIN. *(aside to Bottom)* At least the she-ape shows some wit.
DEB. What's the news, paperboy. I'm not in the mood for you.
CLARK. Well, Deb —
DEB. That's Deborah.
CLARK. Okay, Debbie, this paperboy is bringing some bad news. As I
    had guessed, Barry illegally withdrew funds from the employee
    pension.
DEB. You come to my house at night to tell me that? Then pay it back;
    we have the money, don't we?
CLARK. Oh, we've got it, but we're going to get it when our board finds
    out. Plus, there will be stiff fines and our stock will take a beating.
DEB. When our board finds out? Are you now a boy scout, too? If it
    hurts the price of the stock, then don't tell them.
CLARK. Ha! That's a brilliant idea — if we want to commit a felony.
    Look, even though Barry was my brother and your husband, it's
    clear he did this on his own before he died, so we won't be
    blamed — but we've got to come clean right away.
DEB. Or else?

CLARK. Orange jumpsuits, steel-shuttered windows, concrete floors,
    bunkmates. Is that worth a couple hundred thousand dollars?
DEB. You don't want to know what I'd do for that kind of money.

(Clark takes papers out of his jacket.)

CLARK. Oh, I know what you'd do for twenty bucks. But this is a legit
    business. Let me make this simple for your hair color to
    comprehend: sign these papers or go to jail.
DEB. *(turning her back to Clark)* Just lay them there, and when I will, I'll
    look at them.
CLARK. I'm sure you think I came all this way to bask within your
    surgically enhanced glow — but the fact is, I need these papers
    right away.
DEB. I will when I will.
CLARK. *(pulling up a seat and sitting down)* Then so will I. A drink — a
    drink! Whatever you're having is fine.
DEB. When your brother died, I got half a company to keep, but with it
    half a wit to keep me company.
CLARK. Whatever. Sign the papers.

*(Deb picks up the papers and starts to walk offstage while Robin and Bottom
approach Clark and look closely at him. Deb stops and, unseen by Robin or
Bottom, finds Blossom's ring, picks it up, then exits.)*

ROBIN. Oh, what an ulcerous lot!
    They're even more unpleasant in a pair.
BOTTOM. These humans have a most misshapen math
    In which the sum of one plus one
    Is less than either part alone.
ROBIN. These upright monkeys are a craven breed,
    Bankrupt in trust while glitt'ring in suspicion.
    Their eyes — turned inward — see a blackened soul,
    Rife in cruelty, violence, pain, dishonesty.
    Then nose to nose with another of their kind,
    They're paralyzed by what they know themselves
    To be capable of. The beast in the mirror
    Leaves them helpless, hapless and hopeless.
BOTTOM. Napless, capless and sapless.
ROBIN. And yet they would dissemble with a speech
    Of budding virtue, strut and step the boards
    With chests puffed out declaiming their propriety
    In thunder-rumbling speeches spoken on a drum.

And while they vaunt and wag their principles
In stormy tones, their treach'ry mutely slithers
To its true mark.
BOTTOM. I know a girl,
    A boojum of a girl,
Who lost both her mind and her hair.
When her chin disappeared
    She grew a gray beard
        And said, "Call me Jim, won't you dear?"

ROBIN. Ha ha, so true! They are a changeable lot.
BOTTOM. And an unfixable blot.
ROBIN. Watch this —

(Robin makes a howling sound. Clark stands up and looks around fearfully.)

CLARK. What's that?
ROBIN. These barrel fish quail at the slightest noise,
    Abandoning any sense of self or shame.
BOTTOM. "Who am I?" said the fly?
    "Not me," said the flea.
    Though an itchy man he's found to be.
ROBIN. It's all too easy!

(Robin waves his hand and Clark goes into a trance. As Robin sings and waves his hands, Clark stands up and starts dancing as if led by Robin.)

Catchfly, catchfly,
  Caught you one?
The moon's on the tail of the setting sun.

  Little fly a'buzzing, yes,
    Do re mi!
  Little fly a'sticking, yes,
    One, two, three!

Catchyfly, catchfly,
  Caught and done.
A little fly, a little stuck, fun, fun, fun!

(Robin and Bottom step back laughing. Deb re-enters. Her voice snaps Clark out of his trance.)

DEB. Are you okay? If you're going to pass out, take it somewhere else.

CLARK. What? I was — I thought — oh, never mind. Did you sign the papers?

DEB. I can't — I want my lawyer to look over them.

CLARK. Good god almighty, Deb! Your lawyer? Our company lawyers looked over everything and approved it. Why can't you just once do what I ask? Why must you challenge everything I do? Do you think you can take the company from me over this? Is that it?

DEB. Me? I know you're trying to cut me out. Besides, you were at the company when this happened.

CLARK. But you and Barry profited.

DEB. Maybe it was your idea.

CLARK. You're impossible to talk to!

(Deb walks to the one side by herself.)

ROBIN. Bottom, enough of their squeaking voices and
    Their constant squabbling. Do they nothing else?
    Is this the sum and round of it? The whole?
    Crowding the air with taunts, teeth and scowls,
    Sharpening their tongues with barren banter,
    Spiraling noise and confusion?
    And all for what? For what? So one can have
    More paper than the other? Own more geegaws?
    More cares? More worries? Oh, it hurts my ears!
    It's time for us to start our work, best done
    I think, without them here insulting our noses.

BOTTOM. What's wrong with my nose?
    It is a swell nose that smells quite well,
    A neighborly nose, a noble nose, a —

ROBIN. Bloody nose if you don't shut your yap.

BOTTOM. What nose? I knows nothin'!

(A drum beat and/or music rises slowly then gains speed and volume as the song continues.)

ROBIN. *(singing/chanting)*
    Buzz buzz buzz buzz

BOTTOM. Buzz buzz buzz buzz

CLARK. What's that?

DEB. I thought it was you.

ROBIN. Buzz buzz buzz buzz
  Raised from the grasstops
  And fall'n from the sky
  A sound tweaks the ear
  But nothing the eye.

(Robin pinches Deb, who jumps and squeals.)

ROBIN & BOTTOM.
  Buzz buzz buzz buzz
ROBIN. Yet to your eyes
  You spy not a thing
  Until it's too late
  And you feel its sharp sting!

(Bottom pinches Clark. Deb and Clark come together.)

CLARK. Ow! What is it?
ROBIN & BOTTOM.
  Buzz buzz buzz buzz
  Buzz buzz buzz buzz
BOTTOM. From out of the darkness
  From out of night's cold
  From out of the murky,
  And swirling black fold!
ROBIN & BOTTOM.
  Buzz buzz buzz buzz
BOTTOM. The invisible hunter
  He swerves and he kites
  Then fall on his prey
  And takes out a bite!
DEB. Ow! Ow!
CLARK. Ouch! What's going on? Ow!
BOTTOM. They swarm and they swoop —
  Smelling blood draws them quick —
  All gathering and hungry
  They sink their barbed sticks!
ROBIN & BOTTOM.
  Buzz buzz buzz buzz
  Buzz buzz buzz buzz

(Robin and Bottom start pinching Deb and Clark all over, who act as if being swarmed by hornets. They flail their arms, yelling and running around. Robin and Bottom chase them offstage, then return, laughing.)

ROBIN. See how they run! Oh, if Blossom saw
　　　Their frantic flee she wouldn't be so full of praise!

(Still laughing, Robin reaches into his pocket for the ring, but can't find it. He checks his other pockets. Not there. He then checks the patio table. Not there either. With increasing panic, he starts looking around the stage.)

ROBIN. Bottom, the ring! The ring! Where is the ring?
BOTTOM. Ring? Has it gone silent? I don't hear a thing of the ring?
　　　Or have I gone deaf — oh stars! I'm deaf! I'm deaf! Oh!
ROBIN. Blossom's ring, you moss head!
　　　I cannot find it! Help me!
BOTTOM. *(walking around)*
　　　Not here. Or here. Or here. Or here.

(Robin and Bottom quickly retrace their steps on the stage, but cannot find the ring.)

ROBIN. Those humans — it must be. They're thieves
　　　As well as frogs and worms. Bottom, come,
　　　We'll have to find them and the ring.
BOTTOM. And where the tripping winds do blow, I go!

(Robin and Bottom exit following Deb and Clark.)

SCENE 2

(Scene: A shadowy part of the woods. Dumb show: Clark stumbles onstage and then is spooked back and forth by several fairies until the fairies see Robin and Bottom coming, then they leave.)

CLARK. *(panting and confused)* Okay, Clark. Take a deep breath. You're
    not losing your mind — I think.

(Clark kneels to rest. Robin and Bottom enter, unseen by Clark.)

BOTTOM. Robin, there puffs our man-monkey,
    Crouching on his tail
    More like a frightened shrew
    Than a cutpurse or hobnail.
ROBIN. By Oberon, he's camouflaged his thievery well.
    This sputtering plug must be more eloquent
    In his performance than in his retiring.
    Hmm, yes, he looks more nail than hammer.
    Why, who would know that underneath
    Those darting lenses, that quailing cloak,
    That quiv'ring coil of fear there lies
    The Merlin of pickpockets? Perhaps
    He's seen the error of his grave misplay
    And fears our cuffed review.
BOTTOM. To steal from us — and when we're sober too! Tut tut!
    But that's a rip that's easily stitched.
        (sings)
    Come drink to me
    Come drink to my health
        Come drink to me, my Molly and Seth,
    A shot or a twist
    A dram or a nip
        'Cause you know I can't drink in my death.

Let's get that ring, then get that drink!

(Bottom starts to go but Robin pulls him back.)

ROBIN. No, wait you fool. If we simply lift
    The band from him, the human stain attends
    And Blossom learns of our miscarriage.
    To stanch the human stench, he must
    Concede it to us of his own free will.
    Yes, then, and only then, will it be cleansed
    And the body of our error be disposed.
BOTTOM. Of his own free will?
ROBIN. Yes, he must hand it to us on his own,
    Otherwise the ring will save his scent
    And Blossom smell our plot.
BOTTOM. Then say no more, my wit,
    I'll ask him for it.

(Bottom starts to go, but Robin pulls him back.)

ROBIN. Were it that easy! No, you can't be so full-faced.
    A drowning human will claim a desert's thirst
    If asked to spare a drink. Why they begrudge your breath!
    No, sometimes indirection's more direct.
    The woodthrush won't be caught by lunging at it straight.
    No, what we need is something we can trade,
    Some wares that we can proffer for the ring —
    And I know just the trick.
BOTTOM. What's that? We have no gems or gold.
ROBIN. All true, brave Bott, but we possess a thing
    As bright to them as all the baubles of a king.
BOTTOM. What's that?
ROBIN. Why information, bud! Information, yes!
    For crumbs dropped from the lip of gossip,
    They'll rake the sun-baked soil until their fingers bleed.
    Imagine what they'd do to eye the future!
    Now, play the mirror of my part.

(Robin and Bottom move quietly toward the middle of the stage — unseen by Clark. They motion and then swirling music and noises arises.)

CLARK. What's that? Who's there?

(Robin and Bottom circle Clark, making themselves seen.)

ROBIN. Who's there?
BOTTOM. Who's there?

ROBIN. Who's there indeed?
      In body? speech? In tumbling speed?
      It's we who leap the quantum stream.
BOTTOM. It's we who spring the light-year seam.
ROBIN. It's we who pace the sand's down flow —
BOTTOM. And then outstrip time's nimble toe.
CLARK. Wha — What do you want?

(Robin and Bottom stop circling Clark.)

ROBIN. We're ancient prophets, culled from night,
      Some call us seers — diviners, too.
      We have the gift that some call sight
      And so avail ourselves to you.
CLARK. That's, uh, very nice, yes. Can you tell me how to get out of
      these woods?
ROBIN. We truck no such niggling things —
      We're of a greater metric, higher wing.
      We augur what's to happen, all that will,
      And all that won't, and what might still.
CLARK. I was really just looking for a way out —
ROBIN. Inexorable time lays out the beat
      In which our steps our squarely seated.
      Can any man unrifle fate? Why, none,
      But he who cheats the strike of fortune's drum.
CLARK. I —

(The lights dim, there are flashes of light, thunder, drum beats and the sound of wind.)

BOTTOM. Sleep, you partridge, no refrain,
      Silence, swifts, your dusky strain.
      Stop you twinks and glints of night
        And stay your courser's evening flight!

      Be still you eyeless faces, all,
      Desist your droning click clock call —
      Freeze your hands and stop your swings,
        And put on hold your jolting rings!

        Time abate — obey our will!
        Time apprize — now stand still!

(The music and noise crescendo.)

ROBIN. Silence all! Be hushed, be hushed!
                 (it becomes quiet except for a droning hum)
    Now the dreadful wheel of fate
    Is braked, all time's inanimate,
    And we can see within time's veins
    The fates that wax and those that wane.
BOTTOM. What path, my friend, would you fain choose?
    One that leads to wealth and jewels?
CLARK. Would Deb get half of it?
ROBIN. Perhaps you'd like to travel wide
    And see the earth from side to side?
CLARK. Will I run into Deb?
BOTTOM. Perhaps the fairer sex appeals
    T'you more than wealth and weal.
CLARK. As long as it's not Deb —
ROBIN. Stop pratt'ling 'bout that silly woman!

(Thunder cracks angrily.)

    It really puts us off!
    Do you want the gift we offer?
    Say it now, or else be off!
CLARK. Want it? Uh, sure, I guess. What do I need to do?
ROBIN. We are spirits, sky and rain,
    Our needs are simple, our wants are plain.
CLARK. Well, that's very nice.
ROBIN. A token, bauble, trinket, toy,
    Some bit of gratitude we would enjoy.
CLARK. Oh well, this is really a bad time for me — I'm having some tax
    issues —
ROBIN. If it's too much, then walk away
    And take your fate, whatever may!

(Thunder sounds.)

CLARK. *(pulls out his wallet)* Okay, okay! Let me see — I have 50 —
    57 — no, 58 bucks.

(While speaking the following lines, Robin takes one of the bills from Clark's wallet, looks at it, then drops it with disgust. Clark picks it back up.)

ROBIN. What use have we for these?
    These wrinkled, colored leaves?
    Have you any precious metals, stones
    That we'd delight to wear and own?
CLARK. *(pulling change out of his pocket)*
    I have about, um, 61 cents.
BOTTOM. We use have we for cents.
ROBIN. What other tokens do you keep?
CLARK. Tokens? Bus tokens?
ROBIN. Fool! What jewelry have you? What?
CLARK. Jewelry? I have a watch. But it's a Rolex, I mean, my dying
    mother gave this to me, I'd hate —
ROBIN. What need have we of clocks and chimes
    Who see the length and width of time?
CLARK. Good point. Very good point.
BOTTOM. What about a ring?
CLARK. A ring?
ROBIN. A ring?
CLARK. A ring?
BOTTOM. I'm hearing bells!
ROBIN. *(pointing to his finger)*
    Yes, by god, a ring! A ring!
CLARK. But I don't have a ring.

(Whatever remaining music or sounds stop completely.)

ROBIN. If you were not an arrant fool
    I'd say you use us like a tool.
    Search him Bottom — enough charades,
    Let's find out now if we've been made.

(Bottom roughly frisks Clark.)

CLARK. Hey! Whoa! Hey! Hey!
BOTTOM. It isn't here. Well, that's moss in the pants.
ROBIN. It isn't here? Ah! Then you've pinched our time!
CLARK. Sorry! Hey, uh, what about that, uh, future stuff.
ROBIN. You want, you trembling toad?
    Then you will get by lot and load!

ROBIN & BOTTOM.
> *(resuming song from earlier)*
> Buzz buzz buzz buzz —

> When warming flesh meets chilly night
> Our hungry friends will haste—
> From every den and any dale
> To take of you a taste!

(Robin and Bottom start pinching Clark.)

CLARK. Ow — ouch!

(Clark runs offstage, yelling.)

ROBIN. Ah, you fool! The man ape doesn't have the ring!
BOTTOM. Me fool? You fool, too, fool!
ROBIN. No doubt this is the female's sleight of hand.
> Her art I must admire — she's very good.
> To cop the ring and make us blame the man
> Is neatly done, I must confess. But now
> She's been gleaned, and now she's grist!
BOTTOM. *(pointing at the horizon)*
> Look: the time. The midnight dance will soon commence.
ROBIN. You're right, my friend. Then we must hurry hence.

(Robin and Bottom exit.)

SCENE 3

(Scene: Another part of the woods. Again the moon shines brightly. Dumb show: Fairies lead Deb across the stage. She doesn't see them, but they act of if they are leading or tugging her by invisible ropes, and she follows. Deb and the fairies exit just before Robin and Bottom enter from the opposite side.)

ROBIN. Step it up, Bot, step. The wench should be nearby.
BOTTOM. So close as to be near,
    Yet not so near as to be here.
ROBIN. How now, in such a time so short could we
    Misplace her?
BOTTOM. A taller time just might have found her
    Had she a longer tail to trail behind her.
    But that reminds me of a lively tale!
ROBIN. A tale? Oh heavens no!
BOTTOM. What?
ROBIN. "What?" Why that's exactly what I say
    Upon the hearing of your fuzzy tales.
    They have no seam but run interminably
    To a threadbare climax, and then stand naked
    Amid a chorus of "huhs?" and "whats?"
BOTTOM. But this one I have called "The Ladybug's Tryst."
ROBIN. Hmm. That does pique my interest.
BOTTOM. It should, that title has it all!
    Intrigue and sex and ladies, yes!
ROBIN. All right. Let's hear it.
BOTTOM. What? After such a sneer? No, first
    An apology is due my tale.
ROBIN. I'll give your tail a kick, I will.
BOTTOM. Okay, okay.
    Once upon a Thursday eve —
    Or was it Wednesday night?
    It might have been a Monday morning
    But that doesn't seem quite right.
    Maybe so, it doesn't matter,
    Well, not too much I'd say,
    Unless, of course, your calendar
    Depends upon the day.

So, let's just say it's Monday, yes,
It's such a hair to split.
A Monday once a week sounds right

ROBIN. Just get on with it!
BOTTOM. All right, all right, behave, behoove —
    I'll start the tale right now.
    Once upon a Monday eve
    The spider met the cow.
ROBIN. Wait, wait, wait. I thought this tale was spun
    Upon a ladybug.
BOTTOM. Said who, said who? I say I said no such a thing.
ROBIN. You did you didn't? I know you did it was.
BOTTOM. Did not.
ROBIN. You did, you did, you did, did, did!
BOTTOM. Four times a don't' I say I didn't.
    I said — you will recall — that was its title.
ROBIN. Ugh! So I suppose that there's no tryst.
BOTTOM. Well, actually, no.
ROBIN. No sex.
BOTTOM. Not even a tickle.
ROBIN. And no ladybug.
BOTTOM. Nowhere in sight.
ROBIN. Why oh why do I give weight to your ethereal yarns,
    Give props your petering plots, and give leverage
    To your teetering tales? Far better it would be
    To let them fall of their own nonsense
    Than have their frayed foolishness collapse on me.
    Why, cat's paw, do I let this happen?

(Deb, led by several fairies, enters while Robin talks. Then the fairies exit, unseen by Robin or Bottom.)

BOTTOM. Because the mirror is too painful.
ROBIN. Yes — what?
BOTTOM. (seeing Deb)
    She comes! The female there!
ROBIN. That's her? That's her? By thunder, yes it is.
    She lays upon the eye a graceless log,
    Not near as sharp as I recalled, but I
    Suppose the fox that wears the goose's grin
    Will keep his fork the sharpest.
BOTTOM. Unless he cooks his goose.

ROBIN. A tasty irony. But to our destination
    Let's address ourselves, okay?
BOTTOM. I am the stamp and mark. But how
    Shall we proceed?
ROBIN. By progress we'll progress, my friend,
    And from our naked victimhood
    We'll be redressed. But this time no more lofty promises —
    Our last suit oversized a shallow wit.
    This time our grace will be more finely cut.
    A simple deal for simple minds will simply be
    The best. If we're to lead her from these woods,
    Then she's to leave us with the ring.
BOTTOM. Then let us wring her of the ring.
ROBIN. Well said. *(to Deb)* Good evening, lass.
BOTTOM. Good night, my lady.
DEB. What?
ROBIN. What intention steers you in trespass of our land?
DEB. Your land?
BOTTOM. Yes, it's ours. Well, what I mean it's his
    And mine when I say "ours," Not yours and his and mine.
    Just "ours" — we two, just his and mine.
ROBIN. Is it a treacherous wind that blows you to our woods?
BOTTOM. His and mine, that is, not yours and his and —
ROBIN. We got it. There's no need
    To rub your point to dullness.
BOTTOM. *(to Deb)*
    My point, that is, not yours —
ROBIN. Shut up!
DEB. You own this land?
BOTTOM. We do, it's ours,
    Each leaf and limb,
    Every squirrel,
    Ruck and scrim.
DEB. Oh god, oh god! Oh, I'm so sorry, so sorry. I am so sorry that I
    bought a house next to your property. I was promised this was an
    exclusive community — only the best neighbors. Oh my god —
    I've got to sell my house before anyone finds out and its value
    plummets.
ROBIN. My, my, dear lady, what puffing pride you bear.
    But to our point: What's your motive here?
DEB. Look Mr. and Mrs. Short and Rustic, I'm lost. My property runs up
    against your woods and I got lost in the dark. Just point me back
    to Holcombe Estates, and I can begin listing my property.

ROBIN. And what of us? Just insults? No!
    This trespass you'll atone.
    You'll pay us now or spend the night
    Combing these nettles alone.

DEB. Me pay you? I increase the value of your hillbilly heaven just
    standing on it.

BOTTOM. Or being placed in it.

DEB. You rural rubes don't scare me. Just tell me the way back to my
    house and you won't have to answer to my lawyers.

BOTTOM. L-l-lawyers?

ROBIN. Oh Bot, calm yourself. This fool will range
    The length and breadth of night in vain
    Before she lights upon her door again.

BOTTOM. Which might be through here.

ROBIN. Through here.

BOTTOM. Or here.

ROBIN. It doesn't matter — you won't find the way.

BOTTOM. None will press their pillow who doesn't pay.

DEB. Pay? You've got to be kidding me.

BOTTOM. Baby goat or not, the reckoning's the same.
    Within these mazing woods you're lost
    And be it next week or tomorrow,
    You'll gladly pay our cost.

DEB. Okay, okay. I respect your desire to profit from someone else's
    misfortune. That's admirable. Let's just say I might be game.

BOTTOM. "I might be game."

DEB. Now, what might you want if I were in a giving mood. Remember:
    I don't have my wallet.

ROBIN. You have perhaps some jewelry, yes?

DEB. Ha, no way! These earrings could buy a 10-year supply of burlap
    underwear for you and your girlfriend.

ROBIN. Oh, some token, small, would meet our end,
    Perhaps a ring to give a friend.

DEB. A ring I might possess. And if I give this hypothetical ring to you,
    you'll lead me out of the forest?

ROBIN. Yes, for a gift of a ring
    We'll take you out on wings.

(Deb pulls out the ring.)

DEB. I have a ring — a piece of junk —

BOTTOM. The ring! The ring!

(Bottom reaches eagerly for the ring, but Deb pulls it out his reach.)

DEB. Ah-ah! No grabbing! I see this isn't just a ring — it is *the* ring. I
    think I'll have to rethink our deal.

ROBIN. But we're agreed.

DEB. But nothing's done. You know, I think I'll keep the ring. It looks
    like worthless metal. But it might look good on my aussie-doodle's
    collar. I won't be needing your services tonight, boys.

BOTTOM. *(looking to the horizon)*
    Oh Robin — do you see the hour there?
    The midnight dance comes near!

ROBIN. *(nodding, then to Deb)*
    What do you want with something
     So slight and small?
    It's but a bauble worth almost nothing
     To you at all.

DEB. Oh, I don't know. I'm funny like that. But if you two want it so
    bad, it must be worth something.

ROBIN. I assure you that its value
    Is invisible to all but us.
    So what's the worth in holding something
    You'll just have to dust?

DEB. My feral friend. Tut tut. You've much to learn. First, I pay people
    to dust everything for me. And second, it's not the price that I
    perceive in it that gives it value. No, it's the price that you are
    willing to pay. If my junk is another man's treasure, why should I
    sell as trash what another will pay a fortune? Eh? Now, you walk
    me back to my house and we'll negotiate what you'll pay me for
    the ring.

ROBIN. Yap on: Your callow games and plays
    Redounds our anger coming your way!

DEB. What are you going to do, shorty? The choice is yours. You pay
    and you get what you want, or you don't, and you won't.

ROBIN. Be it one or nine
    I want what's mine.

DEB. That's a noble sentiment and one I live by. Oh, these choices offer
    the illusion of freedom — choose any one — but they are shackles,
    and we who would taste the entire menu of life must settle for one
    course and thereafter is the evening of time as singular and
    predictable as a train upon rails. But what can we do?

ROBIN. Oh, foolish, feckless human, be quiet!
　　By your mock'ry, your torments are abetted.
　　Come tempest or tittle, I want what I want
　　And by Oberon's beard, I will get it!
DEB. My terms are clear.

(An angry rumbling noise rises.)

ROBIN. Enough! *(to Bottom)* I say we sprout a thistle from her nose!
BOTTOM. *(pointing to one side)*
　　Wait! Blossom! I see her coming. What now?

(The rumbling suddenly stops.)

ROBIN. Briars and bullocks! The midnight dance must soon begin.
　　Let's go!

(Robin and Bottom exit to the side. Then several dancing fairies enter, led by Blossom. They all sing. Deb watches in amazement.)

BLOSSOM. *(singing)*
　　We flower the midnight pinnacle
　　　Star light, beam and bright
　　There tip and toe the dewy hour
　　　Shade and shape alight
　　In moonflowers garlanded, white bedecked
　　　Brook, a broach, a sprite
FAIRY 1.　　　The moment's here
BLOSSOM.　　To dance
FAIRY 1.　　　　Sing cheer
BLOSSOM.　　To each
FAIRY 2.　　　　　Endear
BLOSSOM & FAIRY 1. And all appear
　　Tra la, tra la, tra lay!

DEB. What are these elfish immigrants?
BLOSSOM. Come, do not fear.
　　　　Come. Come! Come here!
DEB. Where are you from? Yugoslavia? Are you the Walton's new
　　house staff? It's just like them to let the hired help run amok in
　　the neighborhood.

BLOSSOM. We are the nighttime flutter seen askew,
    The sometimes buzzing in your ears,
     The breath unsourced upon your neck —
    We're the forest fairies, dear!
DEB. Forest fairies?
BLOSSOM. We are. The forest fairies.
DEB. You live here?
BLOSSOM. In the air and between the leaves,
    In weeded beds and arbored eaves.
    This sylvan patch we soar and roam
    Is the bowery that we call our home.
DEB. This forest sure has a lot of claims on it. Who owns this land? Do
    you have the deed?
BLOSSOM. The deed? Indeed we don't.
    What need have we for this? We don't.
DEB. That's what I thought. Look, I'm not normally a do-gooder, but let
    me offer some advice: the Walton's can't make you live in the
    woods like animals. You should call the police. Now I suggest you
    move on.
BLOSSOM. Move where? We live upon the swirling airs?
DEB. I know — you're forest fairies. Fairies of the forest, okay, okay.
    (Deb grabs Blossom) Hey! If that's true, you must give me your
    treasure since I caught you.
BLOSSOM. (laughs)
    You're so earnest! I find that endearing.
    But pet, that's a leprechaun you seek!
    We're but humble fairies,
    The midnight wood's our coin and wealth.
DEB. You're into real estate, huh. Cash poor. It figures that I'd find the
    trailer park fairies. Are there any of the Beverly Hills variety out
    here?
BLOSSOM. Who is this Beverly Hills?
DEB. What about wishes? You grant wishes, right?
BLOSSOM. Wishes? From us? From me?
    You're mistaking us with a genie.
DEB. Of all the sprites, I meet the most bereft.
    What do you do?
BLOSSOM. We pollinate the flowers
    And kiss the leaves with dew —
DEB. Swell.
BLOSSOM. We flounce upon the elmwood palms,
    We circle, call and coo.
    At times, in early evening's gloam,

When the rising moon grins full,
We'll put an ugly, noisy babe
In place of its original.
DEB. Does anyone notice the difference?
BLOSSOM. *(dejected)*
Alas, it's sad, these days no more.
DEB. Well, I had to ask. Look, you can pretend to be whoever you want
to be. And if you're here illegally, that's fine by me. But the
Waltons shouldn't let you run loose in the woods. Not that it's any
of my business. However, can you at least tell me how to get out of
here?
BLOSSOM. Here?
DEB. The woods — the forest.
BLOSSOM. The forest? Whatsoever for?
Here our revels soon will take the floor
When the midnight stars coil into place.
You'll stay, relax, enjoy our merry race.
We'll soon begin our midnight dance
In which all the fairies come at once.
DEB. That's nice, but I just want to get back to my house —
BLOSSOM. My dear, you are mulish one,
Focused solely on your want, and that only!
I think it's cute, so sweet!
Perhaps, tra la, you're lonely?
DEB. What's that supposed to mean?

(Two fairies push Clark onstage. He stumbles as he enters.)

CLARK. Deb! Deb!
DEB. Oh, this is nice. From an incompetent fairy, to a fairly incompetent.
CLARK. What's going on here?
DEB. Oh these — you might as well ignore them. They fancy themselves
"forest fairies" but they are potless and wishless. No gold. No
grants. No go. Just pollen and dews.
CLARK. *(staring at Blossom)*
But they are beautiful —

(More fairies, including Robin and Bottom, enter and begin circling Clark and Deb.)

DEB. I think we should stick together or we might never find our way
out.

CLARK. Out of where? Oh yeah. You wouldn't believe what I saw
    earlier.
BLOSSOM. This way.
CLARK. Is this the way out?
BLOSSOM. Patience, patience, awkward ones.

(Blossom leads Deb and Clark to center stage. Music starts playing.)

DEB. Do you hear that?
CLARK. It's music — where's it coming from?

*(Music slowly rises in volume with a simple, slow, but firm beat. The fairies
start to sing and they have Deb and Clark dance with them. As each verse of the
song passes, it becomes faster and louder. By the last verse, it is a raucous row
in which Deb and Clark are pushed and tossed around. In fear, they try to leave,
but the fairies hem them in.)*

FAIRIES. *(singing)*
    From high look down the breathless stars
    Enchased in evening's eboned bar
      And yet a vig'lant eye reveals
      The stars deliberate skip and wheel
    Across the deep and far.

      On toe step high, then make descent,
      In motion spun, in motion sent.
        The world's a'flutter, all's in play
      So leap the loosestrife, dance and sway.

    On high the pride-backed oak looms tall
    Above the forest madrigal,
      Yet dance its ancient arbored wreaths
      Yet wave and twirl its tressled leaves
    Within the tune enthralled.

      On toe step high, then make descent,
      In motion spun, in motion sent.
        The world's a'flutter, all's in play
      So leap the loosestrife, dance and sway.

On high the river's body snakes
In placid grace it swerves and wakes
 Yet brought to boil it laps and leaps
 It spins and twirls, bursts and sweeps
Until its bounds it breaks.

On toe step high, then make descent,
 In motion spun, in motion sent.
  The world's a'flutter, all's in play
 So leap the loosestrife, dance and sway.

On high the wind blows soft and hard
And tickles lips and buildings jar.
 Unseen, it pushes, bucks and burls,
 It swells and billows, bends and whirls
Till all is made or marred.

 On toe step high, then make descent,
 In motion spun, in motion sent.
  The world's a'flutter, all's in play
 So leap the loosestrife, dance and away!

(The fairies laughingly let Deb and Clark escape, followed closely by Robin and Bottom, then by Blossom. The other fairies one by one dance offstage, laughing.)

SCENE 4

(Scene: Another part of the woods, not far from the midnight dance. Several fairies joyfully scamper across the stage looking over their shoulders. Robin and Bottom enter looking for Deb. The stage has two tree stumps at opposite ends of the stage. Not immediately visible to the audience, one stump has a small hatchet, on the other a small machete. Blossom runs onstage to catch up with Robin and Bottom.)

BLOSSOM. Robin! Robin! Wait! Robin!
ROBIN. *(impatiently)*
        What? What? What?
BLOSSOM. I'm sorry I got mad at you.

(Robin and Bottom continue looking around while talking to Blossom.)

ROBIN. Hmm. What's was, is was.
BLOSSOM. I'm going to the falls with Periwinkle
        To dance beneath the spray. Please join us, won't you?
ROBIN. Periwinkle? Ugh! I'd rather lop my ears
        Than brook her shrill, insipid voice. Besides,
        Right now I have more clamorous mouths to feed.
BLOSSOM. Still angry to be working near the humans?
ROBIN. Sort of, yes.
BLOSSOM. Then like Mercury, put the capstone on and join us.
        I'm going to wear my brand-new dress and all
        My favorite jewelry.
ROBIN. *(suddenly attentive to Blossom)*
        What? Your jewelry?
        Well, if that's the case —
        Uh, that sounds —
        That sounds great. I'd love to go!
BLOSSOM. Then it's a date. I must away to prep —
        Now don't be late!

(Blossom turns to leave.)

ROBIN. No wait, wait!
BLOSSOM. For what?

ROBIN. Yes, uh. Well,
> You don't want to —
> Well —
> I think
> That you should first —
> Bottom! What are you doing?

BOTTOM. Me?

ROBIN. Is there more than one Bottom here? Ha ha!

BOTTOM. Well, I suppose there's three.

ROBIN. He's so full of wit and vinegar. Ha ha!

BLOSSOM. I really need go. I want each glint and glim
> In perfect play.

ROBIN. No, wait — I can't imagine you more perfect.

BLOSSOM. That's very nice! But wait until you see
> What I put on tonight — I'll even wear
> My favorite charms and rings.

BOTTOM. Uh oh!

BLOSSOM. What, don't you like my rings?

ROBIN. Of course he likes them. He meant — just meant
> That you should save them for a special day.
> Besides, what if you lost them in the falls?

BLOSSOM. Oh, I'll be careful. It's such a lovely eve,
> I want to sparkle in the moon shine spray.

ROBIN. Why don't you bide me by the honeycomb?
> And then I'll walk you to our nest. But first
> I have loose ends to tack.

BLOSSOM. I don't know. I've got a lot to do.

ROBIN. Come on!

BLOSSOM. I guess that I could wait here till —

ROBIN. Oh, cobwebs, no!

BLOSSOM. You are a most vagarious man — half phlox
> And wine, half spurs and wormwood.

ROBIN. No, no, no, I meant "oh, cobwebs, no —
> There's no need to stay the human stench."
> Let me finish here and I'll be there
> Faster than the moon face meets the rill.

BLOSSOM. All right, but don't be long. If you're not light,
> Then you'll be late and I'll proceed without you.

ROBIN. I'll see you by and by, just wait. Bye bye!

BLOSSOM. Tra la!

(Robin practically pushes her offstage. He returns to Bottom.)

ROBIN. These unctuous beasts, along with Blossom's
    Untimely bells, have ripped my evening's thread.
    My intentions are tangled in a raveling chase
    That's threaded every crook and crawl within the wood.
    From rim to rise, blind happenstance impels
    Me on a rambling race to nowhere. Yes,
    I'm pinned upon the tail of accident
    And cannot let it go. Oh, I'm the folly-wog
    To fortune's claw — a child's toy, a feline's joy —
    And every out I seek it pounced upon with glee.
BOTTOM. At every hem a hurdle,
    At every wall a fence!
ROBIN. Enough, enough of this! My anger swells.
    I will no longer play the meadow lion's seed
    To be sore buffeted across the fields
    By whimsy's breeze. My mood's congealed
    And turned to lead. Enough — this fickle flightiness —
    Enough! I'll snatch the curséd ring right from their hands —
    Be they live or dead, so be it.
BOTTOM. But what of Blossom, won't she see
    The human stain upon her ringery?
ROBIN. Hah! I don't give a jot, old Bot, not a jot.
    My mind has flown its caring cage
    And soars beyond my Blossom's reach.
    But do not fear, some story I'll concoct
    To blunt her prickly darts.
BOTTOM. Back in school
    They taught a rule:
    A lie too cool
    Oft makes the fool!
ROBIN. A'sudden now you're virtue bloated, eh?
    I'll knock some out. (strikes Bottom) Shut up and do your part.
    The fire's hot, let's bring our stew to boil.

(Several fairies, unseen by Bottom or Robin, push Deb and Clark onstage. Robin
then turns and sees Deb and Clark.)

    Ah, the evening's thieves. See how they cluck
    And hum like nervous hens upon the nest?
    But don't misunderestimate them, Bottom.
    Although they have the twist of simp'ring fools,
    And a bovine gait and grace that plods
    Across the sloping meadows, do not be lulled.

For in this dundering frame, this artless visage,
This monstrous-weird connivance, resides a power
For ruinous confusion, spoil and wrack.
With but a single bungling note from them
All harmony's discordant and the night
Turned shrieks and sevenths.
Before their calamitous wake, all creatures flee,
Their nests upended, left to where fate blows.
BOTTOM. And where fate sucks.
ROBIN. Hush now! They near —
CLARK. That eyesore should be visible by satellites.
DEB. Eyesore?
CLARK. Your house is pink for heaven's sake.
DEB. I guess you'd prefer black.
CLARK. White would be inappropriate.
ROBIN. Ugh! Still, their ceaseless bickering.
    Our time is almost up — let's put an end to it and them.
BOTTOM. The end of the end is the end. Amen.

(Enter Blossom by the side unseen by anyone. She hides upstage and watches gleefully.)

BLOSSOM. What's this? More mischief? Ah!
DEB. Eyesore! You're one to talk. I've seen what your girlfriends wear.
    How much do they charge?
CLARK. More than you, more than you.

(Bottom and Robin invisibly lead Deb and Clark to the different tree stumps.)

ROBIN. *(to Clark)*
    What has she done?
    What races won? Or towers tall begun?
      What's she completed
      Or in laurels seated?
    Nothing, naught and none.
BOTTOM. *(to Deb)*
    What's raised him high?
    What skills has he? What genius eye?
      More likely fate
      And dumb luck's date
    Had smiled upon his try.

ROBIN. *(to Clark)*
 What does she know
 Of planting seeds and helping them to grow?
  She knows nothing, naught
  Of that which can't be bought,
 Betrayed or overthrown.
BOTTOM. *(to Deb)*
 He doesn't care
 For your opinions, valuable or rare.
  Alive or dead
  Upon your head
 The company he won't share.
ROBIN. *(to Clark)*
 Why still endure her slings and slurs,
  The endless sleepless nights
  When it could end with her?
 If never from these darkened woods
  She made it to her door,
 If happened some strange accident
 The company would be yours.
BOTTOM. *(to Deb)*
 He stands before you like a wall
  That blocks your way, holds you at bay
  Forever in a lull.
 But if never from these darkened woods
  He made it to your door,
 If happened some strange accident
 The company would be yours.
BOTTOM. *(to Clark)*
 You're in the forest, by yourselves, alone —
CLARK. Alone.
ROBIN. No one's 'round — your acts are all unknown —
DEB. Unknown.
BOTTOM & ROBIN. Once in a lifetime — seize the prize!
CLARK & DEB. Seize the prize!
ROBIN & BOTTOM. It's all before your eyes, your eyes!

(Robin and Bottom step back.)

ROBIN. Ha ha! Let's withdraw and watch our suit unfold.

(Clark picks up the machete from the stump near him, while Deb picks up the hatchet near her. The both try to keep their weapons out of sight of the other. They slowly approach each other, then start circling attempting to be nonchalant.)

CLARK. It's, uh, a nice day.
DEB. Night.
CLARK. Night, right.
DEB. Yes. A nice night, it is.
ROBIN. *(to Bottom)*
    In a moment, the ring will be ours!
CLARK. What do you have in your hand?
DEB. Mmm, nothing. What do you have in yours?
CLARK. Oh me, uh, nothing.
DEB. Oh.
CLARK. *(catching a glimpse of Deb's hatchet)*
    A hatchet? Are you — are you trying to kill me?
DEB. Me? Oh no! Never! Well, maybe. Yes. Are you trying to kill me?
CLARK. Me? Trying to kill you? Uh, yes. I guess we're both trying to
    kill each other. It's kind of funny that we both had the same idea
    at the same time. I guess we're not so different.
DEB. Funny, yeah. It's actually a relief because I thought your hostility
    toward me might have masked a deep-seated, uh, love.
CLARK. A deep — a deep-seated, passionate love?
DEB. Yeah, that crazy kind of love where opposites are irresistibly
    attracted to each other.
CLARK. And they forget who they are.
DEB. And they say something stupid, like "I love you."
CLARK. I love you?
DEB. Yes, I love you.
CLARK. I — I love you, too.

(Deb and Clark drop their weapons, embrace and kiss. Robin jumps up and, waving his hand, puts Deb and Clark in a trance.)

ROBIN. Unholy horrors! Dark as a moonless night,
    Black as a serpent's eye! Oh, baneful scene!
    Of all the things that I expected, this —
    This is the colossus to the flea —
    The sight alone sets my skin on needles!
    Bottom, do not look! It's too, too horrible!

BOTTOM. I am transfixed as if by a witch's spell —
    My eyes snagged on the burrs of shocking disbelief
    And I can't look away!
ROBIN. Have they no decency, no self respect,
    No sense of duty calling them to do
    The honorable deed and kill each other?
    Oh, soon we'll see them in their naked gloss
    And right before our eyes they'll do the deed.
    The horror! The horror!
BOTTOM. For all that's merciful and clean,
    For all the foxglove's nectar,
    For all the soft-bedded leaves,
    For gentle mercy on us,
    Just take the ring and let's be off!
    Who cares what Blossom knows!
ROBIN. At last, a good idea!

(With obvious disgust, Robin separates Deb and Clark and reaches into Deb's pocket. Then her other pocket. Then he grabs her hands and looks at them.)

ROBIN. The ring — it's gone!
BOTTOM. Gone silent missing?

(Robin frantically looks in Clark's pockets.)

ROBIN. It's not here. And he doesn't have it either.
    Ah, these foolish, stupid, bumbling humans —
    They must have lost it. Brambles and briars!
BOTTOM. Blossom will not like that.
ROBIN. There's not need to poke the elephant.
    Blossom will not know a thing.

(Blossom approaches.)

BLOSSOM. Know what? What secrets have you pocketed?
ROBIN. Blossom! Nothing. Oh, he prates and prattles so
    I've caught the bug myself.
BLOSSOM. That so? Your eyes were rolling back and forth
    As if there's something that you lost. Can I help?
ROBIN. There's nothing lost.
BOTTOM. Oh nothing's lost, we know exactly where it is —
    Within an acre or two.
ROBIN. Patch that leak!

BLOSSOM. That's good. You know, I thought you might
  Be looking 'round for this. *(holding up the ring on her finger)*
BOTTOM. The ring! Oh, there it is unlost!
ROBIN. You ass!
BLOSSOM. Imagine my surprise to find my ring
  Upon this human female while we did
  Our midnight dance.
ROBIN. Amazing, yes. I can't imagine how she got it.
  But these are a wily beast, a furtive breed.
BLOSSOM. They are?
BOTTOM. They are?
ROBIN. They are! Why you can't blink at them
  For in the moment that your eyes are closed
  They'll wreak confusion on your plans.
  I just told Bottom that same thing.
BLOSSOM. You did?
BOTTOM. You did? You did!
ROBIN. By Oberon, it's true, it's true! They're brighter than
  Their dull eyes will concede. Why yes, why yes,
  She must have —
  Yes, she must have snuck
  Into our village —
  Right past the elders —
  And the —
  Children —
  And the women —
  Who — the ring — and nobody —
  Ah, thistles on it all! I give up! I give up!
BLOSSOM. You naughty little boys! You cannot use a scarf
  To hide an oak-sized shame. Your pliant words
  Should leave you both red-faced and chastened.
  I dread to think what hardened stares await
  On our return. By then your words had better stiffen
  Or else the elders may lay down a punishment
  Twice-more severe: Perhaps time with the leprechauns.
ROBIN. Augh! Those miserly midgets! But no more lectures —
  I surrender! I'm sick to the heart. These human brutes,
  Unsteady and inconstant, have left me
  In a dizzy green. Within their sight the toy
  Becomes the player and the world of our intent
  A twisted, shambling bolt of shrieks and tears.
  Let them to their gauds and baubles,
  Oh, I can take no more. No more! No more!

BLOSSOM. Oh Robin, come, shake off those gloomy cuffs.
     The daybreak soon unveils and we will rest.
     I'll tell you what: Let's take the streamlet back
     And dance upon its silver-rippled face.
     That's always cheered you up and will again.
BOTTOM. And can we swing upon the bluebells?
BLOSSOM. Yes, we can.
BOTTOM. Okay!
BLOSSOM. (holding out her hand to Robin)
     Robin, come! The minnows are asleep
     And we can shake them from their beds!

(Robin takes Blossom's hand and with Bottom they exit. Deb and Clark jolt as if awakened.)

DEB. My god, what are we doing?
CLARK. I — I don't know. Have we lost our minds?
DEB. Let's make sure this never happens again. I think our first instincts
     were truer.
CLARK. Agreed. But let's not kill each other either. That's too messy.
DEB. Agreed. Obviously, we've spent too much time in these woods.
     Let's not talk about this ever again. Ever, ever, ever again.
CLARK. Talk about it? I don't even want to think about it. Uh! There's
     your house.
DEB. Thank heaven! I'll sign the papers, just so long as you go away.
CLARK. That's fine. I'll wait in the car and you can bring them there.

(Deb and Clark exit. Music starts playing and the fairies enter.)

FAIRIES. (singing)
     The earth and sun in rhythmed 'brace
     Draw fluent circle's time apace
          From there we turn, we turn, we turn.

     The stars a'quiver fade and pale
     As daylight slowly draws its vale
          From there we fly, we fly, we fly.

     The warbler wakes, unstops her throat
     And cuts the cool with twitt'ring note,
          From there we spin, we spin, we spin.

Unfurls the hyacinth's broad yellow,
The morning milkweed, dewy meadow,
  From there we flee, we flee, we flee.

Soon the lights will all be raised,
Our tales all told, our lines all played,
  And so we say goodnight, good day.

(The fairies exit and the lights go down, ending with a lighted horizon in the distance.)

FINIS

MURDER OUTSIDE THE CATHEDRAL

A One-Act Search for the Perfect Fish Sandwich

CHARACTERS

Sheriff Pym, a man in his mid-thirties
Kevin, a woman in her twenties impersonating a man
Corpse, a sickly-looking young man

Women, two or three middle aged and older women
Wife, an older woman, larger than Sheriff Pym

Archbishop Thomas Beckett, an old man, tall, distinguished, very clean
Archbishop Thomas Becket, a man bent over with age in ragged, musty clothes
Priest 1, Priest 2, middle aged men wearing cassocks, extremely clean and well pressed

Knight, middle-aged man in light armor

TIME / PLACE

Backstage of a contemporary production of T.S. Eliot's
Murder in the Cathedral
~ and at the same time ~
A road near Canterbury Cathedral circa. 1170

(Scene: Backstage of a play with props and various theatre detritus laying about — trunks, racks of clothes. An old backdrop hangs center stage with a picture of a medieval cathedral in the distance with a dirt lane running to the main gate. One side of the stage exits to the "stage," the other to the town/cathedral. A Corpse lays in the front-center stage with a noose around his neck. Sheriff Pym enters from the "town" side of the stage and stops center stage near where Kevin stands, not far from the Corpse but Pym doesn't see him. Sheriff Pym and Kevin are dressed in standard medieval/ renaissance garb, with Sheriff Pym better dressed in a low-ranking official's outfit and Kevin dressed like a peasant or apprentice. Applause is heard offstage from the "play" side of the stage. Sheriff Pym looks toward the sound. Kevin stares into the sky.)

SHERIFF PYM. They're at it again, Kevin.

KEVIN. *(staring blankly into the sky)* What?

SHERIFF PYM. What? Their hand-wringing bickering, their mind-numbing dithering, their poses, their primping, their posturing. And all of it's nothing but trouble for me — snake eyes and snarls, and for what?

KEVIN. *(still staring at the sky)* What?

SHERIFF PYM. Who knows? Perhaps how many angels top a pin? Or if a virgin girl can milk a goat the Wednesday before the Passover begins? Or if a bearded man can eat a turnip washed by a menstruating woman wearing a sackcloth blouse borrowed from her sister. But me and you, Kevin, we know what it's really all about.

KEVIN. What?

SHERIFF PYM. Power, Kevin, power! And clean underwear, but that's beside the point. Yes, here stands King Henry, Lord of our earthly England — there Archbishop Beckett — exulted doorman of heaven, and in between our world, this dirt-under-the-fingernails, wax-in-the-ears, strange-growth-between-the-toes of a world.

Yes, this patch of earth is like a can opener laying between two knights outside a loo. Beckett claims god's right, Henry claims his birthright, but only one can impose law and disorder, smite the poor, seduce the pages, slay the weak, lord the weary, ride the maids, burn the weird, seduce the horses, and wear white in the spring. It's just not right.

KEVIN. What?

SHERIFF PYM. It's just not right these in-bred, bedroom bunglers can send us off to war because our enemy wipes his nose from right to left, not left to right.

KEVIN. *(snapping out of his reverie)* Did you see that, Sheriff, that cloud that floated past? It looked just like a giant rabbit reading a book. *(Sheriff Pym glares at Kevin)* I think it was Aristotle. *(a pause)* What? Were you talking to me, Sheriff?

SHERIFF PYM. Was I — Was I talking to you? No, Kevin, I always launch into a ranting monologue in front of strangers to explain the plot.

KEVIN. Oh, okay. I thought you might be talking to me.

SHERIFF PYM. *(under his breath)* Moron!

KEVIN. What did I do to you?

SHERIFF PYM. You heard that, *(quieter than before)* you stupid bastard.

KEVIN. What?

SHERIFF PYM. Nothing. I didn't say anything.

KEVIN. Did you tell them that Archbishop Beckett is back after a seven-year absence? That Beckett and King Henry were long-time friends? That once Henry named Beckett archbishop of the English church their friendship ended over who made the best fish sandwiches, or something like that.

SHERIFF PYM. D'you think me some lazy-assed writer who would resort to showing off the plot like a whore who hangs her frillies in her window? Do you think me so imaginatively destitute, so beggarly of brightness, so artfully impecunious, so creatively constipated that I couldn't come up with a better way to say:
> The king wants the archbishop dead?
> That we're standing on the road to Canterbury Cathedral?
> That we expect old Beckett to come by any time?
> That we expect some knights to kill him?

What oil-well of depravity do you take me for to think that I would gush the plot in such a sloppy way?

KEVIN. That would be poor, but it's a pretty poor plot.

SHERIFF PYM. It is. It is. But the playwright, like our god, is doing the best he can. But sadly, yes, that's not too good.

KEVIN. It was a cobbler built the house, who should have been a carpenter.

SHERIFF PYM. Aye, and now we're addled tongues and soles. For sure, for sure. Now, where is he?

KEVIN. Who? God?

SHERIFF PYM. God? Our locusts don't need leprosy, I'm on to the subplot, you bulbous sot. Read the script. Where's the dead man?

(Kevin leads Sheriff Pym to the Corpse.)

KEVIN. Ah, right here he's taken seed. It looks like he's been stabbed, oh 30, 40 times, suffocated, poisoned, drowned, lacerated, hanged and had his heart cut out.

SHERIFF PYM. *(closely examining the body)* He certainly hit a rough patch there, I'd say. Hmm, yes, yes.
  (after a pause, standing up)
Well, it's obvious isn't it?

KEVIN. Yes, I would think —

SHERIFF PYM. A suicide.

KEVIN. A murder — *(incredulously)* a suicide?

SHERIFF PYM. Precisely, sir. A suicide, a murdered self, he skipped the slow boat to the choir eternal and went express. He rang his bell, he checked his claim, picked up his hat and said "Farewell my love. Goodnight!" A suicide: it's all there screaming at you.

KEVIN. I can't hear a thing. Are you sure?

SHERIFF PYM. *(looking at the Corpse more closely)* A suicide as surely as the Pope wears a funny hat.

KEVIN. But don't you think it strange that he would stab himself so many times? I mean, there toward the end he'd be simply showing off.

SHERIFF PYM. *(standing up over the corpse)* Oh, Kevin, in passion's sickly fever, who knows what height of showboating a man aspires to? I've seen a man rip out his own esophagus!

KEVIN. Oh my god! You have?

SHERIFF PYM. Well, I didn't see it myself, but his rival for a woman saw the whole thing.

KEVIN. I guess — but to cut your own heart out? Is that even possible?

SHERIFF PYM. Posh! I've seen a woman rip her head off.

KEVIN. You did!

SHERIFF PYM. Well, I didn't see it myself. But her husband saw her do it when he caught her with a lover.

KEVIN. Yes. But you'd think his heart would be around here somewhere.

SHERIFF PYM. Ah Kevin, to one schooled in the dark motives of men, in the shadows of desperate deeds, in that vast and turbid sea of suffering within us all, what seems random ones and b's to most is code for just another human heart gone lost, a mind unhinged by passion's tormenting throes. And to that drowning woe, that moldering moss, comes the thought to end it all — to cease the breath, and thus the stale, to cease the heart and thus the break. Yes, driven by manic passion's whip they seek the final curtain.

But believe me when I speak — as sheriff I have perused an illustrated encyclopedia of suicides: People hanging themselves, drinking poison, beating themselves with a board, hacking off both hands —

KEVIN. Oh come on now!

SHERIFF PYM. What?

KEVIN. If you cut off one hand, how could you cut off the other?

SHERIFF PYM. An easy thing for the man possessed by passion's wraith. Why, I've seen a man chew his own torso in half.

KEVIN. Oh my god! You did?

SHERIFF PYM. Well, I didn't see it myself. But that's what his bill collector saw.

KEVIN. You really haven't seen too much yourself, have you, Sheriff?

SHERIFF PYM. Sadly, no. But let me tell you, Kevin, suicide is now our country's plague — well, other than the real plague, of course. But all who's born will die, so, just by climbing from of the womb, it's suicide bye and bye.

KEVIN. But doesn't the mother push the baby out?

SHERIFF PYM. Good point, my friend! And thus is every daughter's mother her bald murderer.

KEVIN. Oh, mother: heartless fiend!

SHERIFF PYM. (looking at the corpse again) But I can't blame poor souls like this, considering the sundered state of things 'round here: The horrible conditions we live in, the dirt and disease, the ignorance and the dirt, the fear and the hopeless dirt, and the dirt, and the distinct lack of a good fish sandwich.

KEVIN. And the dirt.

SHERIFF PYM. Yes, but suicide is wrong, so saideth somebody, and if somebody saideth it, it must be because no one in his right mind would say "saideth" unless he meanteth it.

KEVIN. But can't we call this murder? As a suicide, he can't be buried in the churchyard.

SHERIFF PYM. What? And lie? Why he's the fourteenth suicide this month. If I did that for every stiff I found, we'd have the bumpkins thinking that a mass murderer is on the loose in town. And that, my friend, would be a terrible mess, a terrible mess! I'd never get a moment's sleep, and you know how the bags droop from eyes if I don't sleep. And I get that terrible rash beneath my armpits —

KEVIN. Yes, I suppose —

SHERIFF PYM. All right then. Oh, I'm not a man without a heart. I have pity for the dead, compassion for the unfortunate, empathy for the fish sandwichless. I'll tell you what: Let's take the corpse and dump him in the river, there. We'll send the problem downstream to Sturry — if anybody finds him.

KEVIN. I like that. Okay.

(Kevin and Sheriff Pym walk to either end of the Corpse and start to pick him up. They stop when he speaks.)

CORPSE. *(sticking up his head)* You're proposing to throw me in the river?

SHERIFF PYM. Uh, yeah.

CORPSE. And let me there to rot?

SHERIFF PYM. Hmm, yeah. Is that a problem?

CORPSE. You're suggesting to throw the temple of my spirit, the flesh of my soul, the throne of my reason into a dirty old river to spend eternity nibbled by fishies and other aquatic quibblers?

SHERIFF PYM. *(looking at Kevin and nodding)* Yep, that's the plan.

CORPSE. Well — you can't do it. You can't! The dead have rights, you know.

SHERIFF PYM. Yeah, last rites.
     Ashes to ashes,
     Dust to dust,
     Into the river
     Your carcass must.

(Sheriff Pym and Kevin laugh.)

CORPSE. Laugh laugh laugh. Oh yes! But you'll be dead someday and we'll see how you like it when they dump your arse into the river, or worse.

KEVIN. It's really best for all.

CORPSE. Best for all? Best for all! I hardly see how this will benefit me.

SHERIFF PYM. Oh, stop being a crybaby. You lived, you died, now make way for the breathing.

CORPSE. A crybaby? If I weren't dead I'd — I'd — I'd give you the what for.

SHERIFF PYM. Grab his legs and let's get rid of him. *(picking up the Corpse)* You'd think the dead would be happy but all they do is piss and whine about how they'd do things better. Well, they had their chance didn't they? Geeze! Let's go.

(They just start to walk away then stop.)

KEVIN. Wait, somebody's coming.

SHERIFF PYM. Oh crap, it's the priests. They're always coming around when you're trying to get away with something.

(They drop the Corpse.)

CORPSE: Ouch! Just because I'm dead doesn't mean I have no feelings!
KEVIN. And they don't like fish sandwiches.
SHERIFF PYM. Obviously.

(Two middle-aged Priests enter from the "play" side, wearing the long, dark monkish-type robes but very well pressed and very clean. They appear immaculate compared to the others, perhaps wearing a bit too much makeup. Sheriff Pym and Kevin try to keep between the priests and the Corpse.)

PRIEST 1. … And you know what he's done? Oh, you won't believe what Archbishop Beckett has done now.
PRIEST 2. What?
PRIEST 1. Now with the King just frantic and the Lords all up in arms and calling him foul names — I mean, really! They want Archbishop Beckett dead, the vile little things. But what's he do? He leaves the door to the cathedral hanging wide open!
PRIEST 2. No way!
PRIEST 1. Wide open! I grow near faint to even think of it. Wide open — so that anyone can just walk in!
PRIEST 2. Tell me about it. Just yesterday, I had to push my way through the pack of cripples to say my prayers. Really!
PRIEST 1. Me too!
PRIEST 2. And it really makes a mess of the vestibule. They're tracking in all kinds of dirt and body parts in the church.

(The Priests nod in agreement. Sheriff Pym and Kevin look at each other and shrug.)

PRIEST 1. Ah, look who comes — the Archbishop!

(From the "town" side of the stage comes a group of Women and Archbishop Thomas Beckett. They stop and the Priests join the group. Woman 1 comes over to Sheriff Pym and Kevin.)

WOMAN 1. It's the archbishop, it's the archbishop, ah! Isn't he just wonderful?
SHERIFF PYM. Really?
WOMAN 1. Oh yes, isn't he just grand, so swell?

SHERIFF PYM. That head, it's too big for his body.

WOMAN 1. His face, so glowingly clear and handsome — see how it shines!

SHERIFF PYM. The makeup does a good job of hiding his acne scars

WOMAN 1. And trimmed so neat and proud!

SHERIFF PYM. The clothes do hide his hump quite well.

WOMAN 1. *(suddenly angry)* Okay, you're killing my buzz. What's your problem?

SHERIFF PYM. D'you praise your husband like this man?

WOMAN 1. My husband? Lordy! He collects urine to make paper. He's a urine collector!

SHERIFF PYM. So, it's a living —

WOMAN 1. And we can't afford no bucket.

KEVIN. Then how's he —

WOMAN 1. You don't want to know! Now here's the bishop: A man of god, a man of keen judgment, tall and handsome, and he's got teeth and clean clothes, he does. His every thought and deed is pure goodness.

SHERIFF PYM. Hmm.

WOMAN 1. Now you should talk to him, yes talk to him and quench your thirst upon his cup of wisdom. Archbishop Beckett! Here, Archbishop Beckett! Here, my lord, is our town sheriff, Sheriff Pym. He'd like to talk to you.

(Sheriff Pym, caught off guard, gives an awkward bow. Beckett looks down his nose at him.)

SHERIFF PYM. Your highest bishopness, your holiest … roller … sir.

BECKETT. *(impatiently)* Well, sir?

SHERIFF PYM. Yes, well, you're a man of the world — well not this world, I guess, the other world, the higher world I mean of course. Yes. But, I guess, in some cosmically godly way, they're all one world — you, know, this world and that. You know that, right? Right. Well. I mean, you have been around the world — Well, not literally, but figuratively I mean you're a man of the world. But maybe you have been, I don't know —

BECKETT. *(grimly)* Your point?

SHERIFF PYM. My friend and I are on a search — a quest you might call it — a holy quest — that's taken us far across this land, this Earth, and several times around this town, looking for the perfect fish sandwich. Well, he doesn't eat no sausage, but he does eat fish. Now not a lot, yes, not as much as me. Well, I don't eat as much as I would like, in fact, I haven't eaten a fish sandwich in fifteen years because I cannot find a good one and I refuse to lower my standards —

BECKETT. Fish! Sandwich!

SHERIFF PYM. Yes, that's it. Exactly! Well, I mean, I'd say it fluently, like "fish sandwich," kind of blending the words together. Do you know where I could find one?

BECKETT. Shut up, fool!

(Beckett strikes Sheriff Pym with his crosier, buckling Sheriff Pym over and stunning him.)

SHERIFF PYM. Ow! You rotten bastard!

BECKETT. Don't speak to me of such ridiculous things. Fish — sandwiches!

KEVIN. No, no, sir, "fish sandwiches." "Fish sandwiches."

(Beckett strikes Kevin and he hollers.)

BECKETT. Let's leave these clowns to their clownishness.

(Beckett and the Women walk offstage toward the cathedral.)

SHERIFF PYM. *(holding his head)* You're a dead man, Beckett! Yes you are! I've seen this play before and it doesn't end well for you! The son of a bitch.

KEVIN. They kill him every night but he keeps coming back.

(Sheriff Pym's Wife runs on stage.)

WIFE. Archbishop! Wait! Archbishop! Was that the — oh, it's you.

SHERIFF PYM. *(holding his arms open as if expecting a hug)* Your loving husband.

WIFE. *(pushes him away)* Get back, fish head. Was that the archbishop who was just here?

SHERIFF PYM. What do you see in that overstuffed old crow?

WIFE. The light, it ripples from his eyes like pools of morning sun. His hair flows black and soft in waves just like a stallion's mane. His voice is like the song of angels — soft yet strong.

SHERIFF PYM. The man just beat me with his crosier!

WIFE. (*slaps him up side the head*) What did you do? Did you insult him? Huh? Were you complaining 'bout fish sandwiches? I knew't! You ale-soaked sot, you puss-headed fool! Archbishop Beckett is the pureness of morning and the mystery of night. He is the zenith of man. Our stars and our moon of the Milky Way.

SHERIFF PYM. What's wrong with you women? He's just a man like me.

WIFE. A man? You call yourself a man? Don't even pair your fest'ring, rat-faced self with him. When I get back, I want the bandages on mother's wounds replaced, you hear me? They're getting black and goopy.

SHERIFF PYM. I am the Sheriff, you know. I've got to work —

WIFE. Sheriff, ha! (*slapping him up side the head*) You're the assistant deputy to the deputy assistant of the sheriff's secretary. But you go 'round all acting like a big shot — I know exactly who you are.

SHERIFF PYM. Yes, but —

WIFE. (*slaps him again*) Just shut your moldy yap. And don't forget to clean the chicken cage and feed the cow. If you don't get your dingle-berried butt to work on that tonight, I'm going to give your scabby, worthless hide a thrashing that will knock fish sandwiches from your head.

(*Wife pushes him out of the way and leaves in the direction of Beckett.*)

SHERIFF PYM. (*rubbing his hands together*) Well, that went pretty well, I think.

CORPSE. (*sits up*) You're pathetic.

SHERIFF PYM. Me?

CORPSE. Duh, yeah you.

SHERIFF PYM. Me, pathetic? Not me, right Kevin?

KEVIN. That was pretty lame.

SHERIFF PYM. Oh, now I'm lame. Yes, first a dead man calls me pathetic. A dead man! Now my friend says that I'm lame!

CORPSE. (*standing up*) Your wife treats you like dirt, man. You have got to stand up for yourself

SHERIFF PYM. You are both single and fools — most singular fools. It shows how little you have thought 'bout love, 'bout life and marriage. Yes, I could have had a pretty one, a tame one, a pleasant one — and where would that have left me? Worrying about her leaving me, cheating on me, working myself to the bone to make sure she's happy. And they all change after a while, the pretty looks sag, those smiles turn sneers, those pleasant airs begin to reek. Who needs it? So I picked the meanest, ugliest, nastiest one I could find. And now, I have no cares in the world. Nothing I do will please her, so I do nothing. My mind is at peace. I go to bed unafraid of death.

CORPSE. Hmm, you have a point there. Though horrifying.

SHERIFF PYM. Of course I do.

(Enter a Knight dressed in light armor, obviously drunk.)

Ah, look who's here, one of the four knights. Thank god there's only seven in a week.

KEVIN. It makes one weak to smell'em. Hoo!

KNIGHT. I say — what did I say? Oh, I forgot it. Ha ha! *(to Kevin)* You are a spindly creature. You — you need to fatten up. Ha ha!

SHERIFF PYM. Dear lord! You smell just like a chamber pot soaked in a skunk and wrapped in a fart.

KNIGHT. Yes, well, it couldn't be avoided. Better smell like this than blood, because we've bloody business, yes.

SHERIFF PYM. I'd say! You're giving me a nosebleed.

KNIGHT. Yes, well you know, you sweat a lot in this iron overcoat. But it's blood we seek.

CORPSE. D'you need a corpse? I can do a first-rate job.

KNIGHT. No, no, no. We can't have just any corpse.

CORPSE. Just any corpse! I'll have you know I played both Romeo and Juliet in a dinner theater production three years ago.

KEVIN. Aren't they on the stage together?

CORPSE. It was my most demanding role.

KNIGHT. No, no, no. We have — have bitter business here. We shan't be arguing with someone silly.

CORPSE. Silly? It's hard for corpses to find good parts, you know.

KNIGHT. Yes, yes. But we've important work to do. We've come to kill Tom Beckett, you know. It's for the good of all.

CORPSE. It doesn't sound so good for Beckett.

KNIGHT. Of course, of course. That's given, isn't it? Eh? Now if we say we need to kill a person for the well-being of all, it's understood the killee is excluded.

SHERIFF PYM. But I don't think the priests will like it either.

KEVIN. Yes, or the pope. He's rather 'gainst these kinds of things — killing archbishops and all.

CORPSE. And I don't think the clerics will like it.

KNIGHT. Yes, well, that's obvious. I mean, when I say it's best for all, I mean it's best for all except for those for whom it's bad. I mean, that's understood. Right?

KEVIN. That makes no sense.

KNIGHT. Yes, yes. Well. Be that as it may, don't try to stop us, don't hold us back from our bloody intention.

SHERIFF PYM. Nobody's stopping you.

KNIGHT. It's a horrible deed that must be done.

SHERIFF PYM. And you're doing a horrible job of it

KNIGHT. No, no, we must! Don't try to tell us otherwise. We are implacable.

KEVIN. Is that contagious?

KNIGHT. I know, I know — the man's almost a saint. So it's not lightly that we do this act, but with a heavy heart. But do not beg us for his life.

SHERIFF PYM. The bastard beat us with his crosier. I say "good riddance!"

KNIGHT. Oh, loved by millions, well respected, a paragon of virtue, yet the man must die and we're the men to do't. Not gladly. No, we are uneven assassins, regretful killers. But your tears will not deter us from the job.

SHERIFF PYM. Who's crying? Are you crying Kevin?

KEVIN. It's that smell — it's burning my eyes!

KNIGHT. We bear the heavy quill of history. Why? Because it is a difficult result we seek, yes, the most difficult thing we'll ever do.

SHERIFF PYM. What? Kill him? Ha! He doesn't have a bodyguard, just a bunch of priests and clerks. The man's unarmed, for heaven's sake, and he's left the door wide open!

KNIGHT. The challenges we challenge, the risks we risk —

SHERIFF PYM. (making a throat-cutting gesture) Look, just barge in, then grab him by hair and skzz.

KNIGHT. Oh England, what a day, a sad and sullen day for god and country.

SHERIFF PYM. If you want me to do it, just say the word and I'm all over it. That swelled headed prima donna's got it coming.

KNIGHT. Ah, don't you see, it must be us knights, it must be us noblemen who rid the isle of this most pleasant-seeming plague, although a damnéd deed it is. No, do not try to stop us.

SHERIFF PYM. Geeze! Are we back there again?

KNIGHT. I know, I know — he is a man of god. But your entreaties are all deaf to us.

SHERIFF PYM. Because they have no voice and you no ears.

KNIGHT. Yes, you can protest, but you don't know, nay, you can't truly understand the danger this man brings to our fair isle.

SHERIFF PYM. For heaven's sake, I heard your cue. Stop your gab! Get the other three knights and get on stage!

(Sheriff Pym starts pushing the Knight to the side of the stage.)

KNIGHT. No, don't try to stop me.
SHERIFF PYM. You're a looney. Get out there and do the deed.

(Sheriff Pym succeeds in pushing the Knight offstage toward the "play" side.)

> And take a bath — you stink! Phew! That is the sorriest knight I've ever seen.

KEVIN. And I'm sure you've seen many.

(Before Sheriff Pym can reply, a rimshot sounds and then a very old, feeble man — Becket — enters from the opposite side of the stage dressed like Beckett, but much shabbier.)

SHERIFF PYM. Uh, who are you?
BECKET. I am that man who men call Becket. Thomas Becket.
SHERIFF PYM. The man who men call Archbishop Becket? What do the women call you?
BECKET. "Am I that man?" I asked the Lord. And he answered me "Thou art the man and all the more the man."
SHERIFF PYM. "That man?" What man? Beckett?
BECKET. I am that man and all the more the man!
SHERIFF PYM. You're the man, but more than the man? What are you, Beckett squared? Are you the ghost of Becketts future?
BECKET. I asked the Lord, "Oh Lord, my god,
> Henry the King has been my friend, my brother,
> And mine uplifter in the world, and chosen me
> For this great archbishopric, believing
> That I should go against him with the church.
> Am I the man?" and the Lord answered me,
> "Thou art the man and all the more the man."
SHERIFF PYM. I don't know anything about the archbishop's prick, but you're kind of all old and rundown and musty. How can you be Beckett? You don't look anything like him.
BECKET. I am that man and all the more that man.
SHERIFF PYM. Wait! *(in sing-song fashion)* "I am the man and all the more the man: I smell me some blank verse! Are you Tennyson's Becket?
BECKET. I am that man and all the more the man.
SHERIFF PYM. Oh dear god! That play's a wretched thing. My friend, this here is Eliot's Murder in the Cathedral — the double-T Beckett. You're in the wrong play, bub.

BECKET. For that I am most sorry. So goodbye.
Forgive my interlude. Adieu, Adieu!
SHERIFF PYM. Goodbye!

(Becket exits toward the "town" side. Absurdly excessive noise and screaming comes from offstage.)

KEVIN. What is that?
SHERIFF PYM. *(looking offstage toward the "play" side)* They are killing
Beckett again.
KEVIN. Still?
CORPSE. Lucky bastard!
SHERIFF PYM. Oh yeah, they're getting him good.
KEVIN. Shouldn't you do something?

(The noise of Beckett's murder stops.)

SHERIFF PYM. Good God, you're right. I should get out of here
before —

(The two Priests run onstage from the "play" side.)

PRIEST 1. Sheriff! Sheriff!
SHERIFF PYM. — they see me.
PRIEST 1. He's dead! He's dead! Archbishop Beckett's dead!
SHERIFF PYM. — ah, shit!
PRIEST 2. Those dark, cruel knights — they killed him — right in front
us! They came right in a pushed me aside — and I think one of
them called me "fatty." Oh, what's wrong with the world? Am I
fat?

(Priest 2 falls into Priest 1's arms.)

SHERRIF PYM. There, there. Now, you're not fat. You're just a little
plump.
PRIEST 2. *(wailing)* It's true — I'm fat!
PRIEST 1. Great. Now look what you've done.

(The Women and Pym's Wife rush onstage from the "town" side.)

WIFE. What happened?
SHERIFF PYM. This one's learned that he's as fat as a holiday goose and
he's not taking it very well.

(Priest 2 cries even louder.)

PRIEST 1. The archbishop has been murdered.

SHERIFF PYM. Oh, that too.

WOMAN 1. Oh oh!

PRIEST 1. Those knights have killed him in a most unmannerly manner. Hacked him down in his prime. Laid him low in is height. Cut his cloth of goodness into threads. They extinguished the bright fire of his life force, they smote his brains, dealt him a deathblow, they raised his ghost —

SHERIFF PYM. He's a stiff — we got it.

WOMAN 1. Oh Sheriff, shouldn't you do something?

SHERIFF PYM. You'd think so, wouldn't you.

WIFE. Well then do something you idiot.

SHERIFF PYM. Oh, oh, before I was some stupid, lazy bumbler who didn't do anything all day. Oh yeah, I just sit on my butt singing la ti da. I'm just the "assistant deputy to the deputy assistant." Well, who wants me to do something now? Eh?

WIFE. *(slaps him)* Shut your yap and get to work!

WOMEN. *(severally)* Arrest the knights! Put'em away! Get'em. Hang'em! Hang'em! Yeah!

PRIEST 2. Especially that tall one, the brute — called me fat! Give it to him good, yeah, give it to him, and keep giving it to him, thrusting your sword in and out and in and out —

SHERIFF PYM. All right. All right. That's enough of the ole' in and out. I'll look into it if that's what everyone wants. But let's keep things civil and explore this in a calm, deliberative fashion.

PRIEST 1. They gutted him like a pig — it's time we stretch their windpipes from the closest tree branch!

WOMEN & PRIESTS. Yeah! Yeah! Hang'em all! Yeah!

SHERIFF PYM. Tut tut. In a calm, deliberative fashion. Do you call stretching someone's windpipe calm and deliberative?

(Women and priests shake their heads "no.")

That's what I thought. Shame on you all. We don't even know if the knights did it. Did anyone actually see what happened?

PRIEST 1. We saw it ourselves, both of us did. We saw the knights cut down the bishop.

SHERIFF PYM. Now we're getting somewhere, right? Calm and deliberative. Okay. The knights were seen killing the bishop. But that's not yet a sign of guilt. Oh no! What of the circumstances? It's circumstances that separate us from fine cutlery.

WOMAN 1. What? That doesn't make any sense.

SHERIFF PYM. Then never mind the cutlery part. What I'm saying is that we need to understand the details of what has happened if we're going to seed the guilt and reap the justice. For a man may kill in self-defense and, thus, be innocent. True?

WOMEN & PRIESTS. Yeah. Sure. Sure.

KEVIN. Unless he kills himself. And then he's guilty of his own murder even though it be in self-defense.

CORPSE. How can you defend yourself from killing yourself by killing yourself?

KEVIN. It makes you wonder, doesn't it?

CORPSE. It makes me wonder what you're smoking.

SHERIFF PYM. May I proceed? A man may be innocent of murder if he kills to defend himself or someone else. That's what we in the law call migrating circumstances.

WOMEN & PRIESTS. Ah.

KEVIN. Mitigating. It's mitigating circumstances.

SHERIFF PYM. Interrupt me one more time and you will get a mitigrating headache. *(to Priest 1)* So tell me, did Beckett strike first?

PRIEST 1. He most certainly did not.

SHERIFF PYM. Did he provoke the attack in any way?

PRIEST 1. No!

SHERIFF PYM. He did not threaten or incite the knights?

PRIEST 2. Certainly not. He almost welcomed the slaughter like a lamb at the altar of god.

SHERIFF PYM. Ah! Now I find that very interesting. Crucial even! Tell me more, tell me more!

PRIEST 1. He knew his life was in danger when he came to England.

SHERIFF PYM. He did?

PRIEST 1. Oh yes.

SHERIFF PYM. But he came anyway?

PRIEST 1. Oh yes, knowing he'd be killed. He openly discussed that likelihood.

SHERIFF PYM. Ah ha! He even discussed it. He, of course, then took precautions to protect himself, did he not?

PRIEST 2. Hmph! He most certainly didn't! He refused all attempts to avoid places of danger or to arm himself. He didn't even lock his doors.

SHERIFF PYM. But clearly he knew someone would try to kill him if he came to England. Is that so?

PRIEST 1. Oh yes, it was assured that he would die if he came.

SHERIFF PYM. But he came anyway and he did nothing to avoid certain death.

PRIEST 2. No. If he died, he would become a martyr to the cause.

SHERIFF PYM. And so the knights just sauntered in and cut him down?

PRIESTS. *(severally)* Yes! Yes! Yes!

SHERIFF PYM. They barged in unprovoked?

WOMEN. *(severally)* Yes! Yes!

SHERIFF PYM. And struck down an unarmed man, a man unable — Nay! — a man unwilling to defend himself?

WOMEN & PRIESTS. Yes! Yes!

SHERIFF PYM. Yes! That's all I need to know!

(The priests and women chatter among themselves excitedly.)

WOMAN 1. *(to one of the other women)* Oh, this is rather exciting!

SHERIFF PYM. Now, quiet, friends. Quiet! After a calm and deliberative process of adjudication, it's clear, friends, what was done, what must be done, what will be done, what we'll do when we're done saying what must be done. And what will be done will be done as such —

WOMEN & PRIESTS. *(impatiently)* Yes? Yes?

SHERIFF PYM. I hereby proclaim that the death of Thomas Beckett, Archbishop of Canterbury, vassal to the Pope, Servant of Jesus, cleric to all England — I declare that his death at the hands and swords of the three knights, under law of man and law of god, not to be murder.

WOMEN & PRIESTS. What the — ? What? Not murder? Surely!

SHERIFF PYM. Nay, good people! Listen! The knights were but the hands, the swords, the dupes, mere puppets of a villain more vile than the villainous villainies of the vilest villainary.

PRIEST 1. Who? What? It cannot be!

SHERIFF PYM. Nay, I absolve the knights of their deed, and doing so indict a higher power and hereby proclaim the true murderer of Archbishop Thomas Beckett to be —

WOMAN 1. Yes? Yes!

PRIEST 2. Dare he say … the king?

SHERIFF PYM. — the archbishop himself. His coming to England was clearly a suicide.

WOMAN 1. A suicide?

WIFE. A suicide? You are an idiot!

(Sheriff Pym's Wife hits him and walks offstage toward the "play" side.)

SHERIFF PYM. It's true — it's true!

WOMEN & PRIESTS. *(pushing him away as exit toward the "play" side)*
Fool! Moron! Suicide? We should suicide him! What a poltroon!
What an ignoramus!

SHERIFF PYM. *(recovering himself)* The wise man's not a welcome one.

KEVIN. I suppose. And neither's the fool.

SHERIFF PYM. The truth, my friend, it hurts.

KEVIN. It hurts as well as lies, as statements, riddles, facts, and
theories — 'bout anything that involves moving your lips, as far as
I can tell.

SHERIFF PYM. What's that I hear? *(applause is heard offstage)* Ah, yes.
The play's been played. Finally. Well, I think we did a smash up
job.

KEVIN. What? We weren't onstage yet. Are we in this play?

SHERIFF PYM. Well, I don't know. I just assumed so. All the world's a
blah blah blah — you know the drill. Of course, I just assumed
that I existed. But I hadn't really thought about it. I guess I should
have. But does it make a difference? I don't know. *(to the audience)*
Does anybody got a script to this? Yo, anybody? No? How about
a playbill? Yes? Am I in it? Sheriff Pym? What? What? Yes? Good.
Thank you. *(to Kevin)* Well, that's a relief.

KEVIN. It would be a stunning blow to learn we didn't exist. I don't
know what I'd do. It sounds rather ... rather lonely.

CORPSE. I'll tell you what you'd do: you'd do what you have to do, it's
that simple.

SHERIFF PYM. Amen, my friend. That's good advice on any day. Here
come our people!

*(Beckett, the Women, the Priests and Knight walk onstage from the "play" side.
Sheriff Pym holds his hand up to them for a high five.)*

High fives all around. Good job, people! Good job ...

*(They ignore Sheriff Pym, casually pushing him and Kevin aside as they walk
past to exit on the "town" side of the stage talking and laughing among
themselves. The Corpse starts talking to Woman 1. Beckett pushes Sheriff Pym
aside as he walks past.)*

Hey! Watch it! *(to Kevin)* Did you see that? He pushed me back
like I was nothing. *(to Beckett)* You're not the star of me, Beckett!
(to Kevin) Damned method actors. He can't push me around. *(to
Beckett)* I may not find a good fish sandwich, but I'm a star, too,
you know! I have principles! Just because I don't go dying over

this or dying over that. Well, I don't go dying over anything, but I stand up for myself, yeah. Well, most time! Some of the time! At least once in a while! I'm part of the union, too. Just because your name is on the marquee doesn't make human decency optional!

(Sheriff Pym sees the Corpse walk offstage with Woman 1. The stage is empty except for Sheriff Pym and Kevin.)

(to Kevin) Geeze, even the corpse is going to get laid. *(to Beckett offstage)* But I'm not going to go anywhere until you apologize, Beckett! I'll sit here forever if I have to! I'll sit here in protest for all the little people that have been stepped all over. All the people that history has forgotten about while noodle-headed titans like you kick up the dust and get dirt in everybody's eyes! I'll sit here all week if I have to! You hear me? I know you do! Sure, act as if you don't care. I'll stay —

(The lights go out. The stage is completely black.)

All week ... if I have to ...

(There is a moment of silence.)

Oh, the hell with this. Let's go home, Kevin. I gotta take care of my mother-in-law.

(In the dark, footsteps can be heard going toward the "town" side of the stage. The steps stop.)

KEVIN. Wait. If the play's over, do I still exist?
SHERIFF PYM. Yes, just darker now. Come on.

(A step or two more, then a door can be heard to open and then slam shut.)

FINIS

THE NAME OF TREASON

The Betrayal of West Point

CHARACTERS

The Innkeeper, a 55+ year-old woman

General Benedict Arnold, 39-year-old war hero and traitor, walks with a distinct limp

Peggy Shippen-Arnold, the 20-year-old wife of General Arnold, renowned for her beauty

Samuel, the Innkeeper's son or servant, a non-speaking part

Patron 1
Colonel Richard Varick, secretary to General Arnold

Patron 2
Joshua Hett Smith, lawyer, friend of General Arnold
General George Washington, commander of the American army

Patron 3
William Tittle, local clergyman
Colonel Alexander Hamilton, General Washington's chief of staff

Patron 4
Mr. Jackson, local apothecary
Captain Murtha, aide to General Washington

TIME/PLACE

October 1780, several weeks after the discovery of Arnold's treason

A rustic inn within the British lines in New York state

NOTES

£10,000 in 1780 would be equivalent to several million dollars today.

Part 1

(Scene: A shadow-filled inn on a stormy evening — the sound of thunder, wind and rain. Occasionally lightning flashes. A fireplace burns in the background. The Innkeeper sits at the front, nearby Sam does chores. The four patrons sit silently in the background shadows occupying the few tables. Their looks are dour and gloomy — they hardly move. The Innkeeper looks up as if she heard something. She smiles.)

INNKEEPER. Look alive, Sam, come — our guests are here!

(Samuel is unmoved. There is a rattling at the door and it opens. A man and a woman enter. They appear wealthy although they are concealed behind long coats, scarves and hats.)

ARNOLD. We'll stay until the storm subsides.
SHIPPEN. *(looking around disapprovingly)*
       At least it's dry.
ARNOLD. It's odd. I don't recall this inn being here before.
INNKEEPER. *(coming to them)*
       Good evening, my lord — my lady.
       Such a vexing night to be outside — the wind howls
       Like a jury of devils. Doesn't it?
ARNOLD. It does. We simply need an hours'
       Shelter till this driving rain subsides.
INNKEEPER. *(leading them in)*
       Of course! Of course! You're welcome. Come!
       My rustic inn may not be what gentle folk
       Are accustomed to, but it is warm and dry.
       Yes, very warm.
       My husband left us some years ago; and since,
       It's only been the boy here and myself.
       We do the best we can.
SHIPPEN. "The Stand?" That's an unusual name for an inn.
INNKEEPER. Well, my husband was unusual, ma'am.
       He loved to watch the trials, and rather
       Fancied himself a lawyer. Of course, he talked
       Unendingly of sin — the original and the ordinary.
       He wasn't what you'd call a merciful man.
       So it was what it was.

Let me take your coats — they're soaking wet!
We'll set them by the fire to dry. Sam, come —
Come take the gentleman's coat.

(The Innkeeper takes Shippen's coat. Sam slowly makes his way to Arnold.)

My oh my, what a beautiful woman you are!
A rare gem in this rough setting!
SHIPPEN. Thank you!

(Sam tries to take the man's coat.)

ARNOLD. *(gruffly)*
I'll leave it on.
INNKEEPER. But it's so wet — here, let me hang it by the fire!
ARNOLD. Thank you, no.
INNKEEPER. Of course, of course. You want to wear a dripping coat?
Well, that's your business. Isn't it?
ARNOLD. Yes, it is, thank you. Please don't ask again.
INNKEEPER. Although it seems you'd rather catch your death.
But that's your choice.
ARNOLD. It is my choice.
INNKEEPER. We do have freedom in this country. Yes.
Wet coats and all.
ARNOLD. Will you stop harping on my coat!
INNKEEPER. Of course, of course. I meant no disrespect.
ARNOLD. Come, Peggy, let's find a seat in back.

(Arnold and Shippen turn to sit in the back, but see the other patrons sitting at the tables. The only table is near the front.)

We'll just sit here.
INNKEEPER. Can I get you something to eat or drink? Mr. — ?
ARNOLD. Jones, Elliott Jones.
INNKEEPER. *(emphasizing "Jones" every time she says it)*
Ah, Mr. Jones it is.
ARNOLD. Is that a problem?
INNKEEPER. No, Mr. Jones. One name's as good as many.
ARNOLD. Give us two brandies.
INNKEEPER. Very good, very good, Mr. Jones. That will warm the soul
On a cold rainy night. Get them their drinks, Sam.
Hurry, hurry! The Joneses want a drink.

SHIPPEN. *(cheerfully)*
>Oh, we're not in a hurry.

INNKEEPER. Where are you from, Mrs. Jones?

ARNOLD. From Providence. Originally.

INNKEEPER.
>I know that acre of the world quite well.
>Providence is a lovely town.
>You know the Thomas Jones clan?
>Perhaps they are your cousins?

(Sam brings over the drinks.)

ARNOLD. No, 'fraid not.

INNKEEPER. You don't, Mr. Jones? That's quite a shame.
>Ah, here you go, Mr. Jones, Mrs. Jones.

(She hands them their drinks.)

>Where in Providence did you live?

ARNOLD. You wouldn't know it.

INNKEEPER. I'm sure I would!
>I spent the noon of my days upon those streets,
>Mr. Jones — many happy memories shadow me.

ARNOLD. Williams Street.

INNKEEPER. Ah, you know the Wrights then!

ARNOLD. I don't want to talk about it.

(Crack of thunder.)

INNKEEPER. The Wrights have lived there years, Mr. Jones —
>Joseph and Sarah —

ARNOLD. I said —

INNKEEPER. And the Hancocks lived next door to them.
>It's strange that you don't know them, Mr. Jones —
>Their beautiful daughter. I think 'twas Sybil — no,
>'Twas Liza she was called. Oh, you'd remember her —
>Almost as beautiful as you, Mrs. Jones.
>It's odd you don't remember her —

ARNOLD. *(angry)*
>All right! All right! If you're going to persist,
>Then know me.

(Arnold takes off his overcoat revealing his British general's uniform. The people at the inn mumble indistinctly. Arnold throws his overcoat to Sam who hangs it up. The wind howls loudly.)

INNKEEPER. Welcome from beneath the cloak —
ARNOLD. Yes, I am —
INNKEEPER: The hero of Ticonderoga! The victor of Saratoga!
    Welcome general, Mrs. Arnold.
ARNOLD. How did you know who I am?
INNKEEPER. I know many things, general. It's my *(thinking)*
    Hobby, let me say.
ARNOLD. What party are you of?
INNKEEPER. Oh, general, rest assured. We're of your party.
ARNOLD. *(sitting down)*
    Oh yes?
INNKEEPER. The same as you. Now what do you call it?
ARNOLD. I don't follow you.
INNKEEPER. Are you a patriot? A loyalist? A mercenary? An agnostic?
ARNOLD. I won't stand for this insolence!
INNKEEPER. Well then, what d'you call yourself?
ARNOLD. Misunderstood! Unappreciated!
INNKEEPER. There you are — yes, that describes us, too!
SHIPPEN. Who are you?
INNKEEPER. Me? Well, most say I'm a nobody,
    That's probably true, but some — they won't
    Even acknowledge my existence. Ha!
    But don't mind me, it's just my way.
            (laughs and turns to everyone in the inn)
    We are honored by the general himself!
    The hero of Quebec and Fort Saint-Jean, and his beautiful wife.
    Your timing here is most fortuitous, general!
    We just read 'bout your case here in the paper.
    What do you make of the news?
ARNOLD. What news?
INNKEEPER. What news! *(laughs)*
ARNOLD. I assure you, ma'am, I've no idea.
INNKEEPER. Oh-oh, you jest! It's all that people talk about!
ARNOLD. What use are gossips' dregs?
INNKEEPER. Ooh, this not mere gossip, general!
ARNOLD. What do I care?
SHIPPEN. We've long been made the sticking point
    Of jealous darts.

ARNOLD. So true. Let them pant themselves to death
    In all their lies.
INNKEEPER. But it's the most extraordinary news,
    Striking close to you.
ARNOLD. If Arnold doesn't know of it, it doesn't matter.
INNKEEPER. You really haven't heard?
ARNOLD. Then out with it, old woman! Augh! You're going
    To tell us if we want to hear or not, just say it then!
INNKEEPER. The British Major Andre —
        (she waits for some acknowledgement from them — the wind
        and rain can be heard)
                        He's been hanged.
ARNOLD. *(after a slight pause)*
    And that's your news?
INNKEEPER. Hanged by General Washington!
ARNOLD. We heard you. And you've nothing else?
INNKEEPER. That's not enough?
ARNOLD. What's Major Andre? What's this man to me?
INNKEEPER. Major Andre! He was hanged a spy —
    Caught in civilian clothes transporting papers
    To the British lines, papers you had given him.
ARNOLD. It wasn't my papers but his foolishness
    That got him hanged. The bloody imbecile.
    And nearly got me hanged as well!
INNKEEPER. But didn't he give his life for you?
ARNOLD. For me? Like many men, he gave his life
    For cause and country. Yes, the battlefields
    Are piled with corpses of his kind,
    Many better than him.
INNKEEPER. Yes, I suppose. *(to Shippen)* You knew him too,
    Didn't you, Mrs. Arnold?
SHIPPEN. I did, in Philadelphia. A name and not much else.
INNKEEPER. I heard he was your suitor.
SHIPPEN. *(laughs)*
    As many men would boast they were!
INNKEEPER. I see, I see. You charmed them all I'm sure!
        (to Arnold)
    They say that Andre took his sentence stoically —
    Yes, bravely climbed the steps to reach the gallows' depth.
ARNOLD. Hurrah for him. At least he had some decency
    And didn't make a scene.
INNKEEPER. Don't you ever wonder if he thought 'bout you
    As that coarse rope was dropped upon his collar?

ARNOLD. Why me? He should have thought about his many
    Errors in judgment that led him to the scaffold.
    Bah — this is idle chatter. Thoughts and opinions
    Die with the man.
INNKEEPER. *(laughing)*
    True, that's true. But you —
    You've not a mote of sympathy for that young man?
    One recalled so gallant, so daring, so charming — a poet, even.
ARNOLD. A poet? Well, there's the problem, isn't it?
    Fools and dreamers, all. This world will not be steered
    By verse — their songs unhorse truth's sentinel.
    Besides, I've seen his rhymes. Yes, Dryden need not fear.
INNKEEPER. So you're a literary critic, too! Ha! And so harsh!
ARNOLD. So true! He dug his hole and now he's laid in it.
    What's that to me? He's not my brother, and
    I'm not his keeper. You don't know
    What happened, what was said. The papers strain
    With lies and slanders. No one knows the truth.
SHIPPEN. It's buried in a grave of lies,
    Dug deep by jealous enemies, tamped down
    By timid gossips! No one's heard what actually happened!
INNKEEPER. Perhaps — perhaps you'll tell us
    While we wait the storm's last breath.
ARNOLD. What good is it to talk? To tell? To play?
    To re-create what's done? It won't be changed,
    Undone — yes, I'm not sure
    That it can even be explained.
INNKEEPER. Then for a couple hour's divertissement
    Here let us play the play, and say what's said.
    Here set what's crooked straight again
    So all the world admits the truth.
    I am quite curious, quite curious indeed
    To hear your telling of this 'mazing tale!
    And I'm not one who's easily unpersuaded.
ARNOLD. As I have seen.
        (to Shippen)
                What do you think?
SHIPPEN. Oh, I don't know.
INNKEEPER. Come, come!
        (gesturing to everyone at the inn)
  We'd love to hear the truth.
    And we can help you tell it.
ARNOLD. I guess we'll get no peace until we do.

INNKEEPER. I'm quite persuasive, not?

SHIPPEN. Who are you?

INNKEEPER. Me? I guess you'd call me a collector, yes.
  A collector of men's lives. I search the world's
  Bustling marketplace for people and their stories —
  Oh, their wonderful stories. And when I want one
  I must have it, and they always tell it.
  I have that gift.

ARNOLD. A curse more like. Rather than collecting lives
  Why don't you live one of your own?

INNKEEPER. Oh general, I guess that's just the way I'm made.
  We have our roles, our callings, each of us —
  Some to live bold lives, and some to gather them up.
  I'm a gatherer — and you — your lives —
  They are the blood and ink of history!
  Please tell us — please! Tell us while you wait the storm!

SHIPPEN. Oh, let's just tell her — set the rumors straight,
  Although it does us little good.

ARNOLD. Fine then.

INNKEEPER. Wonderful! That's wonderful!
  My friends here — they will help us play it as
  It should be played!

(*The patrons move from the tables to behind the Innkeeper, staying somewhat in the shadows.*)

ARNOLD. Where shall we start?

INNKEEPER. Let's start at West Point — in medias res!
  We'll catch up on the prologue as we go.
  I hate a slow beginning.

(*As Arnold speaks and stands, one of the patrons takes off Arnold's British coat and replaces it with the blue United States uniform.*)

ARNOLD. I came late summer to the Hudson Valley
  On orders from General Washington.
  You see, the earth-wood walls
  Of West Point Fort act as the mighty Hudson's gate:
  None can pass who can't unlock the fort.
  Now if the British ruled the river from its source
  In the Adirondacks to its outlet near New York City,
  They could combine their arms and cut
  The northern states in half, then one by one

Destroy rebellion's body. That done,
Could our defeat be far behind?
West Point, in truth, is worth its weight in silver.
So there I was assigned, and what a mess
I found. I led an upgrade of the ramparts
And the replenishment of its supplies.
My improvements were immediate and impactful.
SHIPPEN. The fort hummed like a well-kept hive!
The townspeople said they'd never seen the like!
INNKEEPER. Ah, the local residents were pleased?
ARNOLD. Of course, of course. My name they'd heard
My deeds they knew, my improvements they saw.

(Three of the inn patrons come over and start playing their parts. The lights brighten.)

SMITH. Thank you for seeing us, general.
My name is Joshua Hett Smith of Garrison.
And this is the Reverend Tittle,
The minister at St. Matthew's Church at Stony Point.

(Arnold shakes each man's hand as they are introduced. The guests bow to Shippen.)

TITTLE. General, Mrs. Arnold.
ARNOLD. Reverend, thank you for your visit.
SMITH. This is George Jackson, our apothecary at Stony Point.
JACKSON. Welcome to our valley.
ARNOLD. Apothecary, did you say? Before I wore
These epaulettes I did the same in Bridgeport.
JACKSON. Then my profession's honored, sir!
I'm also pleased to meet the lovely Mrs. Arnold.
Your beauty does your husband's bravery equate.
SHIPPEN. May any woman be so beautiful!

(They laugh.)

SMITH. You have a child as well?
SHIPPEN. Oh yes, he's five months old and sleeps upstairs.
SMITH. That's wonderful!
ARNOLD. Welcome friends!
SHIPPEN. Yes, welcome to our home.

SMITH. And welcome to our growing county. We're honored
    To host the American Achilles.
ARNOLD. *(laughing)*
    The American Achilles? How so?
SMITH. Who in all this land is more renowned, more brave,
    More master of the smoke-eyed field than you,
    Our nation's own Achilles? Whose ear
    Has not been warmed to hear of your siege and storm
    Of the North American Ilium, Quebec?
    He must be mute who hasn't told
    How your small band — out-manned, out-gunned,
    Outside in cruel winter —
    Breached Quebec's tall bulwarks, and
    Like a knife thrust to the city's nave.
    And whose heart has not sunk to hear
    Of fortune gone awry, of fate turned against this band?
    Who didn't shake to hear of the general's wounded leg,
    Our soldiers' hunger and exhaustion,
    Of British reinforcements — our retreat?
    Who hasn't told it twice two times and heard
    It two times more?
ARNOLD. Within the tale's a bitter seed:
    Had we the reinforcements I requested,
    The city would be ours.
JACKSON. But don't forget his victory at Saratoga,
    Where — almost single-handedly — he swept
    A mighty British army from the battlefield.
SMITH. Forget it? How? I dread to think what baneful cloud
    Could blot such light. Who can undo
    What's writ in blood upon the field,
    What's locked within the hearts of grateful countrymen?
    We will not lose, nor will the years efface,
    What lightning's etched into the tablets of history!
    We will rejoice as we recount the tale
    For generations to come
    Of two combatants: two great armies
    Who traded quaking blows all day and stood
    In flagging stalemate, heavy limbed,
    Wrapped in one another's straining arms,
    Unable to dispatch his foe but
    Unwilling to let go his poisonous grip.
    And there it stood, the verdict in the balance,
    Till the general here, ordered rear without command,

Defied instruction. Between the peppered lines
He charged, risking deadly shot and blasts
From either side: a sight that awed their eyes.
Was this a man? Or ghost? Or fury sent
By god across the field of death and fire?
A vision, yes, (what else could it be called?)
That raised within our boys the spirit of Mars
And made the British wish their homes' warm hearths.
And then, with but the slightest twitch of the general's sword
Our emboldened troops stormed from their trenches.
Up, up, they rose and raged across the splintered field
Falling full-fisted on the British mass.
There, like a violent autumn wind that strips the leaves,
Our brash Achilles' charge avulsed the field
Of garish colors, sweeping all before his storm.
A victory! An English route! But wait —
There at the battle's peak, atop the British ramp,
The general's horse was struck. Down our hero fell,
His horse's weight collapsing on his leg,
The self-same leg he wounded at Quebec.
To triumph's threshold the general led our troops
But fate inconstant would not let him claim
The vanquished sword!

SHIPPEN. And don't forget: the battle won
    Did win the French to our assistance.
SMITH. It did! Thus expectation's added to our hope.
ARNOLD. What I have done, I've done to serve my country.
SMITH. And in our hearts, you second only Washington.
ARNOLD. You're much too generous with your praise.
    Come, Mrs. Arnold, drinks for our friends.
SMITH. Thank you!

(Shippen walks to the side with Smith. The Innkeeper turns to Arnold.)

INNKEEPER. My — such an outpouring of love.
ARNOLD. Yes, they worshipped me. My deeds rose up
    Above all other's — even Washington's!
    And where I said they praised too much, I spoke
    Of Washington of course! *(he laughs)*
    Were it not for our petty politicians
    I would stand second to none.
    I should have been commander in chief!
INNKEEPER. But for what? What obstacle prevented you?

ARNOLD. What? The petty qualms of gutless leaders,
　　Poisonous rumor, venomous innuendo.
INNKEEPER. And nothing else?
ARNOLD. There were — there were some incidents.

(Shippen and one of the guests walks over and brings them drinks. The rest of the group comes back over.)

ARNOLD. Ah, thank you!
TITTLE. Excuse me, general. If you please, I have a question.
SMITH. Come friend, you know this is a social call.
　　Don't let your business spoil the mood.
ARNOLD. That's quite all right. Please ask. I'm here to serve.
TITTLE. Sir, having been here several weeks you know
　　Some local merchants (sons of Judas who prefer
　　A fist of silver over our salvation)
　　Make commerce with black loyalists who live
　　Behind the British lines. And thus the traitors
　　Enrich themselves and their red hosts
　　While patriots and supporters of our cause
　　Are suffering. What, I ask, are your plans?
SMITH. Reverend, let's keep a festive mood.
ARNOLD. No, a question fairly asked deserves response.
　　　　　(to Tittle)
　　I have no plans.
TITTLE. No plans! And let the traitors buy
　　And sell our lives to British merchants?
ARNOLD. Reverend, sir, I understand your pain —
TITTLE. No, sir, you certainly don't!
　　This is the edge, the half-light of frontier
　　Beyond which nothing breeds but death and chaos.
　　Each day we face new threats: the robber's clutch,
　　The Redcoat's boot, the Iroquois' ax.
　　These constant dangers
　　Could break apart our small community
　　Were it not for our singleness of mind and spirit.
　　Like an army sat in hazard's way,
　　Our might comes not from numbers bare,
　　But from the conform'ty of our wills.
　　Self interest and dissent attenuate
　　The body when it needs to be most dense.
　　Thus the throat of contradiction must be cut —
　　For if selfish interests infect and grow,

Our community is doomed. Like gangrene,
It spreads its poison through the entire body.
Therefore we must excise the foul disease
Completely — decisively and swift!

SMITH. And how do you propose to mark these willful men?
By innuendo? Gossip's prate?
How would you protect an innocent man
From the false accuser's stain, imprisonment?

TITTLE. If for the good of all it means that some
Good flesh must be lost with the bad, so be it.
These are unusual times requiring
Unusual means and vigilance.

ARNOLD. Reverend, you prescribe a cure that kills
The patient with his illness.

SMITH. Amen!

ARNOLD. But even if I wanted to, there's nothing I can do.
I'm dealt a feeble force and poor supplies —
I barely have enough armed men to see
To our defense. I have no troops to spare.

SMITH. An honest answer honest told!
I'm sorry general.

ARNOLD. No, no, that's quite all right. I understand
The reverend's argument, and I admire
The ardor of his case. I will, my friend, increase
Patrols upon the river to squeeze off
Some contraband — if that, you think, would help.

TITTLE. (coolly)
Yes, it's a start.

SHIPPEN. A toast to our cause and our new friends!

ARNOLD. A splendid thought! To friends and cause.

SMITH. And our nation's hero!

(Before Arnold can bring the drink to his lips, the Innkeeper holds his arm and whispers.)

INNKEEPER. Not yet, dear general. No toast — not yet!

(As the Innkeeper speaks, she takes the glass from Arnold who acts as if he's in a spell. The patrons step back into the shadows. The lights focus on Arnold, Shippen and the Innkeeper. Shippen approaches and laughs, waking Arnold from his revery.)

SHIPPEN. What lovely neighbors, yes, what wondrously dim
      And airless lights. Among these smothered coals
      The general was a blazing flare, a sun!
INNKEEPER. So it seems.
ARNOLD. *(to Shippen)*
      The season here is different, eh? In Philadelphia
      Arnold felt December's sneaping winds.
      But here they breathe a gracious June.
SHIPPEN. And here your name's pronounced
      With loving sighs, your value to the nation far
      Beyond their words to frame.
INNKEEPER. You enjoyed the time at West Point?
SHIPPEN. Me? Oh god no. It was a boring place devoid
      Of novelty and interesting people.
      The general had his work, but I had nothing.
INNKEEPER. I guess it isn't like a city.
SHIPPEN. The hours seem to yawn
      To endless weeks. The days were dull and changeless.
      Until the letter came.
INNKEEPER. Letter?
ARNOLD. The reprimand from Washington.
INNKEEPER. Ah, the "incidents." Let me see ...

(The Innkeeper goes through some papers on the bar and pulls one out. She starts reading.)

"From the Headquarters of General Washington ... Dear Sir ... I would be much happier bestowing commendations on an officer who has rendered such distinguished services to his country as you, but in the present case a sense of duty and regard to candor oblige me to say that your conduct in the use of army wagons for personal business was imprudent and improper ...."
ARNOLD. Where did you get that?
INNKEEPER. You didn't think it fair?
ARNOLD. As fair as lies!
INNKEEPER. You didn't use army wagons?
ARNOLD. I — it's all too complicated. Believe me —
      They tried to make my downfall complete —
      It was a spot where they desired a stain —
      But they failed!
INNKEEPER. But why the wagons? To what end?

ARNOLD. I had some personal goods I wished to sell.
    I merely borrowed them. I tell you,
    What these wagons cost did not come close
    To all the money that I've spent upon the cause!
INNKEEPER. Wasn't there a process for repayment
    Without the use of the wagons?
ARNOLD. *(with increasing anger)*
    Ha! I've drawn from these pockets more
    Than I returned to them.
    I've purchased clothes and blankets to defend
    My men from cold, bought food to sate their bellies,
    And muskets to dispatch our enemies.
    And why? Because our nation could or would
    Not meet their basic needs.
    For all the payments I've made
    Not a dime on every dollar have I seen.
    The use of a few old rickety wagons
    Doesn't come near in balancing the scales.
INNKEEPER. But surely —
ARNOLD. For this, our nation home, I've marched all night
    Through winter's wrack,
    And seen men's feet, by frostbite, blackened dead.
    I've faced the bayonet-led charge indifferent,
    Been splattered by the blood
    Of men — once men — struck by the cannon's grape.
    And I have killed, and seen men try to kill me,
    Been struck by angry musket ball and watched
    The blood overflow my boot.
    And in desperate pain I've argued
    With the surgeons not to amputate my leg.
    "For what has Arnold suffered this?" I ask.
    That I should lay those painful months an invalid
    And hear of others lauded for my deeds?
    See those less talented promoted over me?
    That I, when healed enough to recommence
    My duties, should have my every act disparaged?
    My words disfigured 'gainst my purpose?
    My business deals upturned (though not a cent
    I touched while cumbered to that crippled cot)?
    Is that why Arnold risks his life?
    So these cowering caitiffs, these paper patriots
    Can shrink from danger's teeth
    But grow bold upon the field's cold dead?

SHIPPEN. He should have been rewarded, not reprimanded.
INNKEEPER. But didn't you turn down command
    Of half of Washington's army?
ARNOLD. I had my reasons.
INNKEEPER. Oh?
ARNOLD. I would have never been accepted,
    You know that! The other generals,
    Steeped in jealousy —
    They would have plotted on my every word,
    Upturned my every deed. They would have stopped at nothing
    Until they manufactured my disgrace.
    No man has lived beneath the glass like me!
    Besides, it was an office offered tepidly
    But a denial eagerly accepted.
    If they truly wanted me,
    They would have howled with supplications.
    Instead they smiled and walked away.
    Both sides knew they didn't want me for the job.
INNKEEPER. And you petitioned to command
    West Point — which seems a placid post
    For one who thrives among life's turbulent waters.
ARNOLD. It had its value. Plans were made.
INNKEEPER. But still the reprimand was biting?
SHIPPEN. I remember well that day.

(The lights change and the Innkeeper fades to the background. Arnold grabs the paper from the Innkeeper.)

ARNOLD. This letter, this ink and paper — it cuts,
    It cuts me sore as any blade. If my enemies
    Had done me so, so be it — but my friends?
SHIPPEN. Is it the reprimand from Washington?

(Arnold hands it to Shippen.)

ARNOLD. See. Again, my lighted is dampened so
    That lesser flames can blaze. What's Arnold done
    To make opinion's storm blow 'gainst him?
    The fools and cowards — damn them all!
SHIPPEN. Why act so shocked?
ARNOLD. *(angrily)*
    What do you mean, "why?"

SHIPPEN. My general, dear, my love, be calm and think.
      Haven't your expenses gone unpaid?
      Your profits been denied? Haven't you
      Been abused by politicians? Seen soldiers
      Less merited promoted over you?
      So why the scowl to see a letter
      That sustains this unjust theme? Instead,
      It should animate your will to act.
ARNOLD. You're right. Let it be said that I was quit
      Before I said "I quit," and that their hand
      Was taken back before it was refused.
      For all I've done, I've lost, I've sacrificed
      And risked — the blood I let upon the field —
      For all of it I am spurned,
      Left to the cold, shut off from the approbation
      Of my countrymen through no fault
      Of my own except that I have given all,
      But it's not deemed enough.
      And now, what's left of Arnold? Nothing.
SHIPPEN. My love, you still should feel the warmth
      Of your wife's heart, my love, my faith.
ARNOLD. Your ardor's all that sustains me.
SHIPPEN. And as it should. Don't fret this fool dispatch.
      Look at it as an omen calling us
      To larger acts. It is at once a window
      That closes and a door that opens.
      Don't be angry, but resolute
      In what we've planned to do.
ARNOLD. Though I have faced the bayonet unflinched,
      This black design makes me blench;
      An act so final and extreme.
      Ah, damn it all! Why should this blighted choice
      Be laid on me? But for a captious few
      Who blood their tongues like unseen daggers,
      The mass would cluck my name as if a prince.
      Oh, it's not easily that these banns be broke.
SHIPPEN. I, too, will lose friends,
      And turn my back to things I love and know.
      But what's behind us need not sit before
      And block from us a richer path.
      Don't let our history make us who we are,
      But rather let's make history new.

ARNOLD. I'm afraid this deed will leave us
  With a blackened stain;
  A deed as foul — more foul — than murder.
SHIPPEN. That would be true, if what we do is sinful.
  As right, and we are sure it's right, your name
  Is hailed a hero, shouted from the streets.
  (Plus, don't forget: the victors write the histories.)
  What's more, we act not only for our gain
  But to set right an unjust enterprise
  In which the greater get the least, and the least
  Lord over the greater.
  A deed, whatever it may be, that sets
  The tilting world a'right is right.
ARNOLD. Ah, my sweet bird, your words distill the truth
  From the fog of my self doubt. Our cause is just,
  Our act is decorous. This was my choice —
  Why should I dither now like a philosopher?
SHIPPEN. My heart pounds hard —
  But with your support,
  And as your strength, I know that we do right
  And we'll succeed.
ARNOLD. Then it's settled; this reprimand's the final period.
  We've played a perilous game these last few months —
  Traded messages with British high command, supplied
  Information, asked them what they valued most.
  That's why I sought this fort's command.
  In part, I must admit, it was a lark,
  A dangerous dalliance, one I thought
  I'd not see through to wed conclusion.
  But now the time for flirting has to end.
  Once off the edge, it doesn't matter
  If one was pushed or jumped, the fall's the same.
  And so enough of talk, it's time to act.
SHIPPEN. I feel my blood grow warm
  Oh dear, I start to shake! You feel?
ARNOLD. (he laughs)
  My sparrow turns the hawk and yet
  Grows giddy at the height — but it's all right.
  Take a breath.
  It's weeks before the bow is tied upon this gift.
SHIPPEN. What next?

ARNOLD. What next? What next, we must decide.
    I want to meet our British correspondent
    Face to face — your old friend Major Andre.
    So far, our talks have been coquettish;
    Like lovers, passionate and hot — then coy and circumspect,
    Unwilling to confirm or consummate.
    Each side must set aside their passions
    And talk of business like two businessmen.
    But I won't wed on good intentions. No,
    They must promise me, then they must pay.
SHIPPEN. How much you think the fort is worth?
ARNOLD. How much is victory worth?
    They'll pay what I demand.
SHIPPEN. A royal sum befit a prince!
    But won't we need confederates
    To help us? Varick and Tittle
    Count our every blinking eye.
    Someone needs to stand between to pass
    Our messages until the deal is rung.
ARNOLD. I had the self-same thought.
    Joshua Smith might fill the role.
    When drunk, he has confided that he's loathe
    The masses might control the government
    After the war.
    In addition, he's not opposed to a rapport
    With the British. Add his fawning manners and
    These virtues I can play to our purposes.
SHIPPEN. It has a lovely sound —
INNKEEPER. *(stepping forward)*
    And so your plans were set.
ARNOLD. Our plans were set.
    I knew what must be done, and let my hand
    Be guided by my heart.
INNKEEPER. You weren't afraid.
SHIPPEN. Well —
ARNOLD. Fear is the absence of action. A word.
INNKEEPER. From there, I imagine things heated up.
ARNOLD. They did. But not without some obstacles.
    The rendezvous with Andre proved hard to arrange.

(The Patron as Mr. Smith approaches.)

What happened last night, Mr. Smith?
Why wasn't Andre brought to me?
SMITH. Why?
ARNOLD. That's what I said! Why wasn't he
    Brought from his ship to your house
    Where I was waiting?
SMITH. General, I assure you that my reason's sound —
    That once you hear, you'll understand.
ARNOLD. You mar my mood with preamble — out with it!
SMITH. Sir, when I went out with my boat, I found
    The river's current far too strong to row
    The distance myself, and though I tried
    I couldn't find a man to help me —
    For favor or for money. After hours
    Of search, the eastern sky started
    Taking shape and I gave up.
    I sought an hour's rest at the Red Horse Inn
    And then came here.
ARNOLD. Curse the currents! Did you get
    A message to the British ship?
SMITH. No.
ARNOLD. Then we are doubly damned. What word from Mr. Andre?
SMITH. I've none.
ARNOLD. Then three times we go under and may
    Never resurface. Our failures do not make
    Us stronger, but instead weigh down on us
    The suspicion of our guests.
SMITH. But surely we can try again.
ARNOLD. There may not be another try.
    If we're found out, the plan —

(There is a knock.)

    Come in!

(Varick enters.)

VARICK. A letter has arrived for you.
SMITH. How do you do, Colonel Varick?

(Varick nods coolly at Smith.)

ARNOLD. Here.

(*Arnold takes the letter and starts to open it. He looks up to see Varick standing there.*)

Have you nothing better to do?
VARICK. No.
ARNOLD. Then find a job or you'll be cleaning stables!
VARICK. Yes sir.

(*Varick leaves. Arnold reads the note.*)

ARNOLD. The note's from Mr. Andre.
SMITH. Good. I knew our troubles were only prologue.
ARNOLD. Our bungling of the meeting has not changed
    His mind — he wants to meet tomorrow night.
SMITH. Then we will have another chance.
ARNOLD. Then we will have *one* more chance.
    A cat must count his lives though he has nine.
SMITH. I understand.
ARNOLD. Tomorrow, I'll appoint a boat
    From West Point Fort for you to use.
    Find the men you need, and if they should resist
    Inform them they will deal with my displeasure.
SMITH. Yes, yes.
ARNOLD. This time I'll accompany you.
    Then, in the nearby woods, I'll conference
    With our guest.
SMITH. That has a solid sound.
ARNOLD. Until my business is complete, your men
    And you will wait nearby. When we are done
    You'll take our guest back to his ship.
SMITH. Yes, yes. It's all very thrilling.
    I can't imagine what it's all about.
    But I'm glad to see the two sides talking.
ARNOLD. Soon, my friend, you'll hear
    And it will then redound on every tongue.
SMITH. I'm glad to help. Well, the night's been long —
    It's time that I got home.
ARNOLD. Until tomorrow night, good day.
SMITH. Good day.

(As Smith leaves, Shippen approaches.)

SHIPPEN. Good morning, dear.
ARNOLD. Good morning. Did you hear?
SHIPPEN. The most of it.
ARNOLD. That Smith's a fool. But everything's in place
    This time I'll go myself to see that Andre is received.
SHIPPEN. And then our plan sealed.
ARNOLD. Huh? Yes. The time, it's near. The space
    Between the intention and the deed recedes.
SHIPPEN. My dear, you look worn out.
ARNOLD. I spent the night in restless waiting.
SHIPPEN. Are you all right?
ARNOLD. *(almost to himself)*
    Last night, the silent dark let rise
    In me a thought: Perhaps it would be better
    If I didn't meet with Andre — that this act would best
    Be incomplete, this hand unplayed. Perhaps
    These failed attempts are a portent — so I thought.
    But I do not believe in signs, in depths
    Beneath the surface, nor in words' pale prophecy.
    The stars, they have no eyes nor hands nor legs.
    There's nothing in the robe of night except
    For darkness, endless dark — no one or thing
    To comfort us nor to assuage our pain;
    Just stars and emptiness, indifferent
    If not adverse to the white-knuckled wailing,
    And sad, ragg'd-withering moans of men.
    Ah, it's the silence of the night, its stillness
    That so unrests me, that disquiets me,
    That lets arise in me these airy fears, these doubts,
    That fill the emptiness of night
    And from my nighttime pillow speak.
    They are but words, false born, by passive minds
    Concocted. They do nothing but erode the act.
    But one more night and then our plan is set.
    Bold action is the cure — has always been.
    Then words will mean no more; hard deeds
    Will make the day and make my name.
    Let words to the philosophers, the priests, the poets,
    And politicians — dreamers all. I have no use for them.

Although the skies are hollow, our lives are not —
We fill them with the deeds that live on after us.
I have my destiny that I must see
To its completion or the end of me.

(The sound of the storm grown louder. The stage goes dark. Then silence.)

Part 2

(The scene opens two with chairs setting at the front of the stage. A heavy rain and occasional thunderclap can be heard outside. The storm grow quieter as the scene progresses. Shippen and the Innkeeper stand front center, while Arnold stands toward the rear in the shadows.)

INNKEEPER. And so the general left to meet with Major Andre
    And single-handed bend the nation's arc upon his will.
SHIPPEN. He did. While I waited here
    In a fevered dream-wake state. Listening
    To the blind sounds of the night —

(Varick approaches.)

VARICK. Good morning, Mrs. Arnold.
SHIPPEN. *(startled)*
    Oh, oh! Good morning, Colonel Varick.
    I didn't see you there.
VARICK. You look pale. Didn't you sleep well?
SHIPPEN. I didn't, no. I never sleep well when the general's out.
VARICK. The general was out again last night?
    He was out the other night.
SHIPPEN. He had more business needing his attention.
VARICK. About that business, Mrs. Arnold — we need to talk —
    So far my pleas fallen on deaf ears.
    That's why it's urgent that we speak
    Of the general's secret plan.
SHIPPEN. Then — then — we're found out?
VARICK. Yes. Reverend Tittle and I know all about it —
    That's why it's so important that we talk.
    It's Mr. Smith —
SHIPPEN. It's true! Oh!

(Shippen begins to list.)

VARICK. Are you all right? Come, sit down here.

(Varick helps her to the chair.)

You know about this, too? Then you must understand
Our anxiety for you and the general.
SHIPPEN. Is he — is he all right?
VARICK. Yes, so far — and that compounds our fear with urgency.
Stretched upon the tip toe of his reach
What's gained in height is lost in balance.
And if the general falls,
He pulls down infamy upon himself.
SHIPPEN. The shame! I warned him!
VARICK. You spoke to him of this? That's excellent!
Why should he risk his stature
For what would be a few coins of silver?
Besides, the New York merchants are a guileful lot
Who may concede the cozened penny
But slyly lean upon the scale.
SHIPPEN. *(confused)*
The merchants? In New York?
VARICK. Yes, yes. Is Mr. Smith his ally?
SHIPPEN. This plan? What do you mean?
VARICK. The general's plan to purchase goods
From New York merchants before the British pullout,
And sell them at a profit when our countrymen return.
No doubt, it's Smith's reckless plan.
He is a fiend made up to look a friend.
SHIPPEN. *(regaining her composure)*
Oh, oh!
VARICK. We're hoping that your words will hit the mark
Where ours have missed,
And dissuade the general from this scheme
And future deals with Mr. Smith.
SHIPPEN. I'm surprised you're so suspicious of Mr. Smith.
VARICK. Simply put, the man's a traitorous snake.
SHIPPEN. Oh sir, please rest assured the general makes
No secret business deals with Mr. Smith.
They've none. They — they are —
VARICK. They're what? If not a business deal, then what
Of all their secrets and these late-night meetings?
SHIPPEN. Oh, I forget with whom I speak — a friend.
I'm sorry. You're right, they're trying
To contact city merchants through a friend
Of Mr. Smith. The shame
Makes its acknowledgment painful.

VARICK. Reverend Tittle and I are friends. We mean
    What's best for you and the general.
SHIPPEN. I know you do. You're gentlemen
    And kind, dear friends for your concern.
VARICK. The plot, and Smith's involvement, could undress
    The general's reputation.
SHIPPEN. But surely you don't think my husband would
    Do anything dishonorable.
VARICK. No, no. Of course not. But in the affairs of men,
    Our names are but a breath for men to shape
    As they see fit, unfair or fair.
    And who can say what Smith will do?
SHIPPEN. I also have a low opinion of Mr. Smith,
    Both as a gentleman and man of sincerity.
VARICK. Then you will talk to the general, too?
    That's all we ask.

(Shippen stands.)

SHIPPEN. I'll use what little power I have.
    And thank you for your solicitude;
    Your love for the general touches me.
    He's fortunate to have such a noble man
    Upon his staff.
VARICK. Thank you. I am sure your words will stand
    Where ours have fallen.

(Varick exits. Arnold steps forward to the Innkeeper.)

INNKEEPER. *(smiling)*
    The general spins many plots at once!
ARNOLD. The world has many opportunities,
    And we two hands.
INNKEEPER. And so you met with Major Andre?
ARNOLD. I did.
INNKEEPER. We're not going to that conference?
ARNOLD. Why? It was a man dictating to a nation.
    Major Andre was nothing but a well-paid messenger,
    I did the speaking. He the agreeing.
SHIPPEN. We have a deal?
ARNOLD. *(stepping toward Shippen)*
    We do. For West Point Fort they'll pay £10,000.
SHIPPEN. That's wonderful! And your commission?

ARNOLD. As major general in the British army.
    All things went well but one: Major Andre's path
    Back to his ship was blocked by an American patrol boat.
    So Smith's returning him by horse
    To the British lines. He should be there
    By afternoon.
SHIPPEN. Our plan enjoys the provident hand of fate.
    Oh my, I'm worn out.

(Shippen sits.)

    I didn't sleep last night, my mind
    So restless with thoughts about your meeting.
    Is this the way you feel in battle?
ARNOLD. *(pulling the other chair next to Shippen and sitting)*
    Hmm. Not so much in battle but the night before
    When fear feeds on helpless leisure.
    In battle and in crisis, swift action shoves
    Aside the fear.
SHIPPEN. Varick just asked your whereabouts
    And said he knew of last night's business.
ARNOLD. What?
SHIPPEN. The weight of his expression almost pulled
    Me down. I'm glad you're home! I didn't know
    What to do. He said we had to stop our plan.
    My knees began to melt beneath his gaze —
ARNOLD. What does he know?
SHIPPEN. Some deal with merchants in New York —
    But I didn't know that right away.
    His eyes stared into me and I thought
    He'd read the truth of it upon my soul.
    Oh, it's a desperate relief to have you home!
ARNOLD. *(laughing and standing)*
    What a perfect fool! His suspicions
    Read a plot where there is none and miss
    The story where it is. Are you all right?
SHIPPEN. It is at once a terrible and a wonderful
    Sensation — as much exhilarating as maddening.

(Shippen stands as the Innkeeper steps forward. As they speak, a dinner table and chairs are brought in. The table has been recently cleared of food, but there are still drinks there.)

INNKEEPER. And so the plans were set?
ARNOLD. They were. We only waited Smith
    To bring good news of Andre's safe return.
    That's all he needed do.
SHIPPEN. That night, though, Colonel Varick arranged
    A dinner with Reverend Tittle.

(Tittle and Varick sit at the table talking among themselves.)

ARNOLD. The scoundrel. But I had to play the gracious host.
SHIPPEN. Then Smith arrived. It was — it was
    Ill timed, let's say.
INNKEEPER. I can imagine!

(Shippen sits at the table joining their conversation. Smith enters carrying a drink and somewhat drunk and walks to Arnold. Tittle and Varick scowl at him.)

ARNOLD. Yes, but I had to find out what happened.
SMITH. *(to the people at the table)*
    A splendid burgundy! And very strong!
    I feel it unhinge my knees!
        (Smith laughs)
ARNOLD. Yes, yes.
        (pulling Smith aside)
    We can finally speak in confidence here.
    Between the colonel and Reverend Tittle,
    I hardly have a moment's privacy. And now,
    Varick brings the reverend here in hopes
    Of reconciling us. A man so stiff
    Cannot be bent to friendship.
SMITH. Don't give him any heed. His prejudice is set —
    He's fast unalterable.
ARNOLD. But to our business: How'd you leave our guest
    This afternoon? Did you see Andre
    To the British lines and across?
SMITH. I saw him to, but did not see him there.
ARNOLD. What? What's with this riddle?
    You saw him to the British lines, correct?
    I'm in no mood for jests.
SMITH. I did — doubt it not.
ARNOLD. And you saw him safe to his compatriots?
SMITH. To say so I would lie. I didn't.

ARNOLD. You make my head spin!
    Did you follow him to safety?
SMITH. I certainly did.
ARNOLD. And the British were content with his return?
SMITH. That, I cannot say.
ARNOLD. What? Stop teasing me!
    I'm not in the mood for a lovers' game.
    Say what happened — and make it plain.
SMITH. Come, general, and unfurl your brow. Be content!
    The gentleman's receipt's assured.
                (taking a big drink)
ARNOLD. Assured? Sir, offer no more paper promises
    But to your surety speak.
SMITH. I led young Andre near the edge of Tarrytown
    And left him go the last two miles himself.
ARNOLD. You left him unchaperoned — without a guide or guard?
    Didn't you feel the weight of my charge?
SMITH. I did and think I carried it quite well, sir.
    But I also felt on me the weight of prudence
    And knew the avalanche I'd bring down on myself
    Were I seen flirting with the British camp.
    We both know what our neighbors say of me —
    These days a single whisper's quick to ignite
    An angry mob's bloodlust.
ARNOLD. I'm glad to see your interests well protected
    Though my own were left to bankruptcy.
SMITH. But, sir —
ARNOLD. I don't like it, sir! A task half done remains undone
    And lingers over us an unfit noose.
SMITH. But, general, Tarrytown is far within
    The British territory, not two miles
    From their encampment. What inexpectant scrape
    Could our guest meet in such a narrow space?
    Especially when he's guarded by your pass
    As by an angel's wing? Besides,
    What more could I have done — or kept undone —
    Had I accomp'nied him all the way?
    It's certain: He has made it there as if
    My eyes had watched him to their hands.
ARNOLD. I don't know. I thirst for closure but drink dust.
SMITH. The matter's closed — drunk dry — he has arrived.
                (finishes his drink)

ARNOLD. What's left unfinished can't be now made whole.
    Perhaps — perhaps I seek more certainty
    Than could be laid before me.
SMITH. True, true. All things require faith,
    Tomorrow's sunrise, even. But as certain, he's arrived!
ARNOLD. And as you said, what could go wrong
    In that short distance?
SMITH. Indeed, right now he's toasting his companions.
ARNOLD. I've been a fastidious master —
    I must apologize. I should be thanking you
    For all your service.
SMITH. You're welcome, sir! It is my pleasure
    To serve a man as great as you.
    Now let us celebrate the young man's safe arrival.

(They return to the table and sit. Varick and Tittle are visibly annoyed by Smith.)

TITTLE. *(under his breath to Varick while glaring at Smith)*
    The apostate returns.
ARNOLD. What was that reverend?
TITTLE. Oh, nothing, sir.
SMITH. A splendid burgundy, wonderful, yes!
    Ah, Mrs. Arnold, your return brings
    Light and levity to raise from us
    The war's dark, somber clouds. Yes, it's been years
    Since I have so enjoyed an evening
    With such exquisite company, food
    And drink — a sterling burgundy.
SHIPPEN. Such kind remarks! But I believe the burgundy
    Inflates your flattery. Have more!

(Shippen refills his glass.)

SMITH. It does not amplify but makes more honest.
    Yes, I miss the evenings like this,
    Time spent with gentlemen of quality,
    The hours of conversation with young ladies,
    The dinners and the balls, the excellent wines.
    Before the war, this region teemed
    With men of class. But they've all fled —
    Divided against themselves.

SHIPPEN. *(as she pours herself a cup of tea)*
    The same is true in Philadelphia.
    What once was gay and light a mood
    Is sagged by stormy looks and stony faces.
    Oh, this war has wizened spirits
    And hardened hearts.
ARNOLD. *(picking up the sugar bowl for Shippen)*
    Oh damn, the sugar's gone. I'm sorry.
SHIPPEN. We still have honey.
SMITH. It's just as well. The sugar smuggled here
    Is steep in price and flat in quality.
    The war deprives us of the finer product.
TITTLE. This war's not 'bout a decent cup of tea,
    Sir, it's about the liberty of men —
    About their natural right to rule their own affairs.
SMITH. Yes, reverend, that's a sentiment
    That time has frayed and thinned with use.
    The baseness of our sugar is, of course,
    The fault of no one but ourselves. It's true!
    If we had signed the British peace
    Two years ago, we could enjoy today
    A decent cup of tea, as you would say,
    And, too, the pleasures of our homes.
TITTLE. *(angrily)*
    Profanity! How dare you say such trait'rous things
    Among patriots?
SMITH. How so? What did I say? The British peace
    Was honorable, conceding all demands
    That we had listed before the war.
TITTLE. The world has changed, and now
    That the once-tamed wolf
    Has lapped from freedom's spring, it won't return
    To shallow servitude and table beggary.
    We've had a taste of freedom and we like it, sir.
    Would you have us refit to wear the leash
    Of cowering subservience?
SMITH. Were things so bad before this prolonged war?
    Where was this tyranny of which you speak?
    What man here's felt the tyrant's strap?
TITTLE. Such wickedness! *(to Arnold)* Are you aware, sir,
    How you're framed in your association with men
    Like him? A traitor!

ARNOLD. *(to all, including the Innkeeper)*
    Before our god and king, we're traitors all.
SMITH. Are all whose course does not align with yours
    Called traitors? Are men's differences defined
    Like acid and like base — the mixture of the two
    A dangerous volatility? Is there no steerage
    But here to wrack and there to ruin?
TITTLE. A man may speak his mind if he possesses one.
    If he has two, the worse for both.
ARNOLD. *(tiredly and dryly)*
    Gentlemen, enough. Cease your foolishness.
SMITH. Can no man disagree with his king
    That doesn't want to see him overthrown?
VARICK. Mr. Smith — Reverend Tittle —
SHIPPEN. Men, please!
TITTLE. Oh, treason! Heinous, black-mouthed treason!
    If you've not heard, the drum's been beat,
    The musket shot. Men have died —
    Our land is consecrated with their blood!
    Stand in the boat or on the dock — or drown between!
SHIPPEN. Gentlemen! You're causing me great pain!
    Please cease your bickering!
SMITH. I'm sorry, Mrs. Arnold. These close times
    Make men the mouth of their passions.
    But it is time I left. I go to Fishkill tomorrow,
    So an early morning looms for me.
    Thank you, again, for this exquisite meal.
    And general, I look forward to your company.
    Gentlemen, adieu.
SHIPPEN. I'll walk you out.
SMITH. Splendid!

(Smith and Shippen exit.)

TITTLE. The man's a scoundrel and a liar!
ARNOLD. Sir, if I brought Beelzebub to dine with us,
    I'd expect you to treat him with respect.
TITTLE. Sir, had I been at any other table
    I would have sent a bottle 'gainst his head.
VARICK. General, no doubt the reverend's
    Double-charged his speech tonight,
    But his aim is true.
    That Smith's unsound, and his bald arrogance —

To utter such opinions —
Will put the spark to any patriot's pride.
You stain yourself by your alliance with him.
ARNOLD. Enough of your pestering!
Don't speak to me of stains!
Let me disenrobe my thought so it
Is naked: my business is my own
And no one else's. I won't listen to
More lectures on the man. Now leave it be.
VARICK. We're simply trying to paint our concern.
ARNOLD. Enough of your art! The style's out of fashion.
TITTLE. But general, we're compelled
By duty to the nation, to our cause, and to you.
That Smith is poisonous to all around him.
ARNOLD. How's this? Then make a case against the man.
What is it but chatt'ring innuendo,
Gossip, hints and insinuation?
Are these palled sounds the sum of it?
What else, what act, what trait'rous deed
Can you make stand?
What do you say? What? What?
            (slight pause)
Nothing! You strain forbearance. Let it be!
TITTLE. General, we aim to shed light,
Not to burn. If our ardor gives off heat,
It's not directed at you, but at the hood
Of darkness that surrounds you.
If I didn't care, I'd be as
Indifferent as the winter sun upon a freezing man.
My fault's I care too much, sir,
And speak not out of disobedience,
But with love.
ARNOLD. Love? You call it love that so berates,
And belittles its affection?
That lectures me like a callow child?
That disputes my intentions and doubts my plans?
Oh, if that is love, it's love that bleeds
Me with a thousand jabs. No, it's not love.
But what your real ambition is
I do not know.
TITTLE. What's this? What scandalous stink
Has Smith surrounded me with?

ARNOLD. What kind of fool d'you think I am?
    I'm not a puppet mouthing others' words.
    I don't wear strings that men may pluck
    To watch me dance, and I don't need to borrow
    From another's voice. I have my own!
    I no more take commands from Smith
    Than I will take from you. And that, I think,
    Appears the sore. The duty of the local citizenry
    Is not to lecture but to be commanded.
    My conscience needs no congress.
TITTLE. A man who seeds for blind obedience
    Instead of honest counsel soon reaps the bitter fruit.
    Beware, general, beware of what you harvest.
    Let that blackguard, Smith, fill your ears,
    But I will countenance no more insults!

(Tittle gets up to leave.)

ARNOLD. If you don't like your treatment here,
    Let another doctor salve your ego.
TITTLE. The devil take you, sir!

(Tittle exits followed by Varick who tries to console him. There is a pause.)

ARNOLD. *(to the Innkeeper)*
    Well, that ended well, no?
INNKEEPER. Tittle is certainly a man of his convictions.
ARNOLD. Just one conviction is enough to rid me of him.

(Shippen walks up to Arnold and leans on his chair.)

SHIPPEN. The house was full of sound tonight.
ARNOLD. The boors and cretins — such behavior!
SHIPPEN. I didn't realize just how much
    I missed the hum of city life, the noise, the company.
ARNOLD. And Smith — he's seven-tenths a fool
    Dawdling over his perfection.
SHIPPEN. This calm, it is too much like death —
    Cold, drumless, hollow death.
ARNOLD. But good news.
SHIPPEN. The muted immemorial —
ARNOLD. *(getting up from the table)*
    Did you hear me? Peggy!

SHIPPEN. What? I'm sorry.
ARNOLD. Did you hear me? I have good news.
SHIPPEN. What is it?
ARNOLD. Andre is returned, he's back in British hands.
    Soon, soon, we can expect the crowning of our plan.
SHIPPEN. That's wonderful! And when it's done,
    Let it be a noisy joy — loud and long
    To shake the air.
ARNOLD. All ears will ring with it —
    Believe me, our success will shake the world.
SHIPPEN. *(she laughs nervously, then stands and pauses)*
    But it's so quiet now. Hold me.

(Arnold and Shippen embrace.)

ARNOLD. Are you all right?
SHIPPEN. *(sings)*
        The rose and the briar, they grew up together
        Till they could grow no higher —

    I want music to fill every room — loud and continuous.
    What time is it?
ARNOLD. It's getting late, my sparrow, very late.
    You'll soon have music every day. Till then,
    Why don't you rest?

(They continue to hold each other until the Innkeeper speaks, startling them. They separate as the table and chairs are removed.)

INNKEEPER. What happened next?
ARNOLD. By chance, General Washington arranged
    To come the next morning.
INNKEEPER. The next morning?
    His Excellency comes like Andre's shadow,
    You kept a busy schedule.

(The Patrons bring forward a small sofa and desk.)

ARNOLD. It wasn't my desire, but we play the hand
    We're dealt. I'd no concerns.
    That old statue of a fool would have known nothing,
    If —
SHIPPEN. It started with his courier saying he'd be late.

(The Innkeeper steps aside.)

ARNOLD. He won't be joining us for breakfast?
SHIPPEN. That's right. *(she laughs to herself)*
ARNOLD. *(smiling)*
    What's all this twittering for?
SHIPPEN. The confluence of place and men —
    One day Andre, next his Excellency.
ARNOLD. Fate may be rudderless, but has a sense of humor.
SHIPPEN. I'll need to hide my smile from our solemn general
    And act the perfect hostess knowing what's unsaid
    In everything that's said.
    You'll be the only critic of my performance.
ARNOLD. And rave reviews you'll get, my little actress.
    When I am made Viceroy of the colonies,
    I'll build a stage to hold your art.
SHIPPEN. And I'll play Cleopatra!
ARNOLD. But with a happy ending —
SHIPPEN. Of course! We'll have the history books re-written,
    Set the poets to back to the quill and well.
    And then brave Antony
    Wrapped in Cleopatra's arms,
    Will look to the eastern sun that lights
    The empire of their love.
ARNOLD. *(laughs)*
    I'm glad to see your spirits raised.
SHIPPEN. I feel relieved today, for some reason.
    A burden's lifted from my heart.
ARNOLD. Ah, the battle eye — the cooling balm
    That steels the mind for strife and —

(There is a knock.)

    Bloody business — Who's there?
VARICK. It's Colonel Varick, sir.
ARNOLD. Mrs. Arnold's here. What do you want?
VARICK. We just received a message — from Colonel Jameson.
ARNOLD. So what?
VARICK. His courier said it's important — even urgent.
ARNOLD. Slide it under the door. *(to Shippen)* He's probably found
    A Tory goat that needs interrogated.
SHIPPEN. Since the general's running late, why don't
    You join us for breakfast?

ARNOLD. I will. Just let me put away these papers.
    I'll be right there.
SHIPPEN. Good, good. I'll get the table ready.

(Shippen steps aside out of the main light. Arnold takes papers from his coat and puts them away in the desk. He starts to leave, but stops, then returns to pick up the message Varick left behind. He stops in the middle of the room and reads it.)

ARNOLD. *(to the Innkeeper)*
    This message — Andre caught with my papers on him —
    And the news wings it way to Washington!
            (to himself)
    Arnold, ah! Your trap's been prematurely sprung
    And you are caught within its teeth!
    Toppled from the tower of your invention —
    You fall, you fall, you fall! Ah! I must escape.
    But what of Peggy and our child?
    The time damns hesitation, seconds bleed me.
    This very minute, the general speeds here
    Rope in hand. I must be going now.
            (thunder strikes — he stops)
    What's that? Do horses come? Then fight! Then death!

(Arnold pulls out two pistols from the desk.)

    Unbloodied hands will never collar me!
    An unstained shirt stand over me.
    It's better that Mars brings down these walls —
    That His Excellency and Arnold meet,
    Yes, face to face —
    With no more seconds, no more agents propped between
    To mime our intentions.
    It's time to pour the naked light upon this plot
    And show us who we really are —
    Then fix it with a death, yes, his or mine.
            (pause — listening)
    But wait — my ears deceive me. Nothing's there.

(There is a knock on the door. Startled, Arnold cocks his pistols.)

    What's that?
VARICK. *(outside the door)*
    Sir?

ARNOLD. *(aiming the pistols at the door)*
>Varick!
VARICK. Are you okay? I heard some shouting.
ARNOLD. I'm fine, goddamn your nosiness!
>Prepare my horse — my boat.
>I must get to West Point Fort
>Immediately!
>Quick! Quick! It's an emergency!

(Shippen enters from the private door. Arnold frantically gathers his things.)

SHIPPEN. What's all the noise?
>Where are you going? Your breakfast waits.
ARNOLD. Andre has been captured near North Castle —
>>*(the sound of thunder)*
>Wait! Do you hear horses?
SHIPPEN. No I don't. Just order his release?
ARNOLD. *(listening)*
>I thought for sure —
SHIPPEN. Why can't you order his release?
ARNOLD. He's been caught with dangerous papers in my hand,
>And these they've sent to General Washington.
>Once read, the final sentence is my death.
>You don't hear horses?
SHIPPEN. Oh god! Oh god!

(There's a knock on the door and they both jump. Arnold raises his pistol.)

>Ah!
ARNOLD. *(to Shippen)*
>Be quiet! *(to the door)* Who's there? *(pulls back the pistol hammer)*
VARICK. *(outside the door)*
>It's Colonel Varick. Your horse is ready, sir.
ARNOLD. I'll be right there. Resume your duties.
>>*(to Shippen)*
>I must leave right now.
SHIPPEN. What of me — the baby! Take us — you must!
ARNOLD. I have no time! Each second the gallows' noose
>Grows tighter — I must leave right now or choke upon it.
SHIPPEN. *(becoming faint)*
>I'm feeling sick. I must lie down.
ARNOLD. Not here! Take charge of yourself!
>Be strong — I know you have it in you!

Confine yourself to your room.
Tell your servants you're not well and do not wish disturbed.
Say nothing and no one will suspect
Your knowledge of the plot.
I can't loiter any more, each second
Brings me closer to the gallows' hour.
I'll do whatever's in my power for you.
Be gone! Be gone! Be gone!

(Shippen staggers to the Innkeeper and Arnold steps back.)

SHIPPEN. *(to the Innkeeper)*
    And there alone I stood,
    Where Washington closed in —
INNKEEPER. *(taking Shippen in her arms, speaking to Arnold)*
    You left her there? Your infant, too?
ARNOLD. What choice did I have? My death
    Would not have done them any good.
INNKEEPER. Then Washington arrived?
SHIPPEN. *(releasing herself from the Innkeeper)*
    Just minutes later, yes,
    With Colonel Hamilton and Captain Murtha. I hid upstairs.

(The patrons step forward and begin to play their roles.)

VARICK. Your Excellency, General Washington, gentlemen,
    Come, come in and have a seat.
    I beg your pardon for the general's absence.
    He left abruptly for some urgent business at the fort —
    The subject which, I do not know.
WASHINGTON. Sir, there's no need for your apologies.
    The general's absence gives us time to rest.
    But where's his charming wife, the lady Arnold?
VARICK. She is, I'm sad to say, not feeling well
    And confines herself to bed.
    She sends you her regrets.
WASHINGTON. A shame. I hope it's nothing serious.
    My officers wilt beneath the news.
VARICK. *(laughing)*
    No, sir, I don't think it's serious.
WASHINGTON. We'll wait the general's return.
    If you've other duties, please, go see to them.
VARICK. If you'll excuse me then.

(Varick exits. Washington sits on the sofa.)

HAMILTON. *(pacing)*
 I don't like the general's tardiness —
 It shows a disrespect to your office.
 I hope there's not a message in absence.
WASHINGTON. What do you mean, Colonel Hamilton?
HAMILTON. That the general gives a body
 To his displeasure by withholding his.
WASHINGTON. Oh, he's not so petty, do you think?
HAMILTON. General, I don't like the plot, but that's
 The way I read it.
 I've heard your reprimand was ill digested
 Although its recipe was far more bland
 Than most had called for.
WASHINGTON. Come, Colonel Hamilton, you conjure plots
 Among the lilies. Rest that wariness of yours.
 I don't want these rumors to sour the mood.

(Varick returns while Washington is speaking.)

VARICK. General Washington?
WASHINGTON. Yes?
VARICK. Excuse my interruption, but a note
 Has just arrived for you. The courier said
 It should be read before it cools.
WASHINGTON. Take it Colonel Hamilton,
 And thank you, sir.

(Hamilton takes the note and looks at it before opening it.)

HAMILTON. *(to Varick)*
 This note is dated late last night but came
 Only several miles. Why did it take so long
 If it were urgent?
VARICK. I asked the same. It seems the courier
 Believed you at the town of Danbury,
 And finding no one there, has searched the night for you.
INNKEEPER. *(to Arnold)*
 That was a lucky break for you!

(Hamilton starts reading the note.)

WASHINGTON. The man must be exhausted.
    By our change in plans.
    Please see to him, Colonel Varick.
VARICK. I will, your Excellency.

(Varick exits.)

HAMILTON. What's this? Do I read it right?
WASHINGTON. What is it, colonel? What drives
    The color from your face? Say its purpose!
HAMILTON. I know what's in my hand and what I read,
    In parlance, it is honest. But in purpose —
    It addles understanding.
WASHINGTON. Then forget interpretation and describe
    Its contents. Come!
HAMILTON. It's a note from Colonel Jameson,
    Stationed at our outpost near Tarrytown.
WASHINGTON. Yes, near the British line.
HAMILTON. He says a man is in his custody
    On whom were found some papers and a pass.
    These papers, found within his boot,
    Are in the self-same hand as is the pass:
    That is, the hand of the West Point commander.
WASHINGTON. That's odd, but not so odd. The contents?
HAMILTON. The pass allowed the man to travel through our lines,
    At which point he was taken into custody
    While on his way to Tarrytown.
WASHINGTON. (standing)
    What about the papers found? What weight do they have?
HAMILTON. A millstone's weight — enough to crush
    Our faith in man and cause.
    The papers document the fort's resources —
    Its men and arms — even our army's plans.

(In the background, Shippen undresses to her nightclothes underneath.)

MURTHA. It can't be!
HAMILTON. It can and is! The general has betrayed us!
WASHINGTON. Here, let me see! That hand — that hand — it's his!
    Oh, whom can we trust?

HAMILTON. This damning evidence was also sent to him, who,
 Seeing it, ran off before we came.
 How long since he escaped? Did anybody hear?
 We may yet catch the devil!
MURTHA. The two-faced thief! We'd best prepare the fort
 For an attack. But who can we trust here?
 What if he didn't act alone?
HAMILTON. With each second we mar the hunt.
 Let's after him.
WASHINGTON. Be quiet, colonel! Captain Murtha, go to the fort
 And, with discretion, prep it for attack.
 Tell the officers it is a drill at my request.
 I'll be —
HAMILTON. What about the traitor? He may not be too far!
WASHINGTON. I won't spare any men. Not now!

(Washington turns to Murtha to speak but is interrupted.)

HAMILTON. I don't need many — two or three will do.
WASHINGTON. No, I said. *(turning again to Murtha)*
HAMILTON. You'll let the traitor flee, the blood
 Still wet upon his hands?
 Then give me leave to go myself!
WASHINGTON. God damn your prattling —
 My mind is set, Colonel Hamilton!
 We'll arm the fort for battle first.
 Do what I say — and stop your pestering about —
 About that man!
SHIPPEN. *(from the shadows on the side)*
 Oh! Oh! The sand's aflame!
MURTHA. Who puts a voice to sorrow's depth?

(There is a knock at the door.)

WASHINGTON. Come in!

(Varick enters.)

VARICK. Excuse my interruption, General Washington,
 But Mrs. Arnold's in a strange delirium.
 Her eyes stare unblinking,

Then dart and flutter like a moth.
    Her voice, it trembles as she speaks —
    As if within the horn of torment.
SHIPPEN. *(aside the main action)*
    No please! Don't kill my babe!
VARICK. It chills my soul to see her so. She asks
    To see you. If you don't mind,
    Your face — familiar to her — may assuage
    This haunting mood. Please, sir.
WASHINGTON. I am no doctor, but as a friend,
    Perhaps, I can help. Bring her in.

(Varick leaves.)

    Now, Captain Murtha, be quick and see to my
    Instructions. Hurry!

(Murtha quickly exits. Varick returns with Shippen in her night clothes, pretending to hold a baby.)

SHIPPEN. The heat! The heat! I melt into a wash
    Of brine, a trail of tears, a stream of salt.
                (to Colonel Hamilton)
    Oh, General Washington, oh, tell me please:
    Why have you ordered that my child be drowned?
HAMILTON. But Mrs. Arnold —
SHIPPEN. He's but a babe, unknowing of the acid looks
    Of men — but, oh, he will! Why see him smile!
    Look, there is the white and light of innocence.
    Why must he die? Each born will die, it's true
    (That is the saddest of a parent's gifts).
    But why so soon? To one so round and pink?
    I beg you, please! Whatever that you want
    Is yours: my tears, my pleas, my soul, my body!
    You'll have them all! Give me the script to my
    Humiliation and I'll glad perform it.
    But please don't kill my babe!
    I beg you, General Washington!
WASHINGTON. Here, Mrs. Arnold; here I am.
    Don't you remember me? We've met.
    Have you no memory?

SHIPPEN. Yes, memory. That's all I have —
    The glass has been reversed. The greater part
    Of me is what's behind. And looking forward,
    Nothing's seen.
WASHINGTON. I won't harm your child. Why do you think so?
SHIPPEN. I think because I must and, too, because
    I cannot stop. And if I ever did,
    What would become of me? I fear to think it!
    But there I go again. Where am I now?
HAMILTON. You're in your home.
SHIPPEN. No. This is not my home, this scorpion's nest!
    The exile's desert! I fear I'm lost,
    Banished, my child and me, to walk
    The with'ring sands, the sun, the wind and, oh,
    The flames — the flames that scorch my breast!
HAMILTON. These flames — where do they come from?
SHIPPEN. From you and you and you — from all your eyes!
    Your spiteful stares steep over me and scald
    Like boiling oil! Oh! Oh! No more! No more!
    No more your stinging gaze!
VARICK. Come, Mrs. Arnold. We don't want to hurt you.
    We're your friends, and soon your husband will return.
SHIPPEN. No, no, no, no, my mate is mine no more.
    He can't return. He won't — No, no!
    He can't return! Ah, ah! My burning hair —
    A foul and fetid fume. A fire! Fire!

(Shippen throws herself on the floor and Varick and Hamilton pick her up amidst her writhing and moaning.)

VARICK. Please, Mrs. Arnold, you are bringing me to tears —
    I'm afraid you'll hurt yourself.
SHIPPEN. He's gone, his figure shrinking there before me,
    Forever. That which he once was —
    A giant, a statue of a man, a god —
    Is gone, there vanished into the thinning emptiness
    That stretches out in front of me, forever.
    There and there and there, and then — he's gone.
    The twisted spirits, disfigured in their tortured ecstasies,
    Now lay the irons hot upon his head.

(Breaking free from Varick's and Hamilton's hold, she sings.)

The daffodil's a'bloom,
The tulip's opened wide,
　　When spring comes see
　　We'll marry soon
My true love said to me.

I feel the irons glowing sear upon my head —
Oh! Oh! Only General Washington
Can take them from me.
VARICK. Here's General Washington —
SHIPPEN. No, no. That's but his clothes and voice — not him.
　　But what are we? What more's this wretched tale called "life"?

(Shippen laughs wearily and begins to sway, Varick holds her up.)

Now I must rest. The spirits have relinquished me.
WASHINGTON. *(to Varick)*
　　Put her on the sofa here, and call
　　For my physician.
SHIPPEN. *(again pretending to hold a baby)*
　　The desert is so cold at night! There, there my child!

(Varick lays Shippen on the sofa and leaves. Hamilton and Washington step aside.)

HAMILTON. Poor woman — not much more a child herself.
　　Her husband must have told her of his plot.
WASHINGTON. The tale's enormity has crushed her mind,
　　As it has all of ours.
　　He has betrayed his nation and his wife,
　　If either will recover, I don't know.
　　For now, we'll leave her to the balm of sleep.

(Washington starts walking away but Hamilton remains in a reverie.)

Come, sir, don't let amazement paralyze you.
It is a bitter fruit we must digest,
But we must first to the fort and to our duty.

(The patrons exit to the shadows. The Innkeeper sits with Shippen, stroking her face and hair.)

INNKEEPER. *(soothingly)*
> There, there.

SHIPPEN. All fools, fools, fools! Each one his own.
> Fate entwined, we say we know, yet nothing's known.

(Arnold comes and helps her to her feet. She steps aside to get back in her dress with the help of the Innkeeper.)

ARNOLD. I wrote to General Washington asking their return.
> He soon complied.

INNKEEPER. I see. That seemed an honorable thing.

ARNOLD. Honorable? Ha. He always played the part.
> He had to make it seem that he was better
> Than the rest of us — raised above the muck.

INNKEEPER. And yet he didn't offer Andre for you?

ARNOLD. I'm sure he asked. But me? For Andre? Ha!
> Who was Andre, really?
> And aide to camp, a cabin boy, a fetch for General Clinton?
> Hardly worth a peasant's sum, much less a princely one.
> It was his gross mistake that cost us our reward,
> And British victory.

INNKEEPER. What would have happened —

(A patron helps Arnold put on his British army coat as he speaks. The sofa and desk are removed and everything is restored to where it was at the start of the play. The rain outside starts to subside.)

ARNOLD. — Had he not been caught?
> What lives saved? What state restored?
> With West Point fort they needed only press their thumb
> Upon the apple of deceit
> To choke rebellion of its rancid breath.
> And then — and then I could have been the viceroy —
> And all the colonies would have bent beneath my will.
> But for Andre. But for Andre! Andre's
> Bumbling capture spoiled it all! Ah!
> If he'd been less a fool, I'd be more a king!
>> *(brief pause)*
> And yet the British acted like it was my fault
> The plot failed and charming Major Andre caught.
> Who was this charming Andre? What was he?
> Did charming Andre carry magic dust
> That would spell them to victory?

Was charming Andre secretly a demi-Caesar
Who would lead their armies to a crushing success?
Hmm. Their problem was they were more interested
In charm than gory victory.
If they worried less about their burgundies, and more
About quick, bloody acts, this war would end.
But here we are.
And Arnold, who is ostracized where he should
Be heralded, who is treated with contempt and sneers —
Arnold, who at infinite risk lent victory's key to them
To have that clumsy Andre fumble it away,
And all was lost — lost.
Why am I so cruelly and unjustly treated?
SHIPPEN. Why are our stars made dim by blinding fate?
INNKEEPER. Now Andre's dead.
ARNOLD. And we're alive, thank you very much.
    I take much solace in that!

(A short pause. It is silent outside.)

SHIPPEN. The storm — I think it's stopped.
ARNOLD. It has. It's time for us to go.

(Arnold gets his and Shippen's coats.)

INNKEEPER. With Andre's death Washington's decreed
    Your name be razed from all the nation's records,
    Present and past.
ARNOLD. Deeds outlive words, you'll see.
    Men may hate my name, but can't ignore my deeds —
    They live together
    In the unbreakable braid of history.

(They put on their coats.)

    Ticonderoga — Quebec — Saratoga — those acts
    Are carved in history to never be undone.
INNKEEPER. Your name is struck — the bell has no ring.
ARNOLD. Like Washington's river crossing
    They are the stuff of legends — alive upon men's tongues
    Long after they've forgotten how or why.
INNKEEPER. And yet unnamed would be forgot?

ARNOLD. A name's a name — but deeds will out.
    When I restore the kingdom's rule, they'll know
    Whose hand is clenched upon the whip,
    From where its sharp blows drop!
    If not writ in love, they'll speak my name with fear!
INNKEEPER. Yes, but history's kind and it is cruel.
    Eyes turn, myths change to fit the shape of the age,
    One speaker shrieks above the scholar's whispers
    And we can only shake our heads and wonder
    If volume's right, if Nike's scribes are honest.
    For history is word and deed. It is the namer of names
    And the namer of deeds. Achilles fame lives only
    Through blind Homer's verse. What of the heroes there forgotten?
    And if forgotten, did their deeds ever happen?
    Perhaps, though, it is good that history forgets —
    Forgets our shames, our failures, and our Edenic falls,
    That wilting time blots out our sins from memory
    To join the anonymous dust within the hour glass.
ARNOLD. There will be monuments to me, you'll see.
INNKEEPER. And they'll stand nameless — forgot
    And mute.
SHIPPEN. Who are you?
INNKEEPER. You still don't know?
ARNOLD. Monuments with my name — with my name! —
    Will adorn our towns. This is unfinished!
INNKEEPER. But what if it is?
SHIPPEN. What's your name?
ARNOLD. Come Peggy. (*coolly*) Thank you for your hospitality.
SHIPPEN. (*as Arnold almost pushes her out*)
    Who are you?
INNKEEPER. I have many names. Pick any one you like.

(*Shippen and Arnold leave. The characters resume their positions at the beginning of the play. The lights go down.*)

FINIS

The Other Plays

After Words

As dims this day's prospect, hearing sinks along with anticipation.
Yet dreams will whisper, whisper. So, it is necessary, perhaps, for
the playwright to speak his wishes into the silence, and so calls:
speak trippingly, set sparingly, sing broadly.

www.ingramcontent.com/pod-product-compliance
Lightning Source LLC
Chambersburg PA
CBHW022027260626
47156CB00017B/431